# HERCU
# &
# XENA

## THE UNOFFICIAL COMPANION

# JAMES VAN HISE

BOOKS

RENAISSANCE BOOKS
*Los Angeles*

Special thanks to Art Cover, Jim Keegan, Ruth Keegan, Cal Lynn, Kevin Mangold, Wendy Rathbone, and Dan Whitworth.

Library of Congress Cataloging-in-Publication Data

Van Hise, James.
    Hercules & Xena: the unofficial companion / by James Van Hise.
    p.    cm.
    Includes bibliographical references and index.
    ISBN 1-58063-001-4 (pbk: alk. paper)
    1. Hercules, the legendary journeys (Television program) 2. Xena, warrior princess (Television program) I. Title
PN1992.77.H44V36  1997
791.44'75—dc21                                                          97-29093
                                                                             CIP


98  99  00  01  10  9  8  7  6  5  4  3  2  1


Manufactured in the United States of America
First Edition

# CONTENTS

# PART

# I

✧❖✧

# The

# New

# Heroes

# HERCULES
# AND XENA

*"Xena* and *Hercules: The Legendary Journeys* have inspired a following reminiscent of the original *Star Trek* TV series."
—Jim Abbott, *The Orlando Sentinel*

The first official *Hercules* and *Xena* convention was a sell-out! For two days in a row in January 1997, the two-thousand-seat venue in Burbank, California, was full to capacity, and fans had to be turned away at the door. *Star Trek*, the mother of all fan-convention TV shows, took seven years before it could draw a crowd that size.

What's the big attraction? The characters.

Whether it's two hundred years in the future or two thousand years in the past, it's the characters. As fans of the original *Star Trek* series readily admit, even bad episodes were worth watching if only to see the interaction between Kirk and Spock. *Star Trek* was fun to watch, and the characters were embraced by an incredibly loyal viewing audience. In the late 1990s, audiences found the same kind of character interplay between Hercules and his friend Iolaus and between Xena and her sidekick Gabrielle. The two shows are now both experiencing a *Star Trek*–like ground swell of fan support.

In its early days it was said of *Star Trek* that it was like *Wagon Train* in space, referring to the TV western that had been a big hit five years earlier. The producers of *Hercules* and *Xena* have been very open in admitting that the kind of adventure seen on the old *Star Trek* was part of their inspiration. What comes around goes around: On *Wagon Train* the protagonists journey out west bumping into bad cowpokes, on *Star Trek* the protagonists journey into space bumping into bad aliens, and on *Hercules* and *Xena* the protagonists journey around ancient Greece bumping into bad myths.

# MYTH AND METAPHOR

Although *Hercules* and *Xena* both follow the *journeying-and-bumping-into* format, they each journey and bump in their own way. Hercules, for instance, doesn't kill people. He's super strong, but he's got heart. When Hercules bumps into a mythological bad guy, he cold cocks him. Xena, often as not, runs him through with her sword. Her heart, however, is also in the right place.

Minor inter-myth differences on fight strategy aside, what truly distinguishes both *Hercules* and *Xena* from their competitors is that the main characters are heroes at a time when real heroes seem hard to come by. Hercules and Xena live for no other reason than to help people in trouble and to help in grand and exciting ways.

Hercules has pledged to use his mighty strength to help those from whom the gods have turned away even though his vow has cost him the lives of his wife and children. Xena was herself one of the bad guys until Hercules helped her to see the light and to use her mastery of magical martial arts to fight against evil.

It is only by watching several episodes of each series that one can appreciate the larger tapestry of which they are a part. While other action-adventure shows often don't link episodes together by anything other than the opening theme song, *Hercules* and *Xena* are not only linked, they are shaped by what happens to their characters from one episode to the next. Old friends or enemies often return and current actions have consequences that alter the shape of things to come.

After more than sixty episodes of *Hercules* and nearly fifty of *Xena*, the characters and the formats still continue to evolve. A viewer who may have seen only a few of the lighthearted episodes of either series would not understand why another viewer who happened to see "Mercenary" or "Destiny" thinks the shows are action dramas. The first *Hercules* episode of the third season, "Mercenary" (H-38), has no jokes, and the only remotely funny scene is the expression on the face of a pirate when he is being pulled underground by a devouring monster. In the second season of *Xena* (1996–97), there was a flashback episode entitled "Destiny" (X-36) in which Xena is crucified by Julius Caesar who, to prevent her escape, orders both of her legs broken.

*Hercules* and *Xena* are willing to take chances, and in doing so, they continue to attract, surprise, and thrill their viewers.

Between the first five *Hercules* TV movies (1994) and the first season of one-hour shows (1994–95), *Hercules* had been on the air for more than a year before *Entertainment Weekly* gave it a serious review. Even then, *Entertainment Weekly* TV critic Ken Tucker seemed largely baffled by what he saw, and wrote it off as mostly a show for kids: "the plentiful, exaggerated action scenes, combined with Sorbo's low-key, I-know-I'm-a-big-dumb-guy attitude, make this show a magnet for kids and a soothing brain-cooler for adults slack-jawed in front of their TV's." His comments on *Xena* six months later might be construed as a rave, but again, only if you were part of the milk and cookies set: "If I were a ten-year-old, I'd bite anyone who tried to keep me away from an episode of *Xena*."

While critics seem reluctant to credit the creators of *Hercules* and *Xena* with having produced shows of intelligence and artistry, the fans see more than sword fights, armor-plated leathers, and cool mini-skirts in the same way *Star Trek* fans saw more than phaser fights, color-coded double-knits, and cool mini-skirts. The so-called Trekkers were the first to see it, but ultimately the rest of the world began to recognize the subtext of the show, and it became the subject of serious discussion by critics, editorial writers, university professors, and intellectuals of every stripe.

To their fans, Hercules and Xena are much more than a strongman and a leather-babe. They are representations of the qualities we all wish we possessed, and their stories are classic morality tales. They are the modern embodiment of the classic hero. Undisguised, and perhaps not very subtle, *Hercules* and *Xena* are myths made entertaining. They are myths in the guise of TV shows, which still convey the essential truths and insights that the respected scholar Joseph Campbell wrote about in his book explaining the importance of myth in the human psyche, *The Hero with a Thousand Faces*.

If that's true, given the example of *Star Trek*, it won't be long before you start to hear the sound of critics recanting, editorials and theses being written, and *Hercules* and *Xena* fans saying, "I told you so."

# CHAPTER ONE

# THE ORIGINAL MYTH OF HERCULES

The legend of Hercules originated thousands of years ago with the stories of a mighty hero known to the ancient Greeks as Heracles. Later, the Romans adopted the Greek myths and gave the gods and heroes Latin names: Zeus, the king of the gods, became Jupiter (from *Zeus Pater*, meaning Father Zeus), and his son Heracles became known as Hercules. In the television series, as in many history books and mythology texts, the son is known by his Roman name while the other mythological figures are most often referred to by their Greek names.

Zeus was the god of the stormy skies and the hurler of lightning bolts. His wife, Hera, was the goddess who protected wives and legal marriages, an ironic role for a goddess whose husband was known for his innumerable infidelities—and not just with the local goddesses. Zeus also had a fondness for mortal women, one of whom, Alcmene, was descended from the hero Perseus. Her ancestry was important to Zeus because he had devised a plan to conquer the giants, the Olympians' sworn enemies. His plan called for a new kind of hero who would be fathered by a god—him—and whose mother would be mortal but descended from the gods. Alcmene, a descendant of Perseus, the son of Zeus and Danae, fit the bill. Essentially, it is for this reason that Zeus decided upon Alcmene as his next romantic conquest.

While Alcmene's husband, the great warrior Amphitryon, was out of town, Zeus, disguised as Amphitryon, slipped into her bed. Having made the night of triple length, there was enough time for Zeus to father one of a pair of twins and for Alcmene's true, mortal husband, upon his return, to father the other. (It may not make complete sense, but hey, this is mythology not biology.)

# THE BIRTH OF HERCULES

Because of Zeus's magical triple-night trick, Alcmene never suspected any of these comings and goings, and nine months later she gave birth to twin boys: one, Heracles (who will be referred to hereafter as Hercules), was fathered by Zeus and was therefore more than a mere mortal. The other child, Iphicles, was the completely mortal son of Amphitryon. But, and this is the crux of the story, prior to the day of the birth, as part of his master plan to set things up for his illegitimate son, Zeus had prophesied that the next descendant of Perseus that was born would be the high king of all Greece. Figuring out what her husband had been up to, Hera threw a wrench into the works by seeing to it that another woman descended from Perseus delivered a son, Eurystheus, two hours before Hercules was born.

Despite this triumph, Hera's enmity toward her husband's latest off-spring remained unabated. While the twins were still infants, she dispatched two poisonous snakes to suffocate Hercules in his cradle. Iphicles panicked, but Hercules remained calm and strangled both reptiles with his bare hands. As Hercules grew, it became even clearer that he would be more gifted with brawn than mental prowess. Efforts to teach him the finer things in life—art, literature, music—failed miserably, yet he mastered all athletic undertakings with superhuman ease.

Another of Hercules' shortcomings was a distinct lack of patience. Once, frustrated by his music teacher's attempts to instill in him a sense of harmony, Hercules grabbed a harp and broke it over the teacher's head. If they'd had Ritalin in those days, Hercules might have remained in school. (Actually, if they'd had Ritalin in those days, it would probably have been someone's name.) But they didn't, so Hercules was sent off to become a shepherd. Depending upon which version of the myth you follow, when he wasn't tending his flocks, Hercules was either taught archery by Teutarus the Scythian or educated by the wise Centaur Cheiron. Either way, by the time he was eighteen he'd had it with sheep and opted to become a legend instead.

# EARLY ADVENTURES AND MAYHEM

At first he started out small, killing a ferocious lion that had been ravaging livestock in the country ruled by King Thespius. Thereafter, Hercules

Lion.
(courtesy Dover Publications)

wore the lion's skin as his cloak and hood, which, though it never caught on with anyone else, became his personal fashion statement.

While catching his own clothes was impressive, it was nothing compared to the romantic conquest that took place at the king's castle after the lion slaying. Thespius had fifty daughters, and he invited Hercules to bed them all as reward for getting rid of the annoying beast. Unlike the Hercules of the modern TV series, the original was only too happy to oblige. Hercules begot fifty-two children in the process. The first and last of the king's daughters both bore twins.

In most instances this much begetting would be enough to exhaust a platoon. But for Hercules, fatherhood, even of this magnitude, wasn't enough to make him want to go home each night to the wives and kids. Hercules was too busy righting wrongs to get married.

When Hercules encountered some emissaries from the kingdom of Orchomenus (which received tribute from the city of Thebes), some of them mocked his appearance. Apparently the lion outfit craze hadn't yet hit in Orchomenus. To Hercules, that was no excuse for appearance mocking, an act he felt was definitely a wrong that needed some righting. He attacked them, and cut off their hands, noses, and ears; tied them together by their necks; and then sent them scurrying back to their kingdom. This tended to sour relations between Orchomenus and Thebes, causing a war between the two sovereignties, which, with the assistance of Athena (another of Zeus's offspring), Hercules helped win.

Compared to the fifty-daughter victory celebration thrown by king Thespius, the one in Thebes was a snore. Creon, the king of Thebes, could only come up with one daughter to offer to Hercules, and it was clear it wasn't for a one-night-stand. And so it came to be that Hercules married

Creon's daughter Megara, who bore him either three, five, or six sons, depending upon the version of the myth.

Whatever the number of children, Hera had other plans for this happy family. She waited until Hercules and Megara had their three, five, or six sons, and then drove the hero into temporary madness. When Hercules recovered his senses, he discovered that he had brutally murdered his entire family. (In some versions his wife is not harmed. In others Hercules also kills two of his nephews, the children of his twin brother, Iphicles.)

Some tell that Hercules could not bear to live with what he had done, so he went to the Oracle of Delphi for purification. The Oracle decreed that, as penance, Hercules must do the bidding of his cousin Eurystheus for twelve years. Eurystheus, you'll recall, was the child whom Hera had maneuvered into the kingship by arranging for him to be born two hours before Hercules.

Other variations have it that the death of Hercules' family was just Hera's way of reminding him of a bargain made at the time of his birth. Zeus had fought with Hera over her trickery and had made her promise that Hercules could become a demigod if he fulfilled ten tasks for the future ruler, King Eurystheus.

# THE LABORS OF HERCULES

Eurystheus had little fondness for his muscle-bound cousin, so when he found out that Hercules was going to be his slave for the next twelve years or ten tasks, whichever came first, Eurystheus decided to come up with a list of the most impossible tasks he could think of. When Eurystheus's imagination faltered, Auntie Hera was only too pleased to offer helpful hints and malicious suggestions. Between the two of them, they came up with some real winners.

## THE NEMEAN LION

Eurystheus's first demand was for the skin of the Nemean lion. This was no easy task because this lion was a beast far more awesome than the one whose aging remains Hercules currently wore over his shoulders. The Nemean lion had a hide that could not be penetrated. Swords, spears,

Hercules and the Nemean lion. (courtesy Dover Publications)

knives, arrows—nothing seemed to work. Throwing his weapons away, Hercules strangled the monster bare-handed, losing a finger in the process. He then skinned the corpse with one of the lion's own claws, replaced his out-of-fashion lion suit with the new one, and hauled what was left of the carcass back to Eurystheus's throne room.

## THE HYDRA OF LERNAEA

The next task was even more daunting: kill the Hydra of Lernaea. A dog's body with nine venomous serpents heads, the Hydra could only be killed by severing all of its heads—but every time a head was cut off,

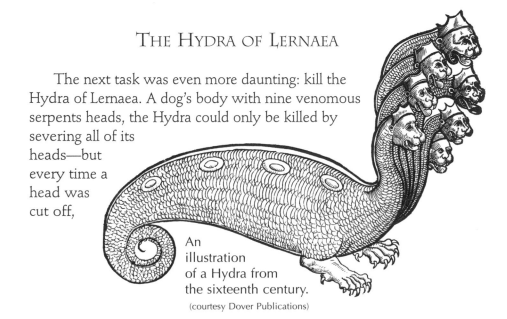

An illustration of a Hydra from the sixteenth century.
(courtesy Dover Publications)

two immediately grew to replace it. He tried crushing the heads with his club, but the effect was the same. After Hera sent a giant crab to bite his foot (which the hero crushed with his club), Hercules enlisted the aid of his nephew Iolaus. (The character of the same name in the TV series is not related to Hercules at all.) Iolaus used a torch to cauterize each neck just as Hercules struck off a head with his sword. After Hercules finished chopping, the monster died in a pool of its own blood.

Hercules took a look at the mess, figured anything as nasty as that would make terrific poison arrows, and dipped the tips of some of his arrows in the Hydra's blood. As you'll see later on, this was not such a hot idea.

## THE HIND OF CERYNEIA

Next, his evil cousin sent him to capture the Ceryneian Hind, a creature sacred to the goddess Artemis. This wily beast with antlers of gold and hoofs of bronze eluded him for an entire year until he pinned its front legs together with a regular, non-Hydra-blood-dipped arrow. This shot was so precise that it did not draw any blood or cause any permanent injury.

Back at court, who should Hercules see but Artemis, one very ticked-off goddess, looking for her sacred hind. It's hard to hide a hind, so Hercules did the next best thing. He blamed Eurystheus. This might not have been such a bad idea except that Eurystheus was the one handing out tasks.

## THE BOAR OF ERYMANTHUS

Eurystheus's next hellish job for Hercules was to capture a massive, wild boar that lived on Mount Erymanthus. Tracking the boar up the mountain, Hercules had a run-in with some hostile Centaurs, and in the course of the fight, the hero wounded one of them with a poisoned arrow. By accident, Hercules had killed his old teacher, Cheiron the Centaur. Hercules then went on to capture the massive wild boar by trapping it in a snowdrift. Trussing it up neatly, he brought it back alive.

Wild boar. (courtesy Dover Publications)

A lion corpse, Hydra heads, a hind, and now a wild boar? Eurystheus was so terrified when he saw Hercules coming, he hid in a large bronze urn.

## THE STABLES OF AUGEIAS

Growing weary of Hercules' success, Eurystheus decided that he'd been giving his cousin far too much time to complete his tasks. After all, Hercules had had a whole year to capture the Hind of Ceryneia. The next task would have to be done all in one day, and Eurystheus found his idea right next door. His neighbor Augeias owned three thousand oxen, and in thirty years had never cleaned their stables. It would take a dozen Herculeses a dozen years just to make a dent in the horrendous mess. Hercules, however, diverted the course of two nearby rivers so that they flowed right through the cattle stalls, and he was out of there by lunch.

## THE BIRDS OF STYMPHALUS

The sixth task pitted Hercules against the deadly, carnivorous birds that dwelt in the Swamp of Stymphalia in Arcadia. Covered with brass feathers and armed with iron beaks, these creatures had been dining on the local citizenry for generations. To make matters worse, the swamp was impenetrable. He could not get to the birds, and even if he could, his arrows were no match for their metallic plumage. The goddess Athena (in some versions, the god Hephaestus) helped Hercules by giving him a bronze rattle, which he used to frighten the birds, causing them to fly about in confusion and expose their unprotected underbellies to Hercules' deadly arrows.

## THE CRETAN BULL

King Minos of Crete had angered the sea god Poseidon. Poseidon had sent a monstrous white bull from the sea as a sign that Minos was king, but when Minos refused to sacrifice the bull to Poseidon, the sea god set it loose on Minos's kingdom where it wreaked great havoc. After a mighty struggle Hercules captured the beast and, perhaps thinking that Eurystheus would jump in the urn again, brought it back to his cousin.

## THE HORSES OF DIOMEDES

The king of Thrace, Diomedes, possessed four vicious mares that lived on human flesh—particularly the flesh of unwanted visitors to that savage kingdom. Assigned the task of capturing them, Hercules sailed to Thrace with his groom, Abderus. Things went smoothly at first. Hercules and Abderus drove the horses out of their stables with little resistance. When Diomedes pursued them, however, Hercules turned to fight, and Abderus, left alone and unprotected, was torn to pieces by the ravenous mares. When Hercules clubbed Diomedes senseless, the insatiable mares ate their master as well. Hercules managed to tame the horses by hitching them to the dead king's chariot and driving it home.

## THE GIRDLE OF THE AMAZONS

The ninth task should have been easy for Hercules. All he had to do was steal the golden girdle of Hippolyta, Queen of the Amazons, and bring it back for his cousin's daughter. When Hercules reached the land of the Amazons, however, the queen fell in love with him and offered him his heart's desire, which, it turned out, was Hippolyta herself, not her girdle. But Hera, never happy to see Hercules having fun, convinced the other Amazons that Hercules was there to kidnap their queen. In the ensuing battle, Hippolyta was accidentally killed by her own people. Heartbroken, Hercules retrieved her girdle and took it back to Eurystheus.

It should probably be pointed out here that an ancient Greek girdle wasn't something to hold your stockings up or your stomach in. (To Amazons, the fashion was to wear girdles on the outside—not unlike in a Madonna video.) Actually, the girdle was a sash, or belt, which had originally belonged to Ares, the god of war, whom the Amazons worshipped.

## THE CATTLE OF GERYON

Geryon, a three-headed or sometimes three-bodied king, lived across the ocean and had a herd of red cows that Eurystheus desired. In that mythological time, Africa and Spain were still joined together, and enclosed the Mediterranean Sea. Hercules decided to cut down on his travel time by making a channel, now known as the Straits of Gibraltar, between the two land masses. He then sailed through, landed at Geryon's island, and hacked and hewed his way through the local denizens until he came face-to-face-to-face-to-face with the three-headed cattle owner himself. Hera tried to blind Hercules, but he defied her magic and shot through all three bodies with a single poisoned-tipped arrow.

The road back to Greece was a hard one. Hera dogged the hero's steps at every turn, sending her minions to misdirect him. At one point he got so turned around, he wound up in Italy before realizing he was lost. Then Hera sent flies to sting the cows, causing them to stampede all the way to Turkey. Eventually, Hercules delivered the cattle to Eurystheus, just before his twelve years of slavery were up.

## THE FLY IN THE OINTMENT

Hercules may have thought he was done, but Eurystheus had an ace up his toga. He claimed that, since Iolaus had helped him defeat the Hydra, the second labor did not count. And because Hercules had diverted a river to clean Augeias's stables, credit for that task should really go to the river god. Hercules would have to perform two more tasks before his enslavement reached its end.

## THE APPLES OF THE HESPERIDES

The first make-good Hercules had to perform was to get the Golden Apples of the Sun from the distant islands in the western seas. Guarded by the Hesperides, daughters of the Titan Atlas, and protected by a hundred-headed dragon named Ladon, the apples were not easy pickings. Any mortal who touched them would die, so Hercules needed to find an immortal to pick the apples for him. He approached Atlas whose punishment for defying the gods was to hold up the sky. Atlas agreed to pick three apples from his daughters' garden if Hercules would hold the sky for him while he did it. Hercules obliged, but when Atlas returned it was obvious that he was going to deliver the apples himself and leave Hercules to take over sky duty on a permanent basis. Hercules agreed, but asked the Titan to take his load back for a moment while Hercules found a more comfortable position. And he did find a much more comfortable position—aboard his ship as he sailed back home with his prize.

## The Dog Cerberus

Finally, the last labor that had to be completed was the capture of Hades' three-headed dog, Cerberus, who guarded the gates of hell. Hercules' trip to the underworld involved much mysterious preparation, and even more mysterious encounters along the way with some spirits of the dead and Charon, the ferryman of the river Styx. When Hercules finally reached the kingdom of Hades, surprisingly, Hades and his wife Persephone were quite willing to let Hercules capture their guard dog as long as he could do so without using any weapons. (Hades was not terribly fond of his sister-in-law Hera.) Hercules seized the dog's heads, choked them into submission, and dragged the dog-like monster back to his cousin's court.

Eurystheus took one look at this addition to his petting zoo and freed Hercules on the spot with orders to send Cerberus back to his master in the Underworld.

## The Olympians Battle the Giants

Finally Hercules' labors were over. He was free of his servitude to Eurystheus and set off on a series of military expeditions and other adventures. Hercules warred against the Trojans, attacked the Spartans, sailed with Jason and the Argonauts, and did a thousand other things, but, most importantly, he fulfilled the destiny that his father Zeus had set in motion when Zeus slipped into bed with a mortal woman to conceive a mighty, yet mortal son: Hercules helped the Olympian gods defeat the giants.

The giants had never forgiven the Olympians for the time when Zeus had imprisoned them in Tartarus. The giants had escaped back to the living world, and the two forces had been at war ever since.

Although the Olympian deities had extraordinary powers, the giants proved to be their equal. The gods could not use their powers to kill giants; they could only wound them. But if there were a mortal man who was strong enough to deliver the blow at the right moment, the giants could be killed. It was because of this that Zeus had plotted the birth of Hercules.

When the final battle came, the gods disabled each of their enemies, and Zeus's mortal son Hercules delivered the final sword thrust that ended each giant's life.

# DEIANEIRA AND HERCULES

Although there are many versions of what became of Hercules' first wife, Megara (one tells that he passed her on to Iolaus), there is no doubt that he did remarry, taking Deianeira as his wife. This marriage came about as a result of his trip to Hades to capture Cerberus. While in the Underworld, the spirit of Meleager had appeared to Hercules begging him to go back to the mortal world and marry his sister, Deianeira.

Upon his return, Hercules set off on more of his many adventures, and along the way he happened upon Deianeira, deflowered her, and promptly departed with the promise that he would be back to marry her.

What with all the labors, wars, giants, and such, something always seemed to get in the way of going back for that marriage. One of the things that got in the way was King Eurytus's archery contest. First prize was the king's daughter Iole. Being somewhat of an expert in both archery and king's daughters, Hercules entered and won, but he missed out on the jackpot. Eurytus wouldn't pay up. The King and Iole's brothers declared that a slave could not claim such a prize as Iole. Grumbling, Hercules killed Eurytus's son, packed up his bow and arrows, and left to go hunt more giants.

After a lot more giant-killing, castle-storming, and general fighting and pillaging, Hercules finally made it back to Deianeira, and they set the date. Hercules married Deianeira, they settled down, and had a son, Tylus. But Hercules wasn't much of a homebody. He got to thinking about the wrongs that had been done to him. Remembering how King Eurytus cheated him out of his prize in the archery contest, Hercules went off to right some more wrongs. He killed Eurytus and sent his daughters, including first prize Iole, back home to be his scullery servants. This didn't thrill his new wife, Deianeira, who knew about the contest and worried that Hercules might still be interested in Iole.

One day while traveling with Deianeira, Hercules came upon an impassable river. Nessus, an all-too-friendly Centaur happened along and offered to carry Deianeira across while Hercules found a place to ford the river. Centaurs, being half-man, half-stallion were in a perpetual state of the hots for Greek maidens. Nessus made a move on Deianeira, and Hercules, being Hercules, whipped out his poisoned arrows and shot Nessus. The dying Centaur, sensing Deianeira's insecurity about her marriage, told her to take some of his blood. If Hercules was ever attracted to another woman, she had only to rub the blood on his shirt and it would work as a love charm.

Once home, Deianeira became more and more preoccupied with the notion that Hercules was falling in love with Iole. When Hercules asked her to fetch one of his best red shirts, she thought he wanted it to impress Iole. Deianeira rubbed the Centaur's blood on the shirt, not realizing that the blood was also imbued with Hydra venom from the poison arrow. As soon as Hercules put on the shirt he began to burn with the poison. As his agony increased, he realized it was his time to die. He fled to Mount Oeta and had his friends build him a funeral pyre. The flames proved less painful than the poison and soon his life was over.

This was just fine with Hera, of course, until Zeus heard the news and decided that his favorite son should come and live with them on Mount Olympus. After he moved in with all the other gods, Hercules married Hebe, who was, surprise-surprise, Hera's daughter, and he took his rightful place among his divine, but eternally squabbling, relations.

# CHAPTER TWO

# HERCULES IN FILM AND TELEVISION

Although the Hercules legend has been a part of western culture for many centuries, the evolution of Hercules into an icon of pop culture can be traced to one film—the 1957 Italian epic *Hercules*. This motion picture was released in the U.S. in 1959 and starred American actor (and former Mr. America) Steve Reeves in one of the first successful Italian imports that wasn't an art film. Apparently *Hercules* was successful at the time because American movie audiences had grown tired of the kind of action films the U.S. studios had been producing. And they'd never seen anything quite like this before.

While big studio pictures with somewhat similar themes such as Ben-Hur had been hugely successful, they had come by their popularity by providing grand spectacle, extraordinary stunts and action, good acting, and excellent scripts. *Hercules* was a sort of low-brow, low-rent *Ben-Hur* with production values that looked like they could have been paid for out of *Ben-Hur's* catering budget.

The star, Steve Reeves, had made his feature film debut in a bit part in the 1954 Ed Wood film *Jailbait*. In the same year he had a role in a major Hollywood production, *Athena*, and it was in that musical that Steve Reeves was seen by some Italian producers who were looking for an actor to play the lead in *Hercules*.

Released in 1957, *Hercules* was a success in Europe and caught the eye of the independent American producer Joseph E. Levine who purchased the U.S. distribution rights. He put a lot of money into promoting the film in the U.S., and when it became a box office hit in 1959, he bought the North American distribution rights for the sequel, *Hercules Unchained*, which had been filmed in 1958. Levine released *Hercules Unchained* in the U.S. in 1960. In 1977 Levine re-released the two vintage Hercules films to theaters as a double-bill.

While box office receipts clearly show that *Hercules* was the right film at the right time, looking at it today, one can't help but wonder how it attracted any attention at all when it was first distributed.

## THE FEATURE FILM THAT STARTED IT ALL

The film *Hercules* opens with someone playing pan pipes as a young woman is bounced around in a runaway chariot as it races across the landscape. Hercules (bulging with muscles and played by Steve Reeves like Superman without a costume) uproots a tree and topples it in front of the runaway horses, bringing the chariot to an instant halt. Interestingly, when we see Steve Reeves open his mouth to speak, we don't hear Steve Reeves talk. Like most foreign-produced films of that era, all the voices of the actors were dubbed by American voice actors even if one of the actors was

Steve Reeves in *Hercules* (1959). In the Greek myth, Hercules was said to wear the skin of a lion. In this movie they went with an off-the-shoulder number with pleated skirt. (photo courtesy Photofest)

speaking English. (This practice may have reached its nadir in 1980 when the Australian import *Mad Max* had the voices of all of the Australian actors dubbed including Mel Gibson's!)

The woman Hercules has rescued is a princess, the daughter of King Pelias whom Hercules has been summoned to help. She warns him to turn back and reveals her childhood memories of the time when her father's brother, the previous king, was assassinated and the Golden Fleece, the symbol of the monarchy, was stolen. The princess suspects terrible truths about that night and fears that things will only get worse in the kingdom if Hercules delivers on his promise to teach her spoiled cousin how to be a proper warrior.

As it turns out, she is dead right. Her spoiled cousin, the king's spoiled son, resents the presence of Hercules. The prince makes the mistake of challenging Hercules to contests that Hercules easily wins, thereby humiliating the prince in front of the kingdom's populace who already despise him anyway. The prince and Hercules have an archery contest in which Hercules teaches another man how to shoot an arrow further than the prince. The prince, having disgraced himself, races off in anger and disgust in his chariot.

Hercules returns to the palace where he sees the dead bodies of some villagers who have been killed by roving lions. Hercules leaves to see what he can do about the local animal-control problem.

The prince has been watching Hercules, and determined to show him up, follows him into the countryside whereupon the prince is attacked by a lion. Hercules pulls the animal off the prince and kills it, but the prince has been mortally wounded.

Astonishingly, King Pelias blames Hercules for the death of the prince! His convoluted logic is that no one asked Hercules to go after the lion and if he hadn't gone, then the prince wouldn't have followed him.

To pay for his crime Hercules is forced to fight the Cretan bull. On the way he visits the sibyl and tells her that his strength is a curse and he wants to be mortal. She seemingly grants his wish, but either the sibyl's powers were off that day or in the original Italian version Hercules must have asked the sibyl for something completely different. In the American dubbed version, there is no further reference made to Hercules having only mortal strength. For the rest of the film he seems to be just as strong as ever, and when he fights the Cretan bull, he knocks it dead with his fist.

Enter Jason, the son of the assassinated king. Jason was spirited away years before, and now he has returned because he wants to retrieve the Golden Fleece from its hiding place and reclaim his crown. Jason goes to

King Pelias and announces his intentions, stating that by finding and returning the Golden Fleece he'll prove his right to the throne.

Jason puts together a crew, including Hercules, to man his ship the Argo. During a storm, one of the Argonauts (a spy sent by Pelias) cuts a line on the mast and part of the cargo falls, smashing a hole in the deck. Hercules goes below and holds up the deck until it can be propped with supports.

The ship lands at an island where the crew is first captured, then coddled, by Amazons. It turns out that all of the men on the island were killed by a volcano years before. Ulysses, who is also one of the crewmen, overhears the queen of the Amazons plotting to kill the men after the women have been impregnated by them. Ulysses and some of the other crewmen drug the Amazons who fall asleep, allowing Jason and his Argonauts to escape. This sequence with the Amazons is proof that it is possible to take action adventure and scantily dressed women and render them both boring.

When the ship reaches the island of Colkis, they are attacked by hairy beast-men whom Hercules and the other Argonauts battle while Jason goes to retrieve the Golden Fleece, which is guarded by a terrible monster. (This is the scene toward which the entire movie has been building.) Unlike the monster in the acclaimed 1963 movie *Jason and the Argonauts*, however, this monster isn't a special effects wonder. This one is a man in an old dinosaur suit! Jason kills the monster quickly in as boring and perfunctory a manner as possible and then returns to the ship.

The reclaiming of the Golden Fleece is the whole point of Jason's voyage, yet the fight scene is over within mere seconds of film time! This is an action movie? This was a hit when it was released in the U.S.?

Anyway, on the backside of the fleece, apparently written in blood, is the dying declaration of Jason's father accusing Pelias of his murder.

Jason and the Argonauts return home, but the fleece is stolen upon landing, prompting Hercules to retrieve it. (At least he does something important since this movie is named after him.) In the course of retrieving the fleece, Hercules is dropped through a trap-door into a dungeon where he is bound in chains. After sitting around the dungeon for a while, he decides that he's waited long enough (why did he wait at all?) and proceeds to break his chains and bust down his cell door. He goes into the courtyard where he knocks guards around with his two lengths of chain, then wraps the chains around two columns which he pulls down to collapse the building on top of the king's guards.

Jason becomes king and the movie finally ends.

Steve Reeves in *Hercules Unchained* (1960). In this low-budget sequel, Hercules still didn't have his lion skin, and it appears that he lost his pleats, too.

# THE SEQUEL AND THE SEQUEL'S SEQUEL AND THE SEQUEL TO THE SEQUEL'S SEQUEL, ETCETERA

*Hercules* was directed by Pietro Francisci who, like Sisyphus condemned to push a rock up a hill only to have it roll back and have to start all over, was hired almost immediately to direct another film on the same subject, the even more inferior 1960 sequel, *Hercules Unchained*. There is actually a third, now almost forgotten, Hercules film starring Gordon Scott called *Hercules and the Princess of Troy*, which was shown in an hour-long version on ABC television in 1965. It was actually a pilot for an unsold TV series produced by Joseph E. Levine, and the full-length version is now available on video tape.

The enormous and unexpected American success of the first *Hercules* did not go unnoticed in Rome. In the early 1960s a wave of Italian imports featuring guys named Hercules hit the theaters. Most of these pictures had actually started off as something else, but when they realized what a gold mine the name Hercules had become, they just stuck the name in the title and rushed them into release. There were two 1960 films: *Hercules Against Rome* and *Hercules and the Masked Rider*, both starring Alan Steel (an Italian actor who used an American sounding pseudonym in films that were

Kirk Morris as Maciste in *Triumph of the Son of Hercules* (1961), another low-budget sequel. This time, not only no pleats, but no shirt budget either. (photo courtesy J. C. Archives)

Reg Lewis as Maxis in *Fire Monsters Against the Son of Hercules* (1962). No pleats, no shirt, and it looks like they borrowed the pants from a *Tarzan* film.

(photo courtesy J.C. Archives)

released in the United States). The 1961 film *Hercules in the Haunted World* starred Reg Park and featured veteran actor Christopher Lee. It's about the only decent one in the pack because it actually contains some visual thrills. In 1963 there came *Hercules Against the Sons of the Sun* starring Mark Forest and *Hercules and the Captive Women* with Reg Park once again in the lead role. *Hercules Against the Moon Men* emerged in 1964, again starring Alan Steel. In 1965 audiences got *Hercules, Samson, and Ulysses*—three strong men for the price of one, starring Kirk Morris, Richard Lloyd, and Enzo Cerusico.

The success of Hercules also started a parade of strongman epics about ancient or mythological characters with different names but who all acted like Hercules anyway. There was *Goliath and the Dragon* with Mark Forest in 1960, *Goliath Against the Giants* in 1961 with Brad Harris, and *Goliath and the Vampires* with Gordon Scott in 1964.

Steve Reeves, who had been the first Hercules, got on the me-too bandwagon. He starred in the 1959 release *Goliath and the Barbarians* with costar Bruce Cabot. This film actually capitalized on his success in *Hercules* before its sequel was released. In 1960 Steve Reeves also starred in *The Giant of Marathon* as well as the sword-and-sandal epic *The Last Days of*

Gordon Scott as Nippur in *Beast of Babylon Against the Son of Hercules* (1964). In this sequel, it looks like they got shirts, but they blew their statue budget to do it. Unlike Steve Reeves, who got to lift a statue in *Hercules*, Gordon Scott had to make do with a telephone pole. (photo courtesy J. C. Archives)

Mark Forest as Maciste with Marilu Tolo in *Terror of Rome Against the Son of Hercules* (1964). No skimping on the shirt budget here. Mark got the shirt and a cape, and it looks like he wants Marilu's too. (photo courtesy of J. C. Archives)

*Pompeii*. In 1961 Reeves was the title character in the films *The White Warrior, Morgan the Pirate*, and *The Thief of Baghdad*. The next year Reeves flexed his muscles in *The Trojan Horse* (still Italian-made) and in 1963 appeared in *Duel of the Titans* with Gordon Scott (who also had made by that time a few Tarzan movies) and in *The Slave*. In 1965 Reeves was in *The Avenger*, an American-Italian coproduction by Hollywood producer Albert Band, and in another Italian film, *Sandokan the Great*. Reeves film career petered out in 1968 with the Italian western *A Long Ride from Hell*. It was released in the United States in 1970 with the name of the Italian director, Camillo Brazzoni, changed to Alex Burks to make the film more palatable to American audiences.

In the midst of this wave of inferior Italian, so-called *big-screen, epics* came a film in which the mythological character Hercules played a supporting role and which provided more visual thrills than all of the other *Hercules*-like films put together. The 1959 Steve Reeves *Hercules* had been partially based on the Greek myth of Jason and the Argonauts. Providing a far better and more exciting version of that tale was the 1963 release *Jason and the Argonauts*, produced by Charles Schneer and featuring the work of special effects wizard Ray Harryhausen.

One of the most famous special effects movies of all time, *Jason and the Argonauts* is considered to be the cornerstone of modern special effects technology and has managed to influence nearly every technician working in the special effects business today. The film had a script strong enough to be interesting even between the spectacular effects sequences. The stop-motion animation by Ray Harryhausen was state of the art for the time, and made the film look like it cost many times its budget (unlike *Hercules* which was made just four years earlier and looked like it didn't cost anything).

Hercules, played by Nigel Green, appears in *Jason and the Argonauts* as a man with great, but still human, strength who is one of the crew aboard the ship, Argo, commanded by Jason (Todd Armstrong). When they reach the mysterious island of Bronze where they battle the Titan Talos, Hercules chooses to remain behind to search for his friend Hylos who has turned up missing. Jason and the rest of the Argonauts continue on their voyage. The cameras go with them, and that's the end of Hercules in this picture.

An actor in his forties was cast in the role of Hercules, which seems to have been done deliberately against type. Even though Nigel Green had a muscular body, his Hercules was a character role rather than a super-handsome warrior.

Six years later, the low-budget film *Hercules in New York* was released in 1969. This ostensible comedy co-starred sitcom actor Arnold Stang and a then-unknown performer named Arnold Strong. Strong was actually a pseudonym taken by an Austrian who had recently won the Mr. Universe title, Arnold Schwarzenegger. Arnold Strong's English sounded so Austrian that his dialogue was completely dubbed for the theatrical release. It is so

Arnold Schwarzenegger—billed as Arnold Strong—in *Hercules in New York* (1970). No pleats, no shirt, no statue, no telephone pole, just a ribbon and a smile. (photo courtesy of Photofest)

bad, however, it can only be the Schwarzenegger angle that gets this film aired on television from time-to-time.

Yet another Italian *Hercules* movie surfaced in 1983, this one starring Lou Ferrigno who had just completed a successful run as the title character in the TV series *The Incredible Hulk* (1978-82). Ferrigno is effective in the part of a strongman, which of course he was in real life and is more than evident in the 1976 feature documentary film *Pumping Iron* in which he is seen competing against Arnold Schwarzenegger for the Mr. Olympic title. The Ferrigno *Hercules* was followed by one sequel, *Hercules II*, in 1985. These two films received virtually no theatrical release in the U.S. and went direct to cable and video.

In 1993 a little known eighty-minute Australian film called *Hercules Returns* was released. The film starred David Argue, but the only actor in the cast that most people would be familiar with is Bruce Spence who will forever be remembered as the Gyro Captain in the 1982 action classic *The Road Warrior.*

## ENOUGH BAD SEQUELS AND SPIN-OFFS, WHAT ABOUT THE HITS?

When *Hercules: The Legendary Journeys* premiered on American television in 1994 as a series of five two-hour TV movies, it was an unknown quantity. There was little similarity between this new television series and the familiar no-budget Italian muscle-man pictures. Instead of starring a

Lou Ferrigno as Hercules in *Hercules* (1983). No pleats and no shirt, but Lou gets to lift Mirella D'Angelo, which beats a telephone pole any day. (photo courtesy Photofest)

former Mr. Something, the series' Hercules was a tall actor who looked like he worked out but who was no Arnold Schwarzenegger. Despite this different approach, the show's mix of humor and adventure quickly proved to be infectious. Both the series of movies and the star, an unknown actor named Kevin Sorbo, became popular almost overnight.

This new Hercules followed most of the classical Greek myth in that Hercules was still the half-mortal son of Zeus and a mortal woman, he still had superhuman strength, he still often found himself battling murderous opponents, and he still embarked on dangerous adventures. By the time the two-hour movie versions of *Hercules* had evolved into the one-hour weekly series, however, the title character was portrayed as being pure of heart, a man of moral as well as physical strength who had devoted his life to helping the downtrodden. Although Hercules had been made over as a do-gooder, he accomplished his new goals with a contemporary and somewhat flip take on all the monster slaying and derring-do that must still be at the heart of any story line derived from mythology.

Adding to the entertainment is a budget that allows for state of the art computer graphic imaging (CGI) effects to present more imaginative monsters than any seen in the previous film incarnations of Hercules. In "The Wedding of Alcmene" (H-34), Hercules and his friend Jason are swallowed by a giant sea serpent and spend several minutes clambering around in its gullet. It is easily one of the most bizarre sequences in the history of television.

The series has also benefited from being filmed in New Zealand. Unlike the many TV series shot in the U.S. and Canada, which have difficulty finding new locations in which to shoot, New Zealand offers a panorama of unfamiliar and often unusual locales.

When this new Hercules series started to rise in the ratings, an event that usually causes people who read *Daily Variety* with their morning lattés to sit up and take notice, a lot of Hollywood still didn't seem to get it. In fact when the producers began crafting a spin-off to be called *Xena: Warrior Princess*, five Hollywood actresses refused the role rather than go to New Zealand during the crucial time when Hollywood was casting new TV pilots. As a result, a local New Zealand actress, Lucy Lawless, became world famous in the role of Xena. Those other five actresses—who knows?

In 1997 two animated films were released starring this hero of Greek legend. June of 1997 marked the successful debut of the Walt Disney Company's latest extravaganza entitled simply *Hercules*. This film, Disney's thirty-fifth full-length animated feature, seemed to take a page from *Hercules: The Legendary Journeys* in that its story line is clearly slanted to appeal to modern audiences. In the Disney *Hercules,* the hero becomes the ancient Greek equivalent of a major league sports hero, complete with merchandise bearing his likeness. Disney's *Hercules* co-director Ron Clements remarked, "Hercules was the common man's hero. Among the Greeks, everyone wanted a vase with Hercules on it. That's how we got into aspects of sports celebrity that have a very contemporary ring." Voice artists in the film include Charlton Heston (Zeus), James Woods (Hades), and Danny DeVito as Phil, Herc's satyr sidekick.

The fall of 1997 saw the direct-to-video release of an animated spin-off of the *Hercules* and *Xena* TV series, starring the voices of Kevin Sorbo, Lucy Lawless, and all the other principal actors from the TV show.

# CHAPTER THREE

# CREATING THE NEW TV SERIES OF HERCULES AND XENA

According to the ancient myths, Hercules was the offspring of Zeus, a mighty god who dwelt upon the lofty slopes crowning the Mount of Olympus. More recent myth has it that Hercules was the offspring of Sam Raimi and Robert Tapert, mighty producers who dwelt among the not-so-lofty, but better-maintained, lawns crowning the Hills of Beverly.

## THE LEGENDARY JOURNEY BEGINS

As everyone knows, in the mythology of Hollywood a producer is bigger than God. And richer. Not only do they get final cut, but producers have enough juice to negotiate a percentage based on gross receipts. In Hollywood, God would have to settle for a net-profits deal.

So, how do such mighty figures rise to their exalted positions? From whence comes this power, this mystical juice that gets them gross-point deals and front tables at Mortons?

In the case of Zeus, he was raised in a cave on the Island of Crete, battled with the Titans for ten years, befriended a Cyclops who helped him defeat his enemies so that he could assume divine powers, and became the god of the skies who threw mighty bolts of lightning.

Unlike Zeus in his Cretan cave, Sam Raimi had to settle for being raised in Michigan and going to high school during the 1970s. He befriended not one Cyclops but two people, Robert Tapert and Bruce Campbell. Michigan having a decided lack of Titans with which to do battle, the three friends developed a movie project instead. They called it *The Evil Dead*.

Zeus fought the Titans for ten years; Raimi, Tapert, and Campbell fought for four years to get their movie made.

When the picture turned out to be a cult hit, the three friends didn't quite assume divine powers and hurl lightning bolts, but it was enough to get them on the lot so they could pitch scripts, which ultimately led to *Hercules* and *Xena*.

# TWO MUSES AND A WANDERING PLAYER

Bruce Campbell, who fifteen years later would play the recurring character Autolycus on Hercules, became friends with Sam Raimi at a high school drama class in their home town of Royal Oak, Michigan. Campbell starred in their first picture, *The Evil Dead*, was co-producer on their second film, *Crimewave*, went back to acting in their sequel, *Evil Dead II: Dead By Dawn*, then went off to Hollywood to look for more acting opportunities. He worked as an actor in a number of horror and science fiction films, had a major role in *The Hudsucker Proxy*, played the lead in the TV series *The Adventures of Brisco County Jr.*, and between acting gigs worked on the production side with Raimi and Tapert.

Sam Raimi and Robert Tapert, the co-executive producers of *Hercules* and *Xena*, originally met because Tapert was rooming with one of Raimi's brothers while attending Michigan State University. Over the following years, Raimi and Tapert worked together on a number of film and television productions. They changed off as executive producers, co-producers, writers, and directors on *The Evil Dead*; its sequel, *Evil Dead II; Dead By Dawn*; the three Darkman films; *Army of Darkness*; *Hard Target*; *Timecop*; and the Sam Raimi directed *The Quick and the Dead*, which Robert Tapert co-produced with Toby Jaffe.

Raimi also wrote and created the short-lived but highly regarded television series *American Gothic* as well as *Spy Game* and *M.A.N.T.I.S.* and wrote the feature film *The Hudsucker Proxy.*

# MYTH MAKING

Everything started when Universal Studios came to Tapert and Raimi and made a deal with them to produce a number of two-hour TV movies. The movies would be broadcast as part of a revolving series of action TV shows to be called the Action Pack. It was decided that one of these revolving properties would involve a modern makeover of Hercules. (Other MOWs in the series included *Rising Son* and *TekWar*.) This modern makeover approach meant that while the new version of the Hercules story would still be set in ancient Greece, the stories would reflect today's sensibilities.

Modern sensibilities or not, it was obvious from the beginning that even though it was a modern take on the story, they were still going to have to deal with the problem of how to bring to life monsters and mythical creatures, and do it on a weekly basis. Only a few years earlier the cost of creating believable special effects of such complexity would have kept the idea from being seriously considered. Recent advances in Computer Graphic Imaging (CGI), however, convinced the producers that a level of realism that would satisfy even the demanding tastes of a technically sophisticated modern audience could in fact be created for a weekly series.

Originally Universal wanted Dolph Lundgren, the Swedish-born karate champion and actor, to play the title role. Tapert and Raimi made Lundgren an offer, but he turned them down. Whether this was because the action actor was concerned with becoming even more typecast or because he wanted a bigger paycheck is not now known. What *is* now known is the name Kevin Sorbo. And it is known as the name of the star of one of the biggest hit syndicated shows in the top 200 television markets in the U.S. and the fifteen major foreign markets where the series is now seen.

Kevin Sorbo won his first TV acting job at age twenty-one. It was three lines on an episode of the nighttime soap opera *Dallas* in 1980. Like all actors waiting for the role that will launch their careers, he got cast in various episodic series including *Murder She Wrote* ("A Virtual Murder") in 1993, and he appeared on the prime time soap *Santa Barbara* in 1986. In films he was seen in the 1992 TV movie *Condition: Critical* and in the 1994 release *Slaughter of the Innocents*. He had also tested unsuccessfully for the lead on *Lois & Clark—The New Adventures of Superman* (1993–97) and was one of the actors who read for the lead in *The X-Files* (1993– ). Finally, fifteen years after his first role at the age of thirty-six, Kevin Sorbo auditioned for a lead role and he got the part of a lifetime—Hercules. Because Sorbo was unknown to audiences, however, Anthony Quinn was cast as Zeus to add promotional power to the first Hercules TV movie.

Doug Lefler, who directed one of the early two-hour *Action Pack: Hercules* movies, remarked in the December 1996 issue of *SFX #19*, "Kevin had never carried a vehicle like this before, so it was good for him to work with somebody like Tony [Quinn]. He really kept us on our toes, because he liked to improvise and didn't necessarily follow the script. And now I can see things that Kevin was able to do later that were enhanced by his association with Anthony Quinn."

The two-hour *Hercules* films caught on quickly and Universal, rather than continuing in the once-a-month format, made the decision to order thirteen one-hour episodes and launch it as a regular series. That was when it was also decided to radically alter the format of the show. It was co-executive producer John Schulian who came up with the new structure that would have Hercules wandering ancient Greece with his friend Iolaus. Zeus's role would be played down while Hera, Hercules' stepmother and nemesis, would move to the forefront. As part of this shifting of emphasis, a story line was developed in which Hera, while attempting to kill Hercules, destroys his family. This plot device was right out of the original Greek myth, and it not only provided the show with an on-going evil antagonist, it also allowed the Hercules character to visit many locales without having to be burdened by a family left behind.

This new approach opened up the story possibilities, and the producers told the writers they should approach it sort of like writing a western with the kind of sensibilities found in the film *Butch Cassidy and the Sundance Kid* (1969). That film employed a light touch with the characters, but the action scenes were still very intense. Commenting on their attitude toward action on *Hercules*, co-executive producer John Schulian told *SFX* magazine, "That's one of our main calling cards. *Hercules* is an action show and we're going to have fights. We obviously don't have guns going off, and Hercules makes a point of saying he doesn't kill people. They may wind up dead when they're fighting him, but it's usually because they're being hoisted on their own petard. It's a fine line, and there were some episodes last year, one in particular, that I think crossed the line. It was much too dark and violent and unpleasant to watch, which is not what we're about. This is escapist fun, the kind of stuff I'd have watched as a kid and I hope that, years from now, people will still be able to enjoy it on any number of levels."

In the *Los Angeles Times* of February 17, 1996, Sorbo described *Hercules*: "There is nothing like it on TV in terms of action and special effects. We pack more into every episode than any other show. We're not 'ER.' We don't try to be based in reality. But we're two hours of make the popcorn and escape from life's bumps and worries for a while."

The special effects in *Hercules* have contributed to the success of the series in a big way. Viewers look forward to seeing how good (and occasionally how bad) the effects will be each week. In some instances the effects are more like a special guest star. For example, in the episode "Once A Hero" (H-27), which has Hercules reunite with the Argonauts, there is a fight scene with sword-wielding skeletons as a kind of tribute to Ray Harryhausen whose classic film, *Jason and the Argonauts,* had mesmerized its audiences with the world's first animated skeleton sword fight. Special effects supervisor Kevin O'Neill made sure that a copy of "Once A Hero" was delivered to Harryhausen who sent O'Neill a letter saying, "Thanks, I'm glad to see that *Jason and the Argonauts* played such an important role." O'Neill proudly announced "That letter obviously hangs up on all of our walls!"

Robert Tapert was asked to comment on the choice of story lines and action from the producers point of view. He said, "When we first started *Hercules* way back when [1993], Sam [Raimi] and I remarked that our favorite shows were the old Captain Kirk *Star Trek* episodes. They were fun and a little sexy and had Kirk in these weird fights, and we tried to deliver that same kind of entertainment value. It is dumb action, maybe, but it is different than anything else on television. More like small feature films each week. The old Hercules myths would have made for bad television because he killed a lot of people. So we decided the best way to go was to find a Joe Montana type with no togas and no Parthenons and all that, someone not so huge and stilted as that old movie guy, someone you would always like to have over to your house. He couldn't be malicious or vindictive because then he isn't your hero. That makes it easier for people to tune in, and we get a lot of fan mail from parents saying, 'It's great to have a hero that my kids can root for who is not an athlete, but someone who actually does good in the world'."

Although few critics had much good to say about either *Hercules* or *Xena,* by the middle of the 1996–97 television season the media could no longer ignore the twin successes. The fans were just too vocal and the ratings were just too good. Suddenly there was a deluge of flashy, fleshy, cover stories, and feature articles appeared in everything but *National Geographic*. Kevin Sorbo and Lucy Lawless usually got the first few paragraphs but there was almost always something about how brilliantly the producers, Sam Raimi and Rob Tapert, had turned this sow's ear of an idea into a syndication silk purse.

If it's true that in the pantheon of Hollywood players, producers are bigger than God, it is equally true that writers are about on the level of trolls. In a reminder that the things that are syndicated in a successful syndication deal are programs, and programs start with scripts, co-executive producer John Schulian made the following remarks to the *Los Angeles Times* on February 26, 1996, regarding the creation of *Hercules* and *Xena*. "With all due respect to the talent and energy of Sam Raimi and Rob Tapert, I believe that Steve Weinstein gave them a bit too much credit in his story on their success in television ('Forget Baywatch: The Action's With Hercules, Xena,' *Los Angeles Times*, February 17, 1996). For one thing, Raimi and Tapert did not create *Hercules*, Christian Williams did. As for *Xena: Warrior Princess*, it evolved out of a script I wrote for *Hercules*, and the credits now say that I created the show with Tapert."

The script that John Schulian referred to was for an episode of *Hercules* entitled "The Warrior Princess" (H-9), which introduced the character of Xena.

## XENA: A HEROINE WITH A DARK SIDE

About the development of *Xena*, Rob Tapert said, "The thing that stands out about the Hercules character is his decency. It's pretty basic and easy to understand. With Xena, we have a character whose way of carrying herself states: 'I have something to say, but I can't quite say it yet.' That will deepen, actually, before it's resolved."

Tapert credits the kind of movies often referred to as "Chop-socky" films with helping to form his vision of Xena. "A lot of the female super heroines you see in Hong Kong fantasy and action films have the same kind of steely resolve we gave Xena. There weren't really a lot of television precedents to draw from, or that we wanted to draw from. I think the last female super heroine on television was Wonder Woman." In the publication *Femme Fatales* Tapert was quoted as saying, "I've always been interested in doing a female superhero show for a whole host of reasons. They tend not to work and I wanted to make one work. And they tended to be kind of mundane and sappy, and I wanted to do a really hard show. *Xena* is for a slightly older audience, although we have a couple of *Xena* episodes that are somewhat lighter. But, I think as a whole, *Xena* has a heavier tone to it."

The spelling of Xena's name with an *X* rather than a *Z* was quite purposeful. Tapert used to work for producer Dino De Laurentiis who once told him that if you spell a word with an *X*, it will be more attractive to children because kids find the letter *X* mysterious and evocative.

Originally, Vanessa Angel (star of the TV series *Weird Science*) had been cast as Xena, but she had become too ill to play the part. Five other actresses were approached, but they turned down the part because they didn't want to travel to New Zealand during the critical Hollywood TV pilot season. So Lucy Lawless won the role of Xena by default. She was already known to the producers for her guest-starring roles as Lyla in the two-hour telemovie *Hercules and the Amazon Women* and the one-hour *Hercules* episode "As Darkness Falls" (H-6). (Lucy also made a special return appearance as Lyla in the *Hercules* episode "The Outcast" [H-18] after she had taken on the role of Xena in her own series.)

When the writers and producers created the character of Xena they specifically chose not to make her simply Hercules in a skirt. In fact in its first season the character of Xena seemed more like the dark side of Hercules—his opposite and his mirror image at the same time.

John Schulian, who wrote the first and the third episodes of the *Hercules-Xena* trilogy, told *SFX* magazine, "I was particularly happy with the first one. I thought that Kevin and Michael were very good, being at odds over this woman, and I thought Lucy was really great as a femme fatale. It's a very simple episode and there are no special effects, but there are some wonderful action sequences and it was shot very well. If you watch closely, though, the ending is a little flat—she just rides away. I wish I'd come up with something a bit better there. But as a whole she was stamped indelibly on the audiences' minds as a great character. She was so evil and treacherous and there was that great scene where Kevin and Michael square off at the end of the second act."

As co-executive producer R. J. Stewart observed, "Looking back on the early episodes, some of them really work well. We got off to a great start, and I think part of the richness of Xena's character is that wonderful conflict she has, of fighting the monster she has inside her. I was speaking to somebody about how we don't do as many monsters on *Xena* as they do on *Hercules*, and I said, 'We do a monster every week; it's the one inside Xena that she's always fighting to keep under control.' This is a wonderfully deep character that we're exploring."

In *Xena*'s second season a more diverse mix of themes was explored, and shows in the vein of the light-hearted romps often seen on Hercules began to appear more frequently.

Given her choice, Lucy Lawless would prefer to see the dark side dealt with even more often. "The truth is, I would like to see Xena go a bit darker. Just when people think they've got her pegged as the 'man in the white hat,' I'd like to shake them out of their comfort zone and display more of the anti-hero. I think this will come through in the schism between Xena and Gabrielle. I've discovered that one of the nice qualities about Xena is that even when she's bad, you love her." Lawless has an interesting way of describing Xena. "She's a good person who doesn't think she is."

What is it that makes Xena so engagingly different? In the March 7, 1997, issue of *Entertainment Weekly*, Dana Eskenazi observed, "There hasn't been a female TV character who is totally independent of a male figure in her life." Not until *Xena*.

With the worldwide success of both *Hercules* and *Xena* it is only natural that the creators are often asked if they have another one waiting in the wings for a time slot to open up. In response executive producer Robert Tapert has stated they were not interested in producing yet another spin-off, particularly with all of the Hercules substitutes already cluttering the marketplace. "I just don't know if we need another mythological superhero. The world has Sinbad and Tarzan…The *Baywatch* people are doing *Sinbad*, and of course there are a bunch of other rip-offs on the way. I mean, what are we going to do: 'Young Moses, Freedom Fighter'?"

Since that statement, a pilot has been announced for what is clearly positioned to be a new spin-off called *Young Hercules*, and an animated version of *Hercules* and *Xena* was scheduled for release in late 1997.

# DETAILS, DETAILS, DETAILS

Both *Hercules* and *Xena* are filmed in and around Auckland, New Zealand, one of that country's four major cities. Auckland is an industrial center, situated on the northern peninsula of the North Island.

The production team that produces both television series is headed by executive producers Sam Raimi and Rob Tapert whose partial credits have been listed previously. Co-executive producer R. J. Stewart worked on the TV series *Remington Steele* (1982–87) and *The Great Defender* (1995). Supervising producer Steven Sears has credits that include *The A-Team* (1983–87) and *Swamp Thing* (1990–93). The producer is Eric Gruendemann whose credits include the feature film *Evil Dead III: Army of Darkness,* and the co-producer is Liz Friedman. Coordinating producer Bernadette Joyce was a part of the Raimi team for the second and third *Darkman* motion pictures. The line producer, Chloe Smith, worked on the New Zealand film *The Piano* (1993) for which Holly Hunter won an Academy Award. The stirring music heard each week is the work of the talented Joseph LoDuca who also scored the *Evil Dead* films as well as the TV series *American Gothic* for Sam Raimi.

# PART

# 2

✧❖✧

# HERCULES:

# THE

# LEGENDARY

# JOURNEYS

# CHAPTER FOUR

# THE CAST

## KEVIN SORBO (Hercules)

Kevin Sorbo, star of *Hercules: The Legendary Journeys*, stands 6' 3", weighs 215 pounds, and has blue eyes and light brown hair. He is by all accounts a modest man. He says that whenever he sees a Hercules action figure in a store window or clutched in a young fan's hands, he has to stop and remind himself: "Hey, that's me!"

The journey from his hometown of Mound, Minnesota, to Aukland, New Zealand, where the series is filmed, while not quite legendary, has had some interesting twists and turns. He was born in Mound on September 24, 1958, the son of Lynn and Ardis Sorbo. His parents, of Scandinavian descent, instilled in him a sense of traditional old-country values. He also inherited from them the good humor that kept him going during the lean years and that has made him such a likable figure both on screen and off.

Raised with four siblings in the suburbs of Mound, Sorbo first realized he wanted to be an actor when he was only eleven years of age. "My parents brought me to a play," he once told a pair of youthful reporters from *Kidsday*. "It was a musical called *Oklahoma!* I saw it, and that was *it*. It made me laugh, it made me cry. That's when I said, 'Wow, I want to do that to people.' I knew then that I wanted to be an actor. I did plays all through junior high and high school."

The high school in question was Mound West Tonka High School, where his father taught biology and mathematics. Sorbo's mother worked as a professional nurse.

## A DIFFERENT PATH

Despite his love of acting, as a young man Sorbo never really considered it a career option. It just didn't seem possible that a guy from the sticks could make a living doing that, no matter how much he loved it. So when he went to the University of Minnesota and Moorhead State, he majored in marketing and advertising instead of acting. The dream, however, refused to die. One day, sitting in a college marketing class, Sorbo found that he couldn't concentrate on his studies. The only thing on his mind was the nagging fact that he wasn't following his dream. It was then that he vowed to give his real vocation a fighting chance.

"I loved MSU and the campus," he later explained. "But personally it was a frustrating period for me. I spent most of my time in lifting weights and playing basketball. To this day I kick myself for not having the guts then to admit what I wanted to do—act."

Following college he went to Dallas where he found work in TV commercials. His first serious acting job on TV was three lines on a 1980 episode of the nighttime soap opera *Dallas* when he was twenty-one. He also appeared on an episode of *Murder She Wrote* ("A Virtual Murder") in 1983.

He fell in love with a model he met in Dallas and, at the age of twenty-four, he went to Europe in order to be closer to her. While on the Continent, he studied acting and did various TV commercials. Like many romances, this one eventually cooled, and Sorbo returned to the U.S. in 1986 and headed for California where he could pursue his career more seriously. Almost immediately he was cast in a commercial that was shot in Australia. He loved the country down under so much he stayed on another six months, doing commercials and appearing in a few plays.

When he returned to the U.S., he landed a small role on the short-lived soap opera *Santa Barbara* as well as a recurring role on the series *First and Ten*, a sports comedy that ran on HBO. He also appeared in the 1992 TV movie *Condition: Critical* and in the 1994 feature film *Slaughter of the Innocents*. He auditioned for, but did not get, the lead roles in the TV pilots for *The X-Files*, *NYPD Blue*, and *Lois & Clark: The New Adventures of Superman*. He did manage to land guest-starring roles on such series as *Cybill* (as Zsa Zsa Gabor's boy toy) and *The Commish*. Even with his mounting list of credits, he kept missing his chance at a major breakthrough role.

"Any actor who gets work is lucky," Sorbo told the *Roanoke Times Spec-*

*tator.* "It's like being struck by lightning to get a job. Also if you get a hit. I got struck by lightning twice, and I lived to tell about it."

## IT'S A LIVING

While he was waiting for his personal bolt of lightning, Sorbo did what most actors do to support themselves. "I didn't even move to L.A. until I was twenty-eight. I used to work as a bouncer and a bartender. Now I don't like being around smoke and drunks at all. I just get this funny feeling in my stomach."

If you brought together all the actors who made ends meet by working as bouncers, bartenders, and waiters, you'd need a restaurant the size of Nebraska. An even larger venue would be needed if you brought together all the actors who did commercials. Kevin Sorbo would be included, having appeared in 150 of them including spots for BMW, Jim Beam, Budweiser, Diet Coke, Pert Shampoo, Lexus, an MTV hockey game, and Target department stores as well as a public service announcement about AIDS.

"When I came out here [to Los Angeles] in 1986, commercials kept me alive. I was very fortunate that I shot a lot of commercials that paid the bills for me. That allowed me the free time to go to acting classes that I wanted to be involved in, to concentrate on the career. I knew the downside of the business when I came out here. I had a good eight years of 'too old', 'too tall,' 'too short.' It's hard to take that rejection and not take it personally. I just sort of reached a space in myself and realized that my time would come, that there's a lot of work out there. I got past the point of being crazy jealous of other people working. The minute I dropped out of acting class and stopped hearing the voices of teachers and other actors telling me how I should be doing things, I started working."

## THE BREAKTHROUGH ROLE

At last he was shown a script for a new show being developed by Sam Raimi and Robert Tapert. It was called *Hercules: The Legendary Journeys.* "When I first got the script I laughed," Sorbo told a reporter from *The Denver Post.* "I thought, 'You have *got* to be kidding.'"

Despite his misgivings, he was encouraged by the call-backs to read and re-read for the part of the ancient Greco-Roman hero. He later joked that the process dragged on so long, "I didn't even want the part any more!"

At first it was a lot of hard work, and the job took Sorbo away from his family and off to distant New Zealand. Long, difficult workdays ensued, many running twelve hours (some running longer than sixteen hours) as he filmed the original *Hercules* TV movies. Sorbo spent eight months in New Zealand filming the five two-hour television movies, which featured veteran actor Anthony Quinn as his divine father Zeus, King of the Gods.

Even after the production team had worked out the kinks and *Hercules* went to series, it still wasn't easy. *Hercules* continues to be filmed in New Zealand for ten months of the year, and the days are filled with stunts, sword fights, and strenuous action scenes. Despite the heavy schedule, Kevin Sorbo still ends his day with a workout. "If I don't get a regular workout, I get irritable," Sorbo has admitted. "It's my personal drug. I don't party a lot. I don't drink that much. I find working out is very relaxing for me, a way to let go of stress."

During the first season of the series, Sorbo was so involved with his work that he didn't have much time to realize the amount of fame he had already garnered. In New Zealand, for example, people often recognized him on the street though they had never seen *Hercules* because it was not on in New Zealand yet. They knew him from a commercial for Jim Beam whiskey with a cowboy theme, a memento from his long years as a commercial actor that caught up with him almost halfway around the world from home. (Kevin Sorbo still gets residuals from that particular job, which was a popular ad in Asia, Australia, and New Zealand long before the *Hercules* mania swept the globe.)

If there is any drawback to being *Hercules*, it is the amount of time Sorbo has to spend away from home. During the two months of the year when the show isn't filming, he likes to come back to the U.S. and spend time with old friends. He even turned down an invitation to appear on *The Tonight Show With Jay Leno* in order to fully enjoy his time off. "I mean Jay Leno, he just seems like the nicest guy, but I just really want to take some vacation with my high school buddies. Hey, they're my three closest friends. I've known them for thirty years."

Right from the start executive producer Robert Tapert felt that Sorbo could take the series all the way, and he told Kevin that he hoped the actor was ready to live in New Zealand for the next five years. When Universal contracted for the show to be a weekly one-hour series rather than a continuation of the two-hour movies, Kevin began looking for a more permanent dwelling in Auckland. "I want three bedrooms, not huge. I need a porch, a verandah, so I can sit and wave to the neighbors and strum my guitar. I mean, I grew up in a small town and it's just a Norman Rockwell, *Saturday Evening Post* kind of thing. Music I like to strum: Eagles, Dan Fogelberg, James Taylor, Garth Brooks, Vince Gill, etcetera. I'm a mellow soul. What can I say?"

As for the inevitable question as to whether Hercules will ever remarry on the TV show, Sorbo was quite candid when he stated, "I don't think the writing team will have Herc remarry. I could be wrong, but I do believe they feel it is the best for the character and I must say I agree. It's that lonesome dove appeal. Major Nelson should have never married Jeannie [on *I Dream of Jeannie*]. Sam marry Diane on *Cheers*? I don't think so. Got to keep the man single. Gives them a better story line to write from."

Interestingly, Hercules does remarry for a brief period in the third-season episode "When a Man Loves a Woman" (H-51), and the actress Sorbo marries, Sam Jenkins, was his real-life girlfriend. (She even went with him to Slovakia when he filmed *Kull the Conqueror* in 1996.) And while Kevin was able to negotiate only a few guest appearances for her before her character was killed off, she was brought back to life again a few episodes later in "The End of the Beginning" (H-55). Those who feel that Sorbo gave an outstanding performance in these particular episodes will now appreciate why.

Recently Kevin Sorbo answered some questions from the Hercules Netforum on the Internet. Regarding co-star Michael Hurst, he revealed, "Michael Hurst and I are good friends off the set as well. He is a good man and a lot of fun to hang out with. We do the dinner thing when we can, grab a few brews, and discuss those manly things like sports and how we could solve the world's problems."

## STUNTS AND ACCIDENTS

Although Lucy Lawless's horseback accident while rehearsing a gag for *The Tonight Show* is perhaps the most famous injury to a cast member, it is by no means the only one. While her injury happened off the set, both Sorbo and Hurst have been battered while filming. During an appearance on *Good Morning America*, Sorbo recalled, "There was a place where I had to fight another actor and he sort of followed my head down too far when my back was turned towards him. And we fight with real swords. They're a little dull, but they're real, and I got a nice three-inch gash and nine stitches to the back of the head."

Sorbo revealed that while he does many of his own on-camera stunts, he doesn't do any that are seriously dangerous. "The only thing I don't do is when they show somebody climbing up some rock, the face of a cliff, or something like that."

In order to help prepare for the role, Sorbo received martial arts training from Douglas Wong including sword and staff training. "Of course in a real kung fu or karate contest I'd get my butt kicked," Sorbo candidly admitted. "But we do connect here when we throw punches—and you feel it. I have learned to pull punches and miss by six inches, but I was just really into this one stunt recently and I threw an elbow out and hit a guy on the nose and he went down. And Michael [Hurst] broke an arm in a stunt about six weeks ago."

## STAR POWER

Initially, when the five two-hour movies were filmed, Anthony Quinn as Zeus brought star power to the program. Since then, the *Hercules* series has become so popular that Sorbo is now arguably more well known to the average television viewer than veteran film star Quinn. In an interview with Kinny Littlefield in the *Orange County Register*, Sorbo explained why the version of Hercules he plays works even though it is quite different from the traditional approach. "I guess I'm Hercules for an entire generation of people under twenty who were never exposed to him before. If you compare this Hercules to the old Hercules films [such as the 1959 and 1960 Steve Reeves flexflicks *Hercules* and *Hercules Unchained*], this one's more affable, more intelligent. He laughs, he stumbles. And he isn't afraid to make fun of himself."

Off the set Kevin Sorbo has contributed his services to the Words of Hope charity by recording an audiotape for BMP Audio entitled *Tales of Young Hercules*. While there is a regular commercial version of this tape available, Sorbo made a point of issuing a limited edition whose profits all went to the charity; he declined any payment for the project.

When Sorbo appeared on the television show *Good Morning America*, hostess Joan London good naturedly took him to task for the fact that Hercules' wife and children were killed off in the first episode of the series even though in the TV movies they were all one big happy family.

"We received a lot of letters on that," Sorbo replied somewhat sheepishly. "We didn't know that the movies would do as well as they did. The movies were received very well. But the producers couldn't have me being married, because if I'm married and I'm gone eleven months out of the year, it's not going to look real well."

In November 1996, when Kevin Sorbo appeared as a guest on *The Rosie O'Donnell Show*, he presented O'Donnell with a child's Hercules costume for her son Parker.

"Well," he joked, "you know I got it at a discount, because it's the day after Halloween."

O'Donnell asked the obvious question: do people ever really think that Sorbo *is* Hercules?

"It's happened a couple of times," he told her. "It happened one time when I was back home for Christmas. I was working out at a club with my brother, and these guys walked by and they were sorta going, 'Yo, Hercules!' But most people that would think I am are little children. I was in the airport in Los Angeles a few months back, and this little girl walked up. I was reading a book. And all of a sudden, this little hand goes on my shoulder and she whispers, 'Hercules, why are you here?' I told her, 'Well, you know, I have to catch a plane. I have to go back. I live in New Zealand now, that's where I shoot the series.' And she said, 'Oh.' She goes, 'You are my hero.' And seriously, I picked up the kid and I handed her back to her mother and said, 'When she's done with my heart, send it to New Zealand to Universal Studios.' She was beautiful."

During this same appearance, Sorbo plugged his extracurricular project, the movie version of Robert E. Howard's *Kull the Conqueror*, which he had just finished filming in Slovakia and Croatia. "The flight to our location was on Air Croatia. You really want to build up your frequent flier miles on that one. It was only about a forty minute flight to Croatia from Slovakia. When we landed, everyone broke into applause. And I looked at the guy next to me and I said, 'Excuse me, but isn't this a normal routine?' The plane goes up and then it comes back down and lands, right? It was just very strange. They erupted in applause!" Apparently, a successful landing was not something his fellow passengers took for granted.

Most would agree that Kevin Sorbo seems like a regular guy. And that's the main appeal of the Hercules character as well. Despite his super-human strength, Hercules projects good will, humor, and honesty—the same qualities that are so obvious in the man who brings him to life on television screens around the globe every week.

Sorbo's first starring role in a feature film was 1997's *Kull the Conqueror*, which also features Tia Carrere and Karina Lombard. Based on the char-acter created by Robert E. Howard, the original screenplay was written by Charles Edward Pogue. However, a dispute with the producer caused Pogue to leave the big-screen project, and the final result was not all that everyone hoped it would be.

When asked why he accepted a role so similar to Hercules, Sorbo said, "Everyone warned me about typecasting because the role isn't unlike Her-cules, but I'd gotten several scripts, and this was the best. If people liked *Conan*, they're going to love this. The action is bigger, and it's better written."

Kevin Sorbo would be the first to admit that though in *Hercules* he finally found his real breakthrough role, he regards it as a start on the road to his ultimate goal. "It's a great launching pad for my career, but I do want to grow beyond this. Eventually I'd really like to do romantic comedy. My heroes are Harrison Ford and Kevin Kline. I want to prove to myself and to others that I can do everything, especially to the people who said I'd never make it."

Sorbo has also tried out his directing skills on a few episodes of *Her-cules*, beginning with "The Apple" (H-30).


# MICHAEL HURST (Iolaus)


Born in Lancashire, England, in 1958, Michael Hurst moved with his family to Christchurch, New Zealand, at the age of fourteen. Michael soon became involved in his new school's theatrical projects and after high school trained at Christchurch's Court Theatre. After moving from Christchurch to the more cosmopolitan northern city of Auckland, he found new acting opportunities and joined Theatre Corporate where he played a variety of roles from Scrooge in *A Christmas Carol* to Mozart in *Amadeus*.

Movie roles also came his way and he appeared in such films as *Constance* (1984), *Death Warmed Up* (1985), *Dangerous Orphans* (1985), and *Desperate Remedies* (1993). In 1992 he played French artist Henri Toulouse l'Autrec in *The Footstep Man*.

## TALENT AND TRAINING

By the time Michael landed a role in the first *Hercules* two-hour TV movie, the 5'7" actor had developed a variety of theatrical skills from traditional singing and dancing to fencing and fight choreography.

Hurst is also a Shakespearean actor. He's played Hamlet and helped mount a production of *Othello*, both in Auckland at the Watershed Theatre, a theater company that Hurst co-founded.

Hurst's depth of experience and training came in handy during the third season of *Hercules* when Kevin Sorbo needed time off to finish shooting his starring role in *Kull the Conqueror*. His absence meant shooting some episodes in which the title character was little seen. But Hurst was up to the challenge.

"Kevin isn't in the episode we've just finished shooting—'Beauty and the Beast' (H-40)—at all. It's been great to explore that action hero thing, but, of course, because I'm Iolaus, I can't do the things Hercules does, so it's a little more quirky. We're doing a sequel to 'King for a Day' (H-32), so I'm going to be playing two characters again, which I'm looking forward to immensely, and the one after that we're calling 'Hercules Lite' (H-48), because Kevin is only in two or three scenes. I've enjoyed it a lot, although I miss Kevin, I must say."

Hurst also got to direct an episode for the first time in the third season. "It's called 'The Mercenary' (H-38), and it wasn't so much a learning curve for me as a learning perpendicular. It's a darker, more serious episode, and I was very comfortable in getting performances out of people. I really had to put my money where my mouth was and trust that my vision would work on screen. I was delighted that the action sequences especially worked out really well." That episode was so well-received by the producers that it became the first episode in the third season even though Iolaus didn't appear in it.

## SERIOUS STORY LINES

While comedy has largely been the mainstay of *Hercules: The Legendary Journeys*, the series does stray into more serious territory from time to time, something that Hurst appreciates. "We recently did a sequel to 'The Enforcer' (H-26) where Iolaus is killed and Hercules has to deal with it, and I think there's a move now to create more of these dramatic situations. This show can bear a lot of extreme, slapstick, over-the-top comedy, but it can also bear the more tragic or serious aspects. In fact, 'Mercenary' has almost no humor in it at all. It's a really serious episode. Hercules gets his arm smashed up right at the start, so he's carrying a major injury the whole episode. That was another highlight for me, not just from the directing point of view, but seeing Kevin move into an area where I saw the kind of real action star in him."

As Iolaus, Hurst is the best friend of Hercules and appears in most episodes. In the episode "The Warrior Princess" (H-9), the evil Xena seduces Iolaus and tries to turn him against Hercules. In "Prometheus" (X-8), the reformed Xena encounters Iolaus once again and apologizes for her earlier misdeeds. Xena's sidekick, Gabrielle, is clearly attracted to Iolaus in "Prometheus" and turns to him when she thinks that Xena is dead in "The Greater Good" (X-21).

Iolaus has shown that he can handle himself without depending on Hercules and has been featured as the main character in the episodes "King for a Day" (H-32), its sequel "Long Live the King" (H-48), and "Beauty and the Beast" (H-40). He encounters an identical cousin named Orestes in "King for a Day" who later is killed in "Long Live the King."

Hercules and Iolaus tend to think alike on many things and he is always ready to fight alongside Hercules and to defend his actions. In "Judgment Day" (H-52) when Hercules is accused of murdering his bride, Selena, Iolaus stands by him and helps devise a plan to expose the true assassin.

The background of Iolaus remained pretty sketchy until the third season when in "Love Takes a Holiday" (H-40) we learn that the father of Iolaus was Skouros who was killed in battle. We actually get to meet Skouros in "Not Fade Away" (H-42) when Iolaus dies and finds himself in the Underworld while Hercules works to get Iolaus released. Skouros was a professional soldier who was away from home a great deal, which his family came to resent. After Skouros was killed in battle, Iolaus' mother remarried, but to a poet, not a warrior. While in Tartarus, Iolaus has a reconciliation with this father.

# BRUCE CAMPBELL (Autolycus)

Autolycus is the self-proclaimed "King of Thieves," a character who has made frequent appearances on both *Hercules* and *Xena* and has become a popular character on both series. Not only has he made a powerful impression on the viewers, but on the star of *Hercules* as well.

"I like Bruce," Kevin Sorbo told Ian Spelling in *Starlog*. "We hang out every time he comes down here. For me, if I were in L.A., we would hang out all the time. He's a great guy and a good friend. He makes me laugh. He's a funny guy, very high-energy on the set. After Bruce leaves the set, people are still quoting things he said months later."

## PERSONAL HISTORY

Bruce Lorne Campbell says that he was born in "the year of the Edsel," June 22, 1958, in Royal Oak, Michigan. He is the youngest of three brothers, and he became interested in acting by observing how much fun his father was having performing in local community theater productions. His first significant role came at age fourteen when he had to step into the role of the young prince in a production of *The King and I* when the regular actor became ill. He continued working in community theater and even appeared with his father in a production of *South Pacific*. Campbell's father directed him in the Tennessee Williams' play *Sweet Bird of Youth* in which he played the role of Chance Wayne.

During one summer Campbell volunteered at the Traverse City Cherry County Playhouse in Northern Michigan, a well known summer-stock theater. Bruce spent long hours building sets, worked as an assistant stage manager, and at one point, while playing bit parts in some of the productions, was a dresser for various visiting actors including Tom Smothers. Years later he would run into these actors, but none remembered the kid from summer stock.

Bruce Campbell's friendship with Sam Raimi, the executive producer of *Hercules* and *Xena*, pre-dates the creation of the series by more than two decades. Bruce and Sam Raimi met in a high school drama class in 1975 and became fast friends.

When Bruce graduated, he went to Michigan State University where he met the guy who was rooming with one of Sam's brothers. His new friend was Robert Tapert who, twenty years later would share with Bruce's old high school buddy, Sam Raimi, the credit of executive producer on *Xena*.

Bruce only lasted six months at Michigan State. Earlier he'd been given a super-eight millimeter camera, which fascinated him to the point that he decided he'd rather make films than go to school.

## FILMS AND THE FUTURE

So Campbell, Raimi, and Tapert made films, amateur films with titles like *The Happy Valley Kid*, *The Blind Waiter*, and *It's Murder*. The one that would actually set them on a career path grew out of a super-eight film they did together in which Bruce Campbell played a monster. It was the core of the idea they would turn into the feature film *The Evil Dead*.

In 1979 the three friends got together with some businessmen and raised $350,000 to make a feature length version of the super-eight horror film they had concocted, which Campbell would star in and Raimi would direct. Campbell also served as an executive producer on the film. It took four years to get *The Evil Dead* completed, but it was worth it. The film became a video hit in England even before they could finalize their U.S. distribution deal.

At the Cannes Film Festival in 1983 it got positive reaction. Horror novelist Stephen King liked the film so much that he wrote an article for *The Twilight Zone* magazine proclaiming that *The Evil Dead* was "the most ferociously original horror film of the year." Largely on the strength of that Stephen King quote, the producers made a deal with New Line Cinema to distribute *The Evil Dead* in the U.S. where it soon achieved cult status.

Sam Raimi then got the backing for a second film called *Crimewave* (1985), which was co-produced by Bruce Campbell and written and directed by Raimi. After teaming up with filmmakers Joel and Ethan Coen, Sam Raimi struck a deal with Dino De Laurentiis to finance *Evil Dead II: Dead By Dawn*. Filmed in 1986 and once again starring Bruce Campbell, it was released in 1987. *Evil Dead II* was almost a satire of the first film. The original had achieved notoriety not only for being truly scary, but also for being truly gory. In *Evil Dead II* the gore was so over the top that the movie looked like a cross between a Three Stooges comedy and a Monty Python film.

With *Evil Dead II* Bruce Campbell began to receive offers to appear in other Hollywood productions. Relocating to Los Angeles, Bruce got cast in featured roles in *Maniac Cop* (1988), *Moontrap* (1989), and *Sundown: The Vampire in Retreat* (1991). On the set of *Mindwarp* (1991), yet another low budget science fiction film, Bruce met Ida Gearon, a costume designer. They later married.

Campbell was co-executive producer of *Lunatics: A Love Story* (1992) and the biker film *Easy Wheels* (1989). He reteamed with Sam Raimi and Robert Tapert to make the third *Evil Dead* entry, *Army of Darkness* (1993) for Universal Studios. Immediately after that, Bruce had a major supporting role in the Coen brothers film *The Hudsucker Proxy* (1994) and landed the starring role on the Fox western series spoof *The Adventures of Brisco County Jr.,* which only lasted one year (1993–94).

## RETURNING TO THE FOLD

Campbell first worked on *Hercules: The Legendary Journeys* as a director. He didn't appear as his signature character, Autolycus, until the episode titled "King of Thieves" (H-14). Autolycus made his transition to *Xena* in "The Royal Couple of Thieves" (X-17) written by Steve Sears. Sears really likes the character as Campbell plays him. He recalled, "When *Xena* first premiered, the *Hercules* episode preceding it was the Autolycus episode, and I remember we all got together at the Universal Hilton and watched it, and I said, 'This guy is great!' I was really pleased when I told Rob I wanted to do a comedy episode, and he said they wanted to bring Autolycus into *Xena*. Then it was a case of putting Xena in a farcical situation where she's subjugated by this guy who's really arrogant and playing the comedy of these two personalities who are forced to work together.

"I remember sitting there watching dailies," Sears added, "and a line would be coming up and I was thinking, 'If the delivery isn't there....' And then he'd give the delivery! I still crack up when Autolycus is running up the stairs at the beginning and Xena pulls the rug out...He falls down and says, 'This is not good!'"

Producer Robert Tapert also likes the Autolycus character. He related, "That was an interesting episode because there were some who didn't like the fact that Xena didn't get back enough at Autolycus. They didn't like to see their hero put as the second fiddle, to constantly be hit upon sexually and not be able to strike back. But our intent was to do a farcical comedy." Even though Autolycus appears often on *Xena*, including in the key episode "The Quest" (X-37), he still turns up on *Hercules* when least expected.

Bruce has tended to play characters who have a strong humorous side to them, but the actor was allowed to show his dramatic capacity on an episode of *Homicide: Life on the Street* in the 1996–97 season. In feature films Campbell has also appeared in *Congo* (1995), *Escape from L.A.* (1997), and *Men in Black* (1997). Fans of the first *Darkman* film will recall that when the title character assumes an unknown face and disappears into the crowd in the final scene of the film, the person we see walking away who turns and looks behind him is none other than Bruce Campbell.

Many fans have asked whether Autolycus has a future in a possible spin-off series. However, executive producer Rob Tapert explained, "I don't want to get into agent politics, but there was an opportunity to make a spin-off with him, and for a whole host of reasons it didn't happen. Bruce has a deal at Disney, and we're at Universal, so he can get out here and there to do an episode, but overall he's working at Disney to develop his own series. I love Autolycus and I talked to Bruce three weeks ago saying, 'Hey, come down and be in one of our episodes!' We need a commitment from Bruce three months ahead of time to write an episode for him, and a lot of times he can't give that, so it's very difficult to write for him."

# SUPPORTING CHARACTERS

The following characters form the supporting pantheon of players in *Hercules: The Legendary Journeys*. Some may have appeared in only one episode, but they are nonetheless an important part of the background and history of Hercules as presented in this television series.

ALCMENE a.k.a. ALCHEME (Jennifer Ludlam, Elizabeth Hawthorne, Liddy Holloway)

She is the mother of Hercules and the daughter of Electryon and Anaxo. Her two sons are Hercules and his half-brother Iphicles. Alcmene is sweet-natured and supportive of both of her sons. She first appeared in "Hercules and the Amazon Women" (HM-1).

APHRODITE (Alexandra Tydings)

Even though she is the goddess of love, she acts mostly like a petulant Valley Girl. She is found on both *Hercules* and *Xena*, but mostly on *Hercules*. Her son is Cupid. She is very protective of her shrines, which Gabrielle is able to use to her advantage in "For Him the Bell Tolls" (X-40). Her first appearance is in "The Apple" (H-30).

ARES (Mark Newham, Kevin Smith)

The god of war and the half-brother of Hercules is introduced in "The Festival of Dionysus" (H-4). It is Ares who takes away the strength of Hercules when Herc wants to marry Serena, the Golden Hind, in "When a Man Loves a Woman" (H-51). After Serena dies, Hercules goes back in time to force Ares to save Serena's life by giving her permanent human form in "The End of the Beginning" (H-55). The relationship between Hercules and Ares has become that of blood enemies.

ARTEMIS (Rhonda McHardy)

She is the Goddess of the hunt and defender of animals, womanhood, and children. She is the daughter of the gods Leto and Zeus and, therefore, the half-sister of Hercules. Her first appearance is in "The Apple" (H-30).

ATALANTA (Cory Everson)

This huntress and blacksmith is almost as strong as Hercules. She wins the first Olympics in "Let the Games Begins" (H-29), and begins the tradition of the Laurel Wreath with the help of Salmoneus. She makes her first appearance in "Ares" (H-5).

ATHENA (Amanda Lister)

This goddess of war and wisdom is sister to Ares who represents the most destructive elements of war. She is first seen in "The Apple" (H-30).

CALLISTO (Hudson Leick)

Hera frees Callisto from Tartarus (the place of punishment in the Underworld) in order to lure Hercules to his death. Callisto poisons the guests at a surprise party for Hercules and offers to give him the antidote only if he comes with her to Tartarus. When she fails to kill him, she is trapped in Tartarus again. Viewers will see her in "Surprise" (H-49).

## CHARON (Michael Hurst!)

The decrepit ferryman of the River Styx in the Underworld realm ruled by Hades first appears in the telefilm *Hercules and the Underworld* (HM-4) and in the series episode "The Other Side" (H-21).

## DEIANEIRA (Renee O'Connor, Tawny Kitaen)

The wife of Hercules is introduced in the telefilm *Hercules and the Circle of Fire* (HM-3). In the following two-hour movie, *Hercules and the Underworld* (HM-4), some years have passed and Hercules and Deianeira have three children. In an attempt to kill Hercules, Hera hurls a fireball at his home, but ends up killing Deianeira and the children instead. After burying his family Hercules leaves on a quest to seek revenge on Hera.

The writers of the series will occasionally come up with some form of magic or time travel that allows Hercules to see his lost family. But it is always only for a brief time and it is painful for him because he knows that until he dies he cannot be truly reunited with them. When Hercules is planning to marry Serena in "When a Man Loves a Woman" (H-51), he goes to see Deianeira in the Elysian Fields to tell her of his marriage plans. At first she is very upset, but she comes to see that Hercules must live his life and she and the children even appear to him at his wedding.

## DEMETER (Sarah Wilson)

She is "Mother Earth" and controls the elements such as wind and storms. She is the sister of Zeus and Hades and the daughter of Cronus and Rhea. Demeter's daughter is Persephone. When Persephone is kidnapped by Hades, Demeter threatens to unleash her fury in the form of mighty storms unless Hercules agrees to go to the Underworld and bring her back. She is introduced in "The Other Side" (H-21).

## ECHIDNA (Bridget Hoffman)

She is known as the Mother of All Monsters. Her children include Hydra, the Serpent, and other creatures slain by Hercules. She is first seen in "The Mother of All Monsters" (H-20). At first Echidna wants to slay Hercules and his mother, but she makes peace with him after Hercules finds and returns her husband, Typhon, to her.

## FALAFEL (Paul Norell)

This salesman has all sorts of business schemes from running a catering business to opening a gift shop near Mount Vulcan. He makes his first appearance in "The Wedding of Alcmene" (H-34).

## GLADIUS (Tony Todd)

This former gladiator is held in bondage by an evil king until he is freed by Hercules so he can return to his wife and child. He is the lead character in "The Gladiator" (H-20).

## HADES (Mark Ferguson; Erik Thompson)

This God is the ruler of the Underworld (which includes Tartarus and the Elysian Fields). Hercules has several encounters with Hades, notably in the telefilm *Hercules and the Underworld* (HM-4) and the series episode "The Other Side" (H-21). Both Hercules and Xena have found themselves at odds with Hades.

## HERA (??)

Although Hera is never seen, her disembodied voice and all-seeing eyes represent this lead antagonist's hatred for Hercules, the illegitimate son of her husband, Zeus. Hera's jealousy manifests itself as an all-consuming obsession with the death of Hercules, which accounts for the numerous attempts on his life that are crucial plot-points in many of the episodes. In fact, the whole structure of the series changed when Hera hurled a fireball that narrowly missed Hercules but killed his wife and children in "The Wrong Path" (H-1). Hera most often makes her presence known as a voice emanating from some magically charged object such as an enchanted mirror. The only times Hera actually *appears* is when she inhabits the body of another as in "Reign of Terror" (H-56), or when she appears as two enormous eyes suspended in space as in *Hercules and the Amazon Women* (HM-1).

IPHICLES (Kevin Smith)

The half brother of Hercules, Iphicles is the son of Alcmene and a mortal man. (Hercules is the son of Alcmene and Zeus.) Bitter resentment is Iphicles defining personality trait. In the episode entitled "What's in a Name?" (H-16), Iphicles masquerades as Hercules to win the love of a woman who, it turns out, actually loves Iphicles for himself. In "The Wedding of Alcmeme" (H-34) when Jason marries the widowed mother of Hercules and Iphicles, Iphicles is crowned King of Corinth [not to be confused with another King Iphicles who is introduced in "The Festival of Dionysus" (H-4)]. To further confuse things, in Greek mythology Iphicles is the father of Hercules' friend Iolaus, a relationship that has been ignored by the TV series.

JASON (Jeffery Thomas)

Hercules sailed with Jason and the Argonauts when they retrieved the Golden Fleece for Hera, but that was years before the period in which the series is set. When we first encounter Jason, he has fallen on hard times and his old crew no longer trusts him. Thanks to the help of Hercules, a traitor is revealed and Jason is redeemed. Jason marries Alcmene, mother of Hercules and his half-brother Iphicles, and names Iphicles as his successor. This legendary hero appears in "Once a Hero" (H-27) and "The Wedding of Alcmene" (H-34).

KEFOR (James Croft)

He is the son of Deric, a Centaur, and Lyla, a human. Although driven into the forest when his house is burned, his family is redeemed with the help of Hercules and Zeus. He is introduced in "The Outcast" (H-18).

LYSIA (Lucy Lawless)

She is an important aide to Hippolyta, queen of the Amazons. She is fiercely loyal, but her dislike of men is tempered after she spends a night with Zeus. She appears in *Hercules and the Amazon Women* (HM-1).

LYLA (Lucy Lawless)

The human wife of Deric the Centaur, Lyla has a son by him called Kefor. Lyla is killed when a bigot sets her house on fire, but she is later resurrected by Zeus. She is introduced in "As Darkness Falls" (H-6) and also appears in "The Outcast" (H-18). As an inside joke, Hercules and Salmoneus comment on her resemblance to Xena.

## ORESTES (Michael Hurst)

The look-a-like royal cousin of Iolaus (also played by Michael Hurst), Orestes is first seen in "King for a Day" (H-32). In a later episode, "Long Live the King" (H-48), Orestes is killed. Iolaus secretly substitutes himself for Orestes in both sequences: the first time when Orestes is drugged by his brother Minos to prevent his royal wedding to the Princess Niobe, the second time when Orestes is assassinated and he must adopt the disguise to unmask the assassin.

## NIOBE (Lisa Ann Hadley)

The bride of Orestes, she is seen in "King for a Day" (H-32) and in "Long Live the King" (H-48). She falls in love with Iolaus when he first masquerades as Orestes. When Orestes is killed, Iolaus confesses that he loves Niobe. He realizes, however, that he cannot remain with her without destroying the social order in her kingdom.

## PERSEPHONE (Andrea Croton)

The daughter of Demeter, Persephone is kidnapped by Hades and taken to the Underworld. As she acclimates to this new world, however, she comes to like it and falls in love with Hades. Hades agrees to allow her to spend six months of the year with her mother if she returns to spend the other six months with him. She is introduced to viewers in "The Other Side" (H-21).

## PROTEUS (Jane Cresswell)

This god can assume the form of any living thing. When a mortal woman rejects his advances, he frames her father for a crime. Hercules figures out the truth and defeats Proteus in battle. He can be seen in "Protean Challenge" (H-33).

## SALMONEUS (Robert Trebor)

A semi-regular on *Hercules*, Salmoneus is a fast-talking salesman with numerous get-rich-quick schemes who is introduced in "Eye of the Beholder" (H-2). In Xena's second appearance on *Hercules* when she makes the change from vicious warrior to defender of the oppressed, Salmoneus is the first to believe that she has truly changed her evil ways. He is also in another *Hercules* episode with Xena, "Unchained Heart" (H-13).

## STRIFE (Joel Tobeck)

He is an underhanded little bootlicker who assists Ares in his nefarious schemes. He is a godling but has no title, which vexes him to no end. He contributes greatly to the anguish of Hercules in "Encounter" (H-50), "When a Man Loves a Woman" (H-51), and "Judgment Day" (H-52). He turns out to be the one who killed Serena and framed Hercules for her murder.

## ZEUS (Anthony Quinn, Peter Vere-Jones)

If a god can be browbeaten by his wife, Zeus is that god. It all started when Zeus had a tryst with a mortal woman, Alcmene, which produced a son, Hercules. Unfortunately for Zeus, he also had a wife back at Mount Olympus who happened to be the most powerful goddess in the universe.

Goddesses do not take infidelity lightly. In the case of Zeus's wife, Hera, that means trying to kill his illegitimate son, Hercules, every chance she gets. And when you're immortal, that's a lot of chances.

Sometimes Zeus intercedes on Hercules' behalf, and other times he refuses to help because his wife wouldn't like it if she were to find out.

Zeus first appears in the telefilm *Hercules and the Amazon Women* (HM-1). His most recent appearance is in "Judgment Day" (H-52) when he restores Hercules' powers to him after Ares has taken them away.

# THE
# MADE-FOR-TV MOVIES

The *Hercules* series of five made-for-television movies, which were each two hours long, became the television series *Hercules: The Legendary Journeys* in early 1995. *Hercules* is a co-production of MCA Television, Renaissance Pictures, and Action Pack.

## PRODUCTION CREDITS

Created by Christian Williams; co-producer: David Eick; producer: Eric Gruendemann; supervising producer: Robert Bielak; co-executive producer: John Schulian; executive producer: Robert Tapert; executive producer: Sam Raimi; music: Joseph LoDuca

## REGULARS

Kevin Sorbo (Hercules); Michael Hurst (Iolaus)

### HM-1: HERCULES AND THE AMAZON WOMEN (1994)

CREDITS: Teleplay by Julie Selbo, Andrew Dettmann, and Daniel Truly; directed by Bill L. Norton

GUEST STARS: Anthony Quinn (Zeus), Roma Downey (Hippolyta), Lloyd Scott (Pithus), Lucy Lawless (Lysia), Jennifer Ludlam (Alcmene)

MYTHOLOGICAL BASIS: There are certain names and events from the original Greek mythology that are key points in this made-for-television movie. Hercules is the illegitimate son of the god Zeus and the mortal woman, Alcmene. His half-brother is the mortal Iphicles, his stepbrother is Ares, the god of war, and his stepmother is the goddess Hera. Because Hercules is her husband's illegitimate son, Hera resents Hercules and makes many attempts on his life. Occasionally, Zeus intercedes on his son's behalf, but more often he allows events to take their course.

The central action of this television movie draws its inspiration from one of the famed Labors of Hercules, his quest for the Golden Girdle. This girdle is a sash, or belt, which originally belonged to Ares but is in the possession of the Amazon queen, Hippolyte (spelled *Hippolyta* in the credits). The Amazons are daughters of Ares who worship their war-loving father, and Artemis, the goddess of virginity and feminine power. When Hercules comes to steal the girdle, Hippolyte falls in love with him and he with her. Hera intervenes and causes the other Amazons to attack Hercules. During the fighting Hippolyte is killed.

In the original Greek myth Iolaus is the son of Hercules' half-brother, Iphicles (and therefore Hercules' nephew), who becomes Hercules' charioteer and accompanies him on many of his labors and later war campaigns. The Iolaus who appears in the first made-for-TV movie is not related to Hercules, but he does fill a similar role, that of sidekick and traveling companion.

STORYLINE: Hercules and Iolaus encounter a ferocious tribe of Amazons, and in the ensuing battle Iolaus is killed. Hercules escapes and comes up with a unique defense strategy for the nearby village. When the Amazons attack, they find that their opposition is not an army of vicious killers, but friendly men. Very friendly men. The warrior women cease their attack on what has turned out to be such an attractive enemy.

Hera takes over Hippolyta's body and commands the Amazons to leave no man alive. Hercules realizes that Hera has taken control of the queen's body and refuses to defeat Hera by killing Hippolyta. Hera hurls Hippolyta to her death in a waterfall.

Although the accidental death of Hippolyta is common to many versions of the original myth (in some she is accidentally killed by an arrow shot by her sister), in the television movie Hercules appeals to Zeus to use his special powers to undo the deaths of both Hippolyta and Iolaus.

OBSERVATIONS: This first Hercules adventure establishes that Zeus, king of the gods, can alter time. It is made clear, however, that this deity is reluctant to do such a deed very often. (When Hercules embarks on time-travel again—in the series' third season—it has nothing to do with Zeus.) Veteran actor Anthony Quinn, a two-time Academy Award winner, was contracted to appear as Zeus, presumably because Universal Studios felt that a prominent performer such as Quinn was necessary to provide the star power necessary to attract TV viewers to watch a movie filled with so many unknowns. Ironically, thanks to the success of the *Hercules* series, Kevin Sorbo is now probably better known than Anthony Quinn.

In this first *Hercules* TV adventure the death of Iolaus does not have the impact it might because it is not clearly established that he will be the hero's faithful sidekick and will appear in most episodes of the series.

In this first movie the design for the costume that Hercules will wear is not fully established and will be refined in the future. It does establish that Hercules never carries a sword and must rely on his ingenuity and sheer strength when combating his foes.

HIGHLIGHTS: Good-natured Hercules horses around with his childhood friend Iolaus and, in a lighter moment, lifts him off the ground and holds him over his head.

The special effects used in creating the Hydra and its battle with the son of Zeus are the first of many gems of visual magic to be seen throughout the series. There are actually many more monsters in the early productions.

TRIVIA: For those intrigued with Kevin Sorbo's hunky anatomy, this episode has a screen moment when he is buck naked.

The supporting role of Lysia the Amazon is played by an actress named Lucy Lawless. At this point, you may not have heard of her. But you soon will. As for Roma Downey, cast here as Hippolyta, she will gain greater fame as Monica, one of the heavenly beings in the fantasy TV series *Touched by an Angel*, which began its successful run in the fall of 1994.

# HM-2: HERCULES AND THE LOST KINGDOM (1994)

CREDITS: Teleplay by Christian Williams; directed by Harley Cokeliss

GUEST STARS: Anthony Quinn (Zeus), Renee O'Connor
(Deianeira), Robert Trebor (Waylin), Eric Close (Telmon),
Barry Hill (King Ilus)

SUPPORTING CAST: Nathaniel Lees (Blue Monk), Onno Boelee
(Gargan the Giant), Elizabeth Hawthorne (Queen Omphale)

MYTHOLOGICAL BASIS: This made-for-television movie makes use
of a number of familiar mythological characters, events, and places, which
have been slightly altered as they are woven into the story. In this movie
Troy is a mist-shrouded, lost kingdom. In the Hercules myth most often
associated with Troy, it is not a lost kingdom by any means, but a major
city-state in the throes of a terrible drought. The ruler, King Laomedon, has
offended Apollo and Poseidon who have caused the drought and un-
leashed a sea monster to menace the coast. Laomedon has his daughter
Hesione bound to a rock as a sacrificial offering to the sea creature in hopes
of appeasing the gods. Hercules offers to kill the monster in exchange for
two magical horses, but after he kills the beast and rescues Hesione,
Laomedon refuses to pay. In retaliation Hercules conquers Troy and kills
Laomedon and all his sons except one who later becomes known as King
Priam, ruler of Troy during the time of the Trojan War.

In the television movie Deianeira is introduced as a feisty young
maiden who admires Hercules. In the Herculean myth Deianeira, the half-
sister of a famous warrior, Meleager, is sought out by Hercules to become
his wife. When Hercules goes to Tartarus to perform his last labor, the capture of Cerberus, he encounters the spirit of Meleager who asks him to go
back to the land of the living and marry his sister, Deianeira.

Omphale is another character with roots in the original Hercules myth.
In one version as penance for killing his wife and children, Hercules
becomes Omphale's slave for eight years during which time she forces him
to wear women's clothing and do the spinning. In another version Hercules wears her clothing to foil Pan who has fallen in love with Omphale.
When Pan sneaks into Omphale's bed to seduce her, he finds that it is
really Hercules, disguised in her clothes, he is in bed with. Hercules
promptly throws Pan out of the palace.

STORY LINE: Hercules intecepts a messenger from the lost kingdom of Troy who has been sent for help. After consulting with Zeus, Hercules goes in search of the device known as the "One True Compass," which will lead him through the daunting mists to Troy.

In his travels Hercules rescues a young woman named Deianeira who is being prepared for sacrifice. In this movie none of Deianeira's mythological back-story is explained, but the groundwork is laid for the future romantic relationship between the two characters. Deianeira accompanies Hercules on his quest.

Hercules obtains the One True Compass from Queen Omphale of Lydia by being her slave for one day (not the three-to-eight years that the myth records). In another echo of the original myth he goes on to battle a sea monster and eventually reaches the lost kingdom where he leads the citizens of Troy against the Blue Cult of Hera.

OBSERVATIONS: Although this episode introduces the character of Deianeira (performed by Renee O'Connor), it is actress Tawny Kitaen who will take over the part in a later installment when she briefly becomes the wife of Hercules.

Also to be noted is that this episode contains the first instance (but certainly not the last) in which Hercules is swallowed on-camera by a sea serpent. It happens again in "The Wedding of Alcmene" (H-34).

This episode introduces the first of many computer-graphic-imaging (CGI) special-effects monsters that will appear often during the first couple years of the series. Whenever the story slows down, up pops a wild-eyed monster. The special effects are surprisingly good, and since the *Hercules* series wasn't initially big on character-driven storylines (until they proved effective on the *Xena* series), monsters were the order of the day. Since this was a new series and an unknown quantity, the monsters were the gimmick used to hook the audience and launch the series.

HIGHLIGHTS: Hercules fights more monsters including Gargan the giant, and his skirmish with the Ninja priest is indeed impressive.

TRIVIA: Hercules is seen in yet another costume. Obviously the wardrobe designers had not yet settled on the official garb for Hercules.

This is the first appearance of Robert Trebor, seen here as Waylin. He will later become the recurring character Salmoneus.

Since Lucy Lawless (later to be known by all as Xena) guest-starred in the first *Hercules* movie, it is an interesting coincidence that Renee O'Connor (Xena's future sidekick) should guest star in this second feature.

## HM-3: HERCULES AND THE CIRCLE OF FIRE (1994)

CREDITS: Teleplay by Barry Pullman, Andrew Dettmann, and Daniel Truly; directed by Doug Lefler

GUEST STARS: Anthony Quinn (Zeus), Tawny Kitaen (Deianeira), Kevin Atkinson (Cheiron), Mark Ferguson (Prometheus)

SUPPORTING CAST: Mark Newham (Antaeus), Stephanie Barett (Phaedra), Christopher Brougham (Janus)

MYTHOLOGICAL BASIS: In Greek mythology Centaurs are half man and half stallion, known mostly for their unruly, brawling behavior and their numerous rapes of Greek maidens. As a youth, Hercules was tutored by a Centaur named Cheiron. Later, when Hercules embarks on his fourth labor, the capture of the Erymanthian Boar, he is attacked by Centaurs and, in defending himself, inadvertently wounds his old mentor, Cheiron.

Another mythological thread woven into the plot is the story of Prometheus who tricks Zeus into giving him the knowledge of fire, which he then shares with mankind. As punishment, Zeus has Prometheus bound to a rock where a vulture eats his liver each day and each night it grows back. It is Hercules who kills the vulture and argues with Zeus for Prometheus' release.

The fight between Hercules and Anteus is a part of the classic Hercules myth. Anteus is the son of Poseidon and Mother Earth, and it is his mother who is the secret source of his strength. Hercules challenges Anteus to a wrestling match, only to find that he can't defeat Anteus because every time Anteus comes into contact with the ground his strength is revived. To defeat Anteus, Hercules has to break his ribs and then hold him aloft until he dies.

STORY LINE: This television movie begins with the Labors of Hercules, which leads naturally to an event adapted from the classic myth, the accidental wounding of Cheiron. In the movie Cheiron is a Satyr (part man, part goat), rather than a Centaur (part man, part horse). Because Cheiron is immortal, if Hercules fails to find a cure for the wound, his old mentor must remain in a state of agony for eternity.

The next mythological thread woven into the plot is the story of Prometheus who tricked Zeus into giving him the knowledge of fire. Hercules now seeks to recover Prometheus' famous Torch of Fire.

Along the way, Hercules once again encounters Deianeira. She has matured considerably since we last saw her. She has matured in real life, too. In fact she has changed from Renee O'Connor, who played the role in the previous movie, to Tawny Kitaen who in this movie plays the role as much more the kind of woman that Hercules could come to love.

As Hercules and Deianeira continue his quest, another myth-based event is introduced: Hercules' fight with Anteus. In this case, however, Deianeira helps Hercules defeat the giant. Ultimately, Hercules must challenge Hera in battle once again, this time in order to retrieve the torch of Prometheus, which lies inside the Circle of Fire.

Running throughout the Herculean myth is the suggestion that Hercules will gain equal status with the Olympians, either through the intervention of his father, Zeus, or through his own merit and achievement. In this movie version Zeus makes the offer outright, which Hercules rejects; this television hero prefers to be a flesh-and-blood savior of humanity rather than doing it from on high.

OBSERVATIONS: This film establishes the desire of Hercules to live among mortals, rather than apart from them in Olympus. This is the opposite of the Hercules seen in the 1997 Disney animated film who wants to prove himself worthy to live among the Gods.

That there is a down side to immortality is demonstrated when Cheiron the Satyr is injured in such a way that his wound will not heal and he'll suffer in pain for eternity unless a cure is found.

The recurring enmity between Hercules and Hera is demonstrated once again. In these early episodes this subplot was used quite frequently, whereas in the later seasons of the series it would only rarely appear and then only when it could be used to good effect such as in the episode "Prince Hercules" (H-45).

This installment is a setup for forthcoming important events in the life of Hercules, most notably his marriage to Deianeira and the family they will have together. Tawny Kitaen, who played Mona Loveland from 1991 to 1993 on TV's *WKRP in Cincinnati*, is exotic as Deianeira.

There are lots of fights in this episode, some humorous and some outrageous. One to watch for is when Hercules must dodge deadly lightning bolts in standing up to his father, Zeus.

HIGHLIGHTS: When Hercules is a guest at an inn, three amorous sisters decide they want to share his bed. Before the bemused hero can convince the trio that this is not a good idea, Deianeira arrives on the scene and dispatches her potential romantic competition.

## HM-4: HERCULES IN THE UNDERWORLD (1994)

CREDITS: Teleplay by Andrew Dettmann and Daniel Truly; directed by Bill L. Norton

GUEST STARS: Anthony Quinn (Zeus), Tawny Kitaen (Deianeira), Timothy Balme (Lycastus), Michael Hurst (Charon), Mark Ferguson (Hades)

SUPPORTING CAST: Marlee Shelton (Iole), Cliff Curtis (Nessus), Jorge Gonzales (Eryx)

MYTHOLOGICAL BASIS: Like the three prior made-for-television movies, this movie is also inspired by the ancient tales of the legendary hero, but the television versions are rarely as raw as the original myths. For instance, in contrast with the contented family man portrayed in the television version, the mythological Hercules is a faithless womanizer who leaves his home for months or years at a time, raping, pillaging, and seeking vengeance on his enemies. It should be noted, however, that the other gods and humans were all doing much the same and many of them were doing it worse.

In the original myth, Nessus is a Centaur whose job it is to carry people across a river. Nessus offers to carry Deianeira across on his back while Hercules goes to check further downstream for a place to ford the river. Being half stallion and finding himself alone with a maiden, Nessus does what Centaurs always do: he attempts to rape Deianeira and is killed by Hercules' arrow, shot from half a mile away. The tip of the arrow had been dipped in the Hydra's blood.

Hercules is married to Deianeira, as he is in this movie, but Iole is a princess he wins as a prize in an archery contest staged by her father, King Eurytus. Even though Hercules wins, Eurytus refuses to give his daughter to him, so Hercules returns at a later time, kills Eurytus, and makes Iole his household servant.

The other mythological event that is adapted for this movie is derived from the Twelfth Labor of Hercules, the capture of Cerberus. Hercules' quest is to go to the Underworld, capture Hades' three-headed dog, Cerberus, and bring it back to Eurystheus.

STORY LINE: In this television movie Hercules is portrayed as a family man who is reluctant to leave his wife, Deianeira, since he has settled into pleasant domesticity. Iole is introduced as a girl whose village is being threatened by poisonous gases escaping from the earth. Hercules and a Centaur named Nessus go with the girl to save her village.

Deianeira learns that Iole is a Nurian maiden, trained to lure men to their deaths. Deianeira hastens to warn her husband. Deianeira's warning and her being sent home in the company of Nessus are devices created to introduce the attempted rape of Deianeira. In this movie Nessus is revealed as one of Hera's minions, so his attack on Deianeira has a slightly less randy motivation than in the original, but the results in both cases are the same: Hercules kills the Centaur with a well-placed arrow and protects his wife's virtue.

The next sequence in the movie owes much to the story of the Twelfth Labor of Hercules, the capture of Cerberus. Hercules finds that the hole from which the gases are escaping leads to the Underworld, and there he learns that Deianeira has committed suicide. Grief-stricken, Hercules makes a bargain with Hades who agrees to return Deianeira to life if Hercules can defeat and capture Cerberus.

In the original myth Hercules is not allowed to use any weapons, so with his bare hands he chokes each neck of the three-headed beast. In the movie he succeeds in his task by treating the animal so gently that it allows itself to be chained up at the gate.

OBSERVATIONS: In the TV movie Iole proves to be no real threat to Hercules or his marriage and all parties happily return to their homes. In the original myth, however, Deianeira knows that Hercules had lusted after Iole, and she becomes consumed with jealousy over the girl. Deianeira's jealousy leads directly to the death of Hercules and the instrument that causes his death is the Hydra-tainted blood of the Centaur, Nessus, which Deianeira smears on Hercules' shirt, thinking it is a love potion.

In this episode we get to see Nessus, our first Centaur. This is the first time a live-action Centaur (half man, half horse) has been presented so convincingly on film or television.

Michael Hurst makes a surprise appearance in this segment, but not as Iolaus; he plays Charon, the Ferryman of the River Styx. However, he's so well disguised that it is difficult to recognize him.

This episode introduces another background element to the TV series, the Underworld of Tartarus. While we tend to refer to the Greek Underworld itself as Hades, the name Hades belongs to the god who ruled there. Tartarus is actually the bad part of the Underworld (i.e. Hell) whereas the Underworld also has a pleasant region where the good people supposedly reside in peace and tranquillity. Tartarus appears to be a series of endless caverns whereas the Elysian Fields (the nice realm) consists of rolling hills and sunny days. The Elysian Fields is a pleasant place where mortal souls live in peace and never grow old, as we'll see in later episodes when Hercules visits his dead family there.

Hades is a character Hercules meets again from time to time, just as he visits the Underworld on other occasions. He's not a two-dimensional villain, however, but then neither is this Underworld quite the special effects extravaganza seen in the 1997 Disney film *Hercules*.

Because the plot focuses so strongly on suicide, death, Hades, and the Underworld, the humor quotient is far more restrained than in most of the shows.

HIGHLIGHTS: Hercules finds himself battling men in the Underworld whom he had previously killed in combat.

## HM-5: HERCULES IN THE MAZE OF THE MINOTAUR (1994)

CREDITS: Teleplay by Andrew Dettmann and Daniel Truly; directed by Josh Becker

GUEST STARS: Anthony Quinn (Zeus), Tawny Kitaen (Deianeira), Andrew Thurtill (Danion), Terry Bachelor (Trikonis), Sydney Jackson (Darthus)

SUPPORTING CAST: Nick Fay (Andius), Geoff Allen (Martan)

MYTHOLOGICAL BASIS: The myth of the Minotaur and the Labyrinth is obviously the genesis of this made-for-television movie. As with much of Greek mythology, the story begins with an angry god. In this case the angry god is Poseidon who vents his displeasure with King Minos by causing Minos' wife, Pasiphae, to lust after a huge white bull. The result of their union is the birth of the Minotaur, a monstrosity with the head of a bull and the body of a man. Minos is so shamed by his wife's actions, he banishes Pasiphae and the Minotaur to the island of Gnosis where they are imprisoned in the Labyrinth, a complicated maze from which none can escape.

In the original myth the Minotaur is killed by Theseus who is the lover of the Minotaur's half-sister, Ariadne. The penetration of the Labyrinth and the killing of the Minotaur can only be accomplished because Ariadne gives Theseus a magical golden thread, which he uses to find his way through the maze and then follows on his way back out after he's killed the Minotaur.

STORY LINE: In the television movie Hercules encounters the Minotaur when he learns that two young boys have accidentally set this monster free from the maze (which is not located on Gnosis, but underground beneath a neighboring village), and the creature is now preying on the village children.

As is to be expected, there is no hint of a woman being seduced by a bull. Here there are two versions of how the half man–half bull got that way, and in both versions the curse is attributed to Zeus. In the first version the Minotaur a century before had been a man who had used his good looks to manipulate people. As punishment, Zeus turned him into this grotesque creature.

When Hercules and the Minotaur have their final battle, the monster reveals the second version of his creation: he claims he is the secret son of Zeus. As the Minotaur is dying, Zeus appears and confirms that the half man–half bull really was a half-brother of Hercules. Needless to say, Zeus does not elaborate on whether a cow figures in the family tree.

OBSERVATIONS: Although the idea of Zeus fathering the Minotaur is a plot device created for the movie, it would not be out of character for the Zeus of Greek mythology who was known to have given birth to his daughter Athene through his forehead; seduced Nemesis while disguised as a swan, which resulted in the birth of Helen; and, in the form of a snake, ravished his own mother, Rhea. With various other goddesses Zeus fathered Apollo, Hermes, and Artemis; he married his twin sister, Hera, and was the father of both King Minos and Hercules (by different mothers), which makes them half-brothers and means that Hercules was actually an illegitimate half-uncle of the Minotaur.

While the Minotaur is a villain, he is patterned in the mold of *Beauty and the Beast* in that he was once a handsome man who was turned into a monster because of his vanity and lack of compassion for his fellow man. He hasn't really learned anything by being punished, rather he's become even more nasty.

That Zeus isn't the doting father he tries to pass himself off as is evidenced by the fact that he stands by as Hercules kills the Minotaur.

This movie is filled out with flashbacks from the first four *Hercules* movies in order to bring new viewers up to speed on who Hercules and Iolaus are, the role that Deianeira has had in the story line, and the information that Zeus is actually Hercules' father. The flashbacks feature such performers as Lucy Lawless, Renee O'Connor, and Robert Trebor.

When the Minotaur captures people, it imprisons them in cocoons in a method similar to the one used by the creatures in the *Alien* movies starring Sigourney Weaver.

HIGHLIGHTS: Noteworthy are Hercules' climactic battle with the Minotaur and the revelation of who the Minotaur really is.

# HERCULES:
# THE LEGENDARY
# JOURNEYS
## SEASON ONE (1994–95)

The episodes created for the television series are all sixty minutes long, the standard length for a drama-adventure series.

## PRODUCTION CREDITS

Created by Christian Williams; co-producer: David Eick; producer: Eric Gruendemann; supervising producer: Robert Bielak; co-executive producer: John Schulian; executive producer: Sam Raimi; executive producer: Robert Tapert; coordinating producer: Bernadette Joyce; line producer: Chloe Smith; associate producer: Liz Friedman; story editor: Chris Manheim; unit production manager: Eric Gruendemann; first assistant director: Andrew Merrifield; second assistant director: Clare Richardson; director of photography: John Marafie; editor: David Blewitt; visual effects: Kevin O'Neill; production designer: Robert Gillies; costume designer: Nigla Dickson; New Zealand casting: Diana Rowan; stunt coordinator: Peter Bell; second unit director: Charlie Haskell; additional visual effects: Flat Earth Productions, Inc.; music: Joseph LoDuca

## REGULARS

Kevin Sorbo (Hercules), Michael Hurst (Iolaus/Charon)

## RECURRING

Robert Trebor (Salmoneus), Elizabeth Hawthorne (Alcmene)

# H-1: THE WRONG PATH

CREDITS: Teleplay by John Schulian; directed by Doug Lefler

GUEST STARS: Clare Carey (Aegina),

SUPPORTING CAST: Mick Rose (Lycus)

MYTHOLOGICAL BASIS: The plot of this first regular television episode is based in part on the story of Perseus and Medusa, along with some of the elements of the classic Hercules myth in which Hera, Hercules' stepmother, is responsible for the death of his wife and children. Sometimes it is Hercules' first wife, Megara, sometimes his second, Deianeira; the number of children varies, but most often their deaths are a result of Hera driving Hercules temporarily insane, causing him to murder his own family.

In the original Perseus myth, Perseus is sent by his future stepfather, Polydectes, to bring the head of Medusa the Gorgon as a wedding gift. Knowing that a mere glimpse of Medusa, a winged monster with serpents for hair, turns mortals to stone, Perseus, armed with Hades' helmet of invisibility, winged sandals from the Nymphs, and Athene's shield, succeeds in decapitating Medusa. He avoids being turned to stone by only viewing Medusa's face in the reflection of Athene's shield.

STORY LINE: In this episode Hercules has married Deianeira and become the father of three children. He returns from his travels to find that his entire family is dead, killed by a fireball hurled from the heavens. No doubt the work of Hera.

Consumed by his desire for vengeance, Hercules ignores a farmer's request that he help a village plagued by a she-demon who is turning people to stone. Iolaus goes by himself to face the menace.

Ultimately Hercules must battle the she-demon, and this is where the story line picks up the Medusa legend but puts Hercules in the role of Perseus. Hercules tricks the monster into seeing her own reflection, which turns her into stone and causes all of her victims to revert to human form.

OBSERVATIONS: As noted previously, by using the death of Hercules' family from the original myth, the series' producers avoided having the hero constantly leave his family while he traipses off to do good deeds.

Although in subsequent episodes Iolaus will act somewhat dimwitted (see: "The Warrior Princess"[H-9]), in this one he proves himself brave to the point of recklessness in foolishly trying to use his mortal skills to defeat a powerful, enchanted monster.

Also to be noted is that this episode establishes the format in which Hercules learns of some menace often as he is just appearing on the scene. Is his arrival really fortuitous, or does evil appear only when Hercules is in the neighborhood? It's a wonder people don't become apprehensive when they see him coming because some fantastic menace or calamity is almost surely right around the corner.

While *Hercules* episodes tend to be light-hearted adventures in which violence isn't very explicit, here we have a true dramatic storyline in which Hercules loses his entire family in one fell swoop. The fact that this isn't just brushed off but affects the character and shapes his actions for much of the episode demonstrates a higher quality of writing. The emotional resonance was only hinted at in the character before as he exhibits now a great sense of loss and seeks vengeance against Hera in spite of the fact that as a mortal he is still in danger. But all Hercules wants to do is knock over Hera's temples.

The fact that Zeus allowed Hera to kill Hercules' family and will not intervene marks the diminishing of Zeus as a character. A later episode unwisely has Zeus bring a minor character back to life, which only begs the question of why he couldn't do the same for his own son's wife and children? Zeus will largely fade out of the series after this and then not be seen at all for some time until he makes a cameo appearance in the third-season episode "Judgement Day" (H-52).

HIGHLIGHTS: The emotionally charged Hercules rages over his family's murder, then later uses his vengeful energies to battle the she-demon who turns men to stone.

## H-2: EYE OF THE BEHOLDER

CREDITS: Teleplay by John Schulian; directed by John T. Kretchmer

GUEST STARS: Robert Trebor (Salmoneus), Richard Moll (the Cyclops), Kim Michaels (Scilla)

SUPPORTING CAST: Michael Mizrahi (Castor), Derek Ward (Ferret), David Press (Glaucus), Ray Woolf (Chief Executioner)

MYTHOLOGICAL BASIS: In Greek mythology Hercules is eighteen years of age when he performs his first act of heroism by slaying the lion that is terrorizing the land ruled by King Thespius. In reward Thespius offers his fifty daughters to Hercules whereupon Hercules proceeds to father fifty-two children.

In myth Salmoneus is the brother of Sisyphus and a most unpopular character who claims credit for many of the accomplishments of Zeus. Though not specifically identified as the mythological personage, the television Salmoneus has similarities in personality and character.

The Cyclopes (as the name is spelled in most mythological texts) were the sons of Mother Earth, and originally there were three of these one-eyed creatures who were builders and blacksmiths. The Cyclopes were banished to Tartarus until Zeus freed them to help him overthrow the Titan, Cronus. In exchange they forged Zeus' thunderbolts. The three Cyclopes were killed by Apollo long before the birth of Hercules, so Hercules must have encountered one of their descendants who, it is said, lost the knowledge of their craft and became shepherds.

STORY LINE: In this television episode Hercules is not only older than eighteen but his libido is considerably more diminished than his mythological counterpart. Here, when Hercules encounters the fifty daughters of Thespius, he rejects the eager maidens and in the process encounters a fast-talking toga salesman named Salmoneus.

Salmoneus accompanies Hercules on a rescue mission to a nearby village that is threatened by a rampaging Cyclops. Hercules finds that the Cyclops is being manipulated by Hera because he has been mistreated by the townspeople his entire life. Hercules arranges a truce between the townspeople and the misunderstood giant, which, of course, brings down the wrath of Hera and necessitates the joining of forces between Hercules and the Cyclops.

OBSERVATIONS: When Salmoneus was introduced in this episode, he was a comedy device created to take care of the king's fifty daughters.

However, this fast-talking salesman with an abundance of get-rich-quick schemes that never work proved popular with viewers and has returned many times to *Hercules: The Legendary Journeys*. He also turns up once in a while on *Xena: Warrior Princess*. This episode features the first of many appearances of Salmoneus.

Hercules gets a chance to help people and give Hera a poke in the eye of sorts at the same time. He even teams up with a monster (a Cyclops) instead of just cutting him down to size. Giants and such do not always turn out to be monsters in this series, but if they're non-human, you can bet that they're evil. This first season has so many monsters in it that they were all turned into toys and merchandised through toy stores. These days one can find them at remainder prices because they are being moved out to make way for the new Hercules and Xena toy lines.

The idea of having the giant Cyclops be the victim instead of the townspeople is an unusual story twist. Richard Moll as the Cyclops is an interesting casting choice. Although Moll is best known as Bull from the TV sitcom *Night Court* (1984–92), he has also appeared in several movies, usually as the villain, including *Metalstorm* (1983) and *House* (1986). In addition, he played the rogue in the first episode of the *Highlander* TV series (1992– ). Here he proves to be equally effective in the sympathetic role of a misunderstood giant.

We never actually see Hera on screen, and in fact even her voice remains uncredited throughout the series. This makes it easy to use whomever is available to do her voice as she speaks out of clouds, mirrors, and idols to whomever she is manipulating at the time.

HIGHLIGHTS: Hercules fights side by side with the Cyclops, making an unbeatable team on the battlefield.


# H-3: THE ROAD TO CALYDON

CREDITS: Teleplay by Andrew Dettmann and Daniel Truly;
    directed by Doug Lefler

GUEST STARS: Norman Forsey (Seer), John Sumner (Broteas),
    Portia Dawson (Jana), Christopher Sunoa (Ixion)

SUPPORTING CAST: Peter Dowley (Epitalon), Sela Brown (Leda), Stephen Papps (Teles), Andrew Lawrence (Odeus), Maggie Turner (Hecate), Bruce Allpress (Old Man)

MYTHOLOGICAL BASIS: The Sixth Labor of Hercules is the killing of the birds of Stymphalus, which have metal plumage and claws and beaks of brass. In order to kill these birds, Hercules uses a rattle to scare them into flight so that he can aim his arrows at their soft underbellies.

Although the name Broteus appears in Greek mythology, there is little similarity between the television character and the mythological character, other than that they both offended goddesses. In the myth Broteus is known as a famous hunter whom the goddess Artemis causes to commit suicide.

STORY LINE: In this episode Hercules arrives at a town in the grip of freakish weather and strange, powerful storms. An old, blind seer reveals that the tempests are a result of the theft of a sacred chalice belonging to Hera. Always willing to annoy Hera, Hercules helps the citizens migrate to the city of Calydon as hellish storms and Hera's shock troops impede their progress.

It is this migration that introduces an event based on the mythological Labors of Hercules, the killing of the birds of Stymphalus. In the television version the Stymphalian swamp has one huge winged creature, which Hercules defeats while saving the life of the refugee leader, Broteas, who reveals that he is the one who stole the valuable chalice.

OBSERVATIONS: This is one of the episodes in which drama outweighs comedy, and there is a believable, eerie atmosphere created for the town plagued by freakish storms.

Also of note is the very good special-effects scene in which Hercules battles a decidedly weird creature, the Stymphalian Bird.

Iolaus is missing from this episode, and the old seer that Hercules encounters temporarily takes the place of his sidekick.

Periodically the series does episodes where Iolaus isn't around and his absence is not referred to. In season two they even do the reverse and have Iolaus be the main character in an episode although Hercules does appear at the beginning and end of the storyline (as well as in its sequel in season three).

In the absence of Iolaus, this might be a good time to point out that his character gradually becomes more and more interesting as he isn't just Hercules without the strength. In fact his fighting ability seems just as good as, or maybe even better than, Herc's since he doesn't depend on his strength to accomplish the end results. This becomes particularly evident in season four in "When a Man Loves a Woman" (H-51), when Hercules gives up his strength and later has a hard time in a fight because he doesn't have his strength to depend on and needs the help of Iolaus to even the odds.

# H-4: THE FESTIVAL OF DIONYSUS

CREDITS: Teleplay by Andrew Dettmann and Daniel Truly; directed by Peter Ellis

GUEST STARS: Noel Trevarthan (King Iphicles), Ilona Rodgers (Queen Camilla), Norman Forsey (Seer), Mark Newham (Ares)

SUPPORTING CAST: Martyn Sanderson (Priest), Johnny Blick (Prince Nestor), Warren Carl (Pentheus), Katrina Hobbs (Marysa), Todd Rippon (Gudrun)

MYTHOLOGICAL BASIS: Although this episode has many of the elements of Greek mythology, there would appear to be no one legend from which it draws its primary inspiration. However, the questing hero being trapped and at the mercy of a serpentine monster is one of the most common motifs in mythology and legend. In this episode the television Hercules is pitted against a classic of the genre, a giant eel-like creature that must be defeated before the hero can continue his quest.

According to Joseph Campbell's *The Hero with a Thousand Faces*, the hero almost always reaches a turning point in his journey when he encounters a wizard, a gnome, a talking frog, or some such magical character who helps him move forward. In this case Hercules meets the seer whom he met in "The Road to Calydon" (H-3), and the wise man assists Hercules to accomplish his quest.

STORY LINE: Once again the story begins when Hercules' assistance is sought—this time by Prince Nestor who fears that his father is in danger. Hercules and Prince Nestor arrive just as the Festival of Dionysus is beginning. Revelers fill the streets, creating just the kind of confusion that could easily mask an assassination plot.

In order to save the king, Hercules must first fight a giant eel-monster, then seek the aid of the wise old seer who assists him to defeat Nestor's brother who is being aided by Ares in his attempt to murder the king.

OBSERVATIONS: In this episode Prince Nestor, who had been considered weak and unfit to rule, becomes more mature and self-reliant. This makes an interesting coda to the adventure because in the ancient Herculean myth there is a King Nestor who is the only one who will help Hercules to purify himself after he has killed Eurytus' son. As repayment for his kindness, Hercules makes him a king.

The story line of Hercules helping a member of a royal family in dire straits is repeated in future episodes including "War Bride" (H-57) in the third season.

The relationship between Hercules and Ares is expanded in future segments to the point where they become blood enemies. Making the situation more complex is the fact that Ares is the half-brother of Hercules. One of their most notable conflicts comes in "The End of the Beginning" (H-56).

The version of Ares as seen initially in this series is very different from the later version played by Kevin Smith. This Ares is an armored monstrosity who looks not only like a warrior ready for war, but like a one man army! He's a truly frightening character, a monster done without CGI effects. In some respects he almost looks like a robot. The human version played by Kevin Smith clearly has a greater range of possibilities, particularly when he turns up on *Xena* in season two as a sympathetic character (however briefly).

In this story Hercules inevitably gets in a trap that he must inevitably get out of. Needless to say he uses his brawn more often than his brains, but at times Hercules is shown thinking his way out of traps as well, so he isn't just a muscle-bound hero.

HIGHLIGHTS: The fight with the giant eel-monster is the most exciting scene of the episode.

TRIVIA: This is Ares' first introduction. He is played by Mark Newham. In later episodes Kevin Smith will take over the role.

# H-5: ARES

CREDITS: Teleplay by Steve Roberts; directed by Harley
    Cokeliss

GUEST STARS: Cory Everson (Atalanta), Peter Malloch (Titus),
    Marsie Wipani (Janista), Callum Stembridge (Aurelius),
    Taungaroa Emile (Ximenos), Mark Newham (Ares)

SUPPORTING CAST: Peter Mueller (Soldier), Kelson Henderson
    (First Child), Nick Clark (Second Child), Rebecca Hobbs (First
    Woman), Rebekah Mercer (Second Woman)

MYTHOLOGICAL BASIS: This episode more specifically sets up what will be the on-going antagonism between Hercules and his half-brother, Ares. In the Greek myth Ares is the only son of Zeus and Hera. He becomes the god of war and takes delight in inciting battles and creating turmoil.

STORY LINE: In this episode a villain is luring boys to a secret altar honoring Ares and turning them into a blood-thirsty army that does the bidding of the god of war.
    As fate would have it, Hercules is there to inform a young boy about his father's death in battle. The boy easily falls prey to the lure of Ares, and as his first mission, the boy is ordered to slay Hercules.
    When Hercules is attacked, he unmasks his assailant and finds the boy. Hercules then faces both the villainous recruiter and the god of war.

OBSERVATIONS: In this installment the Ares we meet doesn't even look human. He's a huge, hulking figure with fierce, glowing red eyes.
    Having children fight as warriors is a dramatic concept, but even with weapons a twelve-year-old boy is no match for a full-grown man in battle. Battles are decided by the strength of the warriors on either side, and even hypnotized children cannot vanquish their adult opponents.

In spite of what would seem to be a silly premise (teenage boys, some of them quite young, raiding villages as masked warriors), the storyline focuses on the human elements involved. There is a gentle, even melancholy undertone due to the fact that Hercules has arrived in the village to tell a family that a woman's husband, and young boy's father, has fallen in battle. This emphasizes why Hercules hates everything that Ares represents and will do whatever he can to defeat the plans of the god of war. In this way Hercules believes he can prevent the fathers of other children from dying in needless battles.

The friendship between Hercules and the boy's mother hints at possibilities, but they never followed up on them. As it turns out, whenever Hercules does try to get seriously involved with a woman, it either just doesn't work out or has tragic consequences.

HIGHLIGHTS: There are good dramatic scenes here in which the tragic fallout from war is portrayed, rather than just depicting the glory of battle.

# H-6: As Darkness Falls

CREDITS: Teleplay by Robert Bielak; directed by George Mendeluk

GUEST STARS: Lucy Lawless (Lyla), Cliff Curtis (Nemis), Peter Muller (Deric)

SUPPORTING CAST: Jacqueline Collen (Penelope), Mark Ferguson (Craesus)

MYTHOLOGICAL BASIS: This episode features one of the most interesting of mythological beasts, the Centaur. The plot is a variation on a myth in which Ares and his sister Eris become angered that they aren't invited to the wedding of Peirithous and Hippodameia. The two gods send drunken Centaurs who turn the wedding into a brawl.

The Centaurs attempt to rape the bride resulting in a bloody battle in which the Centaurs overwhelm their enemies.

STORY LINE: Hercules is attending a wedding when the festivities are crashed by three Centaurs who kidnap a bridesmaid as well as the bride-to-be.

Hercules and three others pursue the Centaurs, but Hercules' attempt at rescue is impeded by something that happened when he first arrived at the village. He had spurned the advances of a beautiful woman, Lyla (Lucy Lawless), who then drugged his wine with a substance that causes him to slowly lose his eyesight.

After the others in his party are killed or injured, a blinded Hercules is left to face the Centaurs.

OBSERVATIONS: This episode features the return of Salmoneus who has a new occupation—real estate salesman—just as he has each time he is reintroduced in subsequent adventures. In *Hercules*, Salmoneus is sort of a parallel to wacky Kramer on the sitcom *Seinfeld*.

This episode also brings back Centaurs to the *Hercules* TV series mythos, following their introduction in the fourth Hercules telefilm, *Hercules in the Underworld.* These creatures return often on both *Hercules* and *Xena.* (The special effect used to create the Centaurs is one of the best effects in the series.)

Once again Lucy Lawless appears in another (pre-Xena) role. Her character begins like a stereotyped evil schemer, but she learns the error of her ways when she falls in love with a Centaur. We meet her again in "Outcast" (H-18).

Watching many of these episodes of Hercules in a short time one sees that Lucy Lawless was not the only actor to turn up in multiple roles in multiple episodes. Due to the small talent pool of actors in New Zealand, many of the supporting actors on Hercules play roles in subsequent episodes. Even main guest stars turn up in other roles in the same season (such as Kevin Smith appearing as Ares in some episodes and as Iphicles, the mortal half-brother of Hercules, in other episodes). Lucy Lawless herself appears as Lyla in the second-season Hercules episode, "Outcast"(H-18), even after she played  Xena on her own series!

HIGHLIGHTS: The rescue by the blind Hercules and the heroic sacrifice made by the Centaur Nemis are the outstanding scenes in this episode.

TRIVIA: Lucy Lawless appears in her second original role on *Hercules: The Legendary Journeys.*

The plot of the hero losing vision is also used in the *Xena* episode "Blind Faith" (X-42).

## H-7: PRIDE COMES BEFORE A BRAWL

CREDITS: Teleplay by Steve Roberts; directed by Peter Ellis

GUEST STARS: Lisa Chappell (Lydia), Karen Witter (Nemesis)

SUPPORTING CAST: John Dybvig (Rankor), Jeff Gane (Rak), David Stott (Boatman)

STORY LINE: Iolaus is in the middle of a brawl when Hercules steps in to help him. Iolaus is offended that Hercules would think that he cannot defend himself. In a fit of pique Iolaus chooses to go off by himself.

Hercules encounters his old flame, Nemesis, the goddess of retribution. To his dismay Hercules learns that she has chosen Iolaus as her next target because he has so blatantly exhibited the sin of pride.

Iolaus finds himself in a situation where he must help a young woman in a daring escape and defend her from attacking monsters. Nemesis prevents Hercules from assisting his friend, leaving it up to Iolaus to prove he's the man he believes himself to be. And, of course, he is.

OBSERVATIONS: Monsters again, this time a giant eel and a hydra, but monsters aren't what the episode is really all about. The character of Iolaus is the hub on which this story wheel turns. In deepening his character, we're shown that he resents being viewed as the sidekick of Hercules (a theme returned to in the series from time to time). In his anger Iolaus overlooks the fact that his friend was just trying to help as they are truly friends, not just sidekicks. The realization of the truth of this is at the heart of this story.

While Hercules inevitably encounters someone else who needs help, in this case Iolaus is the one being menaced, and the menace comes from someone he knows thereby complicating the dilemma. This complicates the story nicely since he has to defend his mortal friend from his immortal friend.

Iolaus is established as an important supporting character again. The heroic Hercules is a compelling character in stories where he's the lone protagonist. However, he's equally interesting in partnership with Iolaus because they present such contrasting personalities. Iolaus is eccentric and has a hot temper whereas Hercules is more mellow and easygoing in spite of his toughness.

TRIVIA: Iolaus returns to the series. He hasn't been seen since "The Wrong Path" (H-1).

## H-8: THE MARCH TO FREEDOM

CREDITS: Teleplay by Adam Armus and Nora Kay Foster; directed by Harley Cokeliss

GUEST STARS: Lucy Liu (Oi-Lan), Nathaniel Lees (Cyrus), Stig Eldred (Belus),

SUPPORTING CAST: Maya Dallziel (Mother), Joanna Barrett (Pretty Girl)

STORY LINE: Hercules witnesses a young woman being sold into slavery. Knowing the fate that awaits her, he buys her and sets her free. Her fiancé who has already been sold into slavery, escapes his owners and vows to kill the person who bought the girl. He knocks Hercules over a cliff, but both he and the girl are recaptured by the slave traders.
Bruised but safe, Hercules drags himself up the side of the cliff and chases after the captured lovers. He attacks the slave train and defeats the slave traders. With misunderstandings resolved, Hercules gives the couple the land where he once lived with his family, knowing he could never reside there again himself.

OBSERVATIONS: When this episode opens, Hercules is visiting his mother, Alcmene. *Hercules* is one of the few television shows with a virile character shown visiting his mother without making fun of the relationship in some way. In fact mothers tend to be nonexistent on most other action-adventure programs.

In many respects this is a typical *Hercules* episode. It begins with Hercules performing a good deed, which promptly complicates his life as one action leads to another and he has to see it through to the end to get everything untangled. And of course there are misunderstandings, attacks by brigands, and Hercules having to track down and rescue someone when it would have been just as easy (actually easier) to just throw up his hands and go on to the next adventure.

Hercules gives the land he once lived on with his family to these new friends, a touching gesture that seems to mark closure to that part of his life. Had Hercules not been able to get over that tragedy then he would have kept the land and made it a monument to his dead wife and children. On the other hand, how many people are able to visit their dead relatives in the Underworld and return to tell about it?

That Hercules bought the girl from the slave traders in order to rescue her leads one to wonder why Hercules doesn't concentrate on destroying the slave trade since he's so clearly opposed to it. After all, this task would take no more effort than destroying monsters, which he does on a regular basis.

HIGHLIGHTS: The final wild battle between Hercules and the slave traders is outstanding in its action-packed stunts.

TRIVIA: In this episode Iolaus has again disappeared from the proceedings.

## H-9: THE WARRIOR PRINCESS

CREDITS: Teleplay by John Schulian; directed by Bruce Seth
    Green

GUEST STARS: Lucy Lawless (Xena)

SUPPORTING CAST: Bill Johnson (Petrakis), Michael Dwyer
    (Theodorus)

STORY LINE: A power-hungry, evil, warrior princess, Xena, views

Hercules as the only obstacle in her path to conquering all she surveys. Viewing Iolaus as the weak link to Hercules (Iolaus is presented as a bit more goofy in these early shows), she decides to seduce the hero's side-kick in order to drive a wedge between the two friends.

As part of Xena's scheme, Iolaus becomes so infatuated with her that he's willing to fight Hercules to defend her. (Iolaus, unfortunately, can be painfully simple.) When Iolaus inevitably loses this contest of strength, Hercules refuses to finish off his friend. Iolaus sees Xena's true colors. Xena rides off, threatening to return one day to finish the job of eliminating Hercules.

OBSERVATIONS: Iolaus, who has been shown to be brighter and more interesting in past episodes, here is so thoroughly manipulated by Xena that he actually attacks Hercules. He even thinks that Hercules is lying to him when he tries to explain who Xena really is. Has Iolaus been this stupid before? Well, yes. In "Pride Comes Before a Brawl" (H-7), Iolaus stupidly stalks off in a huff when Hercules tries to help him, so he has been shown to be able to make remarkably poor decisions at times. His seduction by Xena is perhaps at the top of the list, however.

This is the evil Xena referred to in various *Xena* episodes and even seen in flashback in the episode "Destiny" (X-36). But this is no flashback and as a result, we see the unvarnished version of the character who is willing to kill anyone who stands in her way and who exhibits no positive characteristics.

Because of the abruptness of the ending (she just rides away vowing revenge), it was decided to bring the character back soon, but this time to groom her for stardom.

Xena is introduced as a typical villainess in an episode that raises the question of how *Xena* ever achieved greatness after this humble introduction. There is nothing in this lackluster introduction that anticipates the Xena we have come to know and love. Here she's just a typical hissing, spitting villainess, chewing up the scenery and her warriors along with it.

HIGHLIGHTS: This is the first appearance of the aggressive Xena and her destructive warriors to whom she grants sexual favors as reward for exemplary service.

# H-10: THE GLADIATOR

CREDITS: Teleplay by Robert Bielak; directed by Garth Waxwell

GUEST STARS: Tony Todd (Gladius), Ian Mune (Menas Maxius), Alison Bruce (Postera), Kyrin Hall (Felicita)

SUPPORTING CAST: Mark Nua (Skoros), Stuart Turner (Leulia), Nigel Harbrow (Turkos), Gabriel Pendergast (Spagos), Tawny Kitaen (Deianeira), Jeffrey Thomas (Dellicus), Ray Bishop (Rankus), Jonathon Bell-Booth (Traveler)

STORY LINE : Hercules and Iolaus rescue a young woman who is being attacked by bandits. They learn that she's the wife of a gladiator champion imprisoned by a corrupt Roman ruler, and agree to help her free her husband.

When the woman is later captured by soldiers, she is bound along with Iolaus and used as bait to force Hercules and her husband to fight each other. Hercules convinces the Galdiator that the only way to save her is to join forces and turn on the Romans.

OBSERVATIONS: As depicted here, the Romans have an outpost in Greece. This is also postulated in the second-season *Xena* episode "Destiny" (X-36). The aspect of Romans in Greece (with their own kingdom no less) manages to fit into the artificial timeline of the series as it has been established in other episodes that the *Hercules* and *Xena* episodes are set roughly around zero A.D., which is prior to the fall of the Roman Empire.

By now Iolaus is definitely entrenched as Hercules' regular sidekick, which allows the character to grow in importance. Eventually, he'll be able to carry entire episodes himself.

Once again Hercules and Iolaus find trouble without looking for it, but since Hercules has vowed to help the downtrodden of humanity, he quickly moves forward under the hero's mantle he has adopted.

While black characters don't appear on either *Hercules* or *Xena* with any great regularity, when they are seen, they tend to be well written and strong protagonists. I believe that this is also a result of the smaller talent pool of actors in New Zealand since, in this case, Tony Todd is an American actor (like Kevin Sorbo) who had to be flown there in order to do both this episode, and the second-season *Xena* episode, "Lost Mariner" (X-45).

TRIVIA: Actor Tony Todd, who plays Gladius, is better known to American audiences from his title role in the two *Candyman* horror features (1992 and 1995), as well as for his appearance in the award-winning *Star Trek: Deep Space Nine* episode "The Visitor."

# H-11: THE VANISHING DEAD

CREDITS: Teleplay by Andrew Dettmann and Daniel Truly; directed by Bruce Campbell

GUEST STARS: Erik Thomson (King Daulin), Reb Brown (Jarton), Amber-Jane Raab (Peona)

SUPPORTING CAST: Richard Vette (Aelon), Chris McDowell (Krytus)

STORY LINE: A battle rages between two armies as two siblings, brother against sister, are determined to fight to the death. Hercules soon determines that Ares has tricked the siblings into a feud so he can enjoy the devastation being wrought. The final confrontation has begun when Hercules and Iolaus track Ares to a cave where Hercules exposes Ares as the true manipulator of the tragic and violent events.

OBSERVATIONS: This is a more downbeat episode, especially as it concerns Ares' canine, the dog of war—a vicious beast who has been eating the bodies of the dead on the battlefield. The concept of a canine eating the dead is pretty horrific. In an interview one of the producers of *Hercules* remarked that one first season episode was so grim that he regrets having made it. He wouldn't say to what segment he was referring, but this may well have been the one.

Ares appears for the third time, thereby making him a more imminent threat than Hera. But in the case of Ares, rather than the villain seeking out Hercules, our hero keeps stumbling across plots and counterplots which the god of war has set in motion.

HIGHLIGHTS: There are two major confrontations: Hercules versus the dog of war and Hercules versus the god of war.

TRIVIA: This episode was directed by actor Bruce Campbell *before* he first appeared on the series in "King of Thieves" (H-14) in the role of Autolycus.

# H-12: THE GAUNTLET

CREDITS: Teleplay by Peter Bielak; directed by Jack Perez

GUEST STARS: Lucy Lawless (Xena), Matthew Chamberlain (Darphus)

SUPPORTING CAST: Dean O'Gorman (Iloran), Peter Daube (Spiros)

STORY LINE: There's treachery in the ranks when Xena's right-hand man challenges her. In a show of force Xena is deposed and compelled to run a brutal gauntlet where she is severely beaten and left for dead. However, the warrior princess is made of tougher stuff than her soldiers apparently realized.

Xena goes to Hercules for help. Although he is naturally suspicious of Xena's motives, Hercules is interested in resolving the situation. In a long-awaited confrontation Xena kills her traitorous lieutenant, Darphus. However, Ares, who has been watching these events, returns Darphus to life so that Darphus is now the one who is out for revenge.

End of part one of this two-part episode.

OBSERVATIONS: The gauntlet Xena runs is pretty brutal, but as we already know, Xena is one tough customer. In the course of this story Salmoneus makes certain that neither we nor Hercules overlook Xena's better qualities. (Can you say "series spin-off"?)

While the producers did accurately predict that Xena would be a popular character, the two sequel episodes were conceived after "Warrior Princess" (H-9) was filmed and did not appear right after "Warrior Princess." Some people believe that the three were originally aired as a trilogy of stories back to back. However, two other episodes were aired before Xena returned in "The Gauntlet" and "Unchained Heart" (H-13) which are the second and third appearances of Xena.

Xena is still very much the evil Xena in this episode. Initially Xena is concerned only with revenge and goes to Hercules with great reluctance, but it is the influence of both Hercules and Salmoneus that begin to bring her around to a different world view.

This is the first appearance of the morally reformed Xena. In addition there is the introduction of the continuing rivalry between Ares and Xena whom the god of war considers a rival.

HIGHLIGHTS: Xena gets the stuffing beaten out of her while running the brutal gauntlet.

# H-13: UNCHAINED HEART

CREDITS: Teleplay by John Schulian; directed by Bruce Seth
  Green

GUEST STARS: Lucy Lawless (Xena), Matthew Chamberlain
  (Darphus)

SUPPORTING CAST: Stephen Papps (Pylendor), Mervyn Smith
  (Village Elder), Robert Pollock (Villager), Shane Dawson (First
  Warrior), Ian Harrop (Camp Boss), Margo Gada (Quintas),
  Bruce Allpress (Eros), David Mercer (Warrior), Gordon
  Hatfield (Lieutenant), Campbell Rousselle (Sentry)

STORY LINE: Xena and Hercules believe that the menace of Darphus has ended forever, but unbeknownst to them, Ares has returned Darphus to the land of the living. Darphus and his army attack and Salmoneus is kidnapped.

Hercules and Xena follow Darphus and rescue the bumbling Salmoneus. Subsequently, Hercules and Xena pit Darphus and his lieutenant against each other, thus removing the threat of both.

A repentant Xena realizes that she has a great deal to make up for and now appreciates that helping people is far more satisfying than burning and pillaging neighboring villages.

OBSERVATIONS: Xena and Hercules, while reluctant partners, play well off each other. She's no longer the embodiment of corruption that she appeared to be when introduced in "The Warrior Princess" (H-9). In fact she officially reforms in this episode as she realizes the error of her ways and makes apologies all around, even to Iolaus.

This episode is key because it shows the turnaround of personality in Xena. What's important is that this personality change is grudging. Xena comes to realize that she had indulged in extremism in the name of protecting her home kingdom, but that in doing so she'd become as big a menace as the enemies she was protecting her people from.

While her personality change may seem a bit abrupt, she displays more sides to her personality now. One interesting characteristic is that, unlike many other guest damsels on the series, she doesn't just fall into the arms of Hercules.

This episode is where the spin-off series *Xena* all began.

HIGHLIGHTS: Because of the underlying humor in most *Hercules* episodes, a comical scene was inserted into this installment that many Xena fans find grating in which her character, made to look rather bizarre with frizzed-up hair and so forth, serves as a cheerleader for Hercules.

# HERCULES: THE LEGENDARY JOURNEYS:
## SEASON TWO (1995–96)

The episodes created for the television series are all sixty minutes long, the standard length for a drama-adventure series.

## PRODUCTION CREDITS

Created by Christian Williams; co-producer: David Eick; producer: Eric Gruendemann; supervising producer: Robert Bielak; co-executive producer: John Schulian; executive producer: Sam Raimi; executive producer: Robert Tapert; coordinating producer: Bernadette Joyce; line producer: Chloe Smith; associate producer: Liz Friedman; story editor: Chris Manheim; unit production manager: Eric Gruendemann; first assistant director: Andrew Merrifield; second assistant director: Clare Richardson; director of photography: John Marafie; editor: David Blewitt; visual effects: Kevin O'Neill; production designer: Robert Gillies; costume designer: Nigla Dickson; New Zealand casting: Diana Rowan; stunt coordinator: Peter Bell; second unit director: Charlie Haskell; additional visual effects: Flat Earth Productions, Inc.; music: Joseph LoDuca

## REGULARS

Kevin Sorbo (Hercules), Michael Hurst (Iolaus/Charon)

## RECURRING

Robert Trebor (Salmoneus), Liddy Holloway (Alcmene)

## H-14: THE KING OF THIEVES

CREDITS: Teleplay by Doug Lefler; directed by Doug Lefler

GUEST STARS: Bruce Campbell (Autolycus), Martyn Sanderson
   (King Menelaus), Lisa Chappel (Dirce)

STORY LINE: Iolaus is falsely accused of stealing a box of jewels. As
Iolaus is subjected to three seemingly inescapable trials, Hercules searches
for the true thief—Autolycus, the King of Thieves. Hercules tracks Autolycus to an empty castle where they both fall into a booby-trapped dungeon
and become partners in peril. Escaping together, they return to Scyros
where Autolycus returns the prized Dragon's Eye Ruby. Iolaus is freed
from the executioner's blade and Autolycus escapes in the confusion.

HIGHLIGHTS: Foremost in this episode are the labors of Iolaus who
must use his wits (in the absence of Hercules' brawn) to accomplish three
amazing feats called the Erebus Test. In the first test his feet are tied to a
huge stone to see if he'll float in a pond. In the second he must carry a
plank piled high with stones without dropping any. And in the third he
must share a pit with a wild boar for three hours without losing so much
as one drop of blood.
   It's not unusual for an episode to have two parallel, but interlinked,
storylines. In this case it's a toss-up as to which is more interesting. While
Hercules and Autolycus in the castle is a lot of fun, it's also wild seeing the
three *labors* that Iolaus has to endure in Hercules' absence. Since Iolaus is
mortal, he must use his wits and skill to survive these challenges. The challenges themselves are cleverly imagined and demonstrate why this series
remains superior to its low grade, unimaginative imitators.

TRIVIA: Autolycus, who makes his *Hercules* debut here, would soon
be featured more often on *Xena*; in "The Quest" (X-37), for example,
Autolycus is the main character. Another engaging return appearance by
Autolycus is in the third-season *Hercules* episode "The End of the Beginning" (H-55) in which the rascal travels back in time a few years and meets
himself! Bruce Campbell really shines in this showy role.

# H-15: All That Glitters

CREDITS: Teleplay by Craig Volk; directed by Garth Maxwell

GUEST STARS: Jennifer Leah-Ward (Voluptua), Tracy Lindsey (Flaxen), Noel Trevarthan (King Midas), Terry Bachelor (Segallus)

SUPPORTING CAST: Margaret-Mary Hollins (Hispides), Max Cryer (Barker), Alexander Gandar (Tacharius), Joseph Greer (Romanus), David Scott (Paraicles), Peter Rowley (Buffoon), Dale Corlett (Thaddeus), James O'Farrell (Eisenkopf), Ray Sefo (Alee)

MYTHOLOGICAL BASIS: King Midas is perhaps one of the best known names in Greek mythology, but the significance of the myth is often missed. Dionysus granted his wish that anything he touched would turn to gold. But it was a curse, not a blessing. When literally everything he touched turned to gold, he could not eat or drink. Midas was the living embodiment of the warnings "The gods are jealous" and "Be careful what you wish for, you may get it."

STORY LINE: In this episode there are subtle echoes of the subtext, but mostly Midas is portrayed as a Las Vegas sort of character. Hercules and Salmoneus visit King Midas' Touch of Gold gambling palace where Hercules observes gamblers making life or death wagers. When Hercules intervenes, he impresses a casino owner who wants Hercules for her showroom headliner.

Caught in the middle of casino rivalries and the kidnapping of Midas, Hercules is manuvered into an arena fight, which he wins, inspiring the townspeople to rise up and destroy the casino.

OBSERVATIONS: Every TV series seems to eventually get around to an episode dealing with *wicked* Las Vegas, but who would have ever thought this would happen on *Hercules*? By combining the legend of King Midas with the clichés of the lore of the gambling capital, we get an average Hercules episode that is pretty much by the numbers.

Voluptua, one of the casino bosses, is a name that rings in the mind like the kinds of women's names that Ian Fleming used to devise for his James Bond spy novels (e.g., Honey Rider and Pussy Galore.)

One truly funny element in this segment is that not only does the plot line parody the gambling and greed aspects of Las Vegas, but it even goes so far as to include a version of arena boxing, a spectator sport made famous by the Nevada mecca.

This episode is very much a template of a typical Hercules episode. Hercules encounters adversity, moves to do something about it, becomes entangled in the subterfuge of the villains and then turns the tables on them in order to free the oppressed. Take one fight from column A and another fight from column B and when in doubt add a free-for-all. In spite of the fact that Hercules possesses greater than human strength, his fighting doesn't just consist of throwing his antagonists twenty feet away, he also performs acrobatic moves in attempting to deal with a dozen men attacking him at once. Some fights are routine but others are cleverly choreographed performances. Amazingly they also consist of action more than violence (fist-fights being uncommon in these bouts).

HIGHLIGHTS: Hercules is ganged up on by vicious opponents when he's tricked into being the main arena attraction.

## H-16: WHAT'S IN A NAME?

CREDITS: Teleplay by Michael Marks; directed by Bruce
    Campbell

GUEST STARS: Kevin Smith (Iphicles), Kenneth McGregor
    (Gorgus), Simone Kessell (Rena), Ross Duncan (Pallaeus), Paul
    Glover (Josephus)

SUPPORTING CAST: Lewis Martin (Priest), Jon Watson
    (Hawker), Simon Prast (First Soldier), Jason Garner (Young
    Soldier), Bernard Moodi (Old Man), John Mcnee (Soldier)

MYTHOLOGICAL BASIS: In Greek mythology Iphicles is the half-
brother of Hercules, born of the same mother, Alcmene, but fathered by

Amphitryon. In the original myth it is Iphicles whose crying saves Hercules from the snakes Hera has sent to kill him. As an adult, Iphicles helps Hercules in his hunt for the Calydonian Boar.

STORY LINE: Hercules finds that Iphicles is impersonating him. Hercules attempts to get his sibling to admit he's an impostor, but Iphicles refuses because he's in love with a woman and he's afraid she will reject him if she learns the truth.

In interrelated subplots, Hercules must battle an evil warlord, save Ioluas from death-trap-laden catacombs beneath the castle, and battle a monster.

In the end Iphicles saves the girl and regains her admiration while Hercules, forever everyone's champion, defeats both the monster and the warlord.

OBSERVATIONS: The idea of someone imitating Hercules is an obvious notion, but that it would turn out to be his half-brother is an interesting twist because this plot device allows for other issues to be explored beyond the typical "Hey, you're not me!" stuff.

Hercules' mother was initially introduced in the original two-hour movies, but this is our first encounter with his earthly half-brother. Iphicles clearly harbors resentment toward Hercules, what with his half-brother being the son of the king of the gods. However, most of these problems are resolved by the end of this episode. In fact the two of them are clearly on the best of terms when we next see them together in "The Wedding of Alcmene" (H-34).

This episode offers a treasure trove of intriguing special effects including catacombs filled with death traps and for good measure a deadly monster. In act four, as Hercules and his brother are engaging in a lot of vital exposition, a monster is introduced in order to bring the story to a rousing conclusion.

Kevin Smith as Iphicles is quite interesting without the beard he wears when playing Ares. In fact Smith looks so different without a beard that many fans didn't originally realize that the actor who plays the half-brother of Hercules also plays Ares.

HIGHLIGHTS: The catacombs of death are awe-inspiring with ingenious pitfalls everywhere. The fight scene with the raptor-like monster is also an exciting sequence.

TRIVIA: Kevin Smith, seen here as Iphicles, would later replace Mark Newham as Ares.

# H-17: SIEGE AT NAXOS

CREDITS: Teleplay by Darrell Fetty; directed by Stephen L. Posey

GUEST STARS: Brian Thompson (Goth), Ray Woolf (Bledar), Rebecca Hobbs (Elora)

SUPPORTING CAST: Patrick Smyth (Charidon), Robert Harte (Dax), Richard Adams (Argeas), Zo Hartley (Patron)

STORY LINE: Hercules and Iolaus capture a warlord and are forced to retreat with their prisoner into an old fortress. The specter of a young woman who was the warlord's former lover inhabits the stronghold. However, because he betrayed her once, she is less than ideal material to mold into his co-conspirator.

One of their attackers discovers that Hercules and Iolaus are defending the fortress alone. While the army prepares their final attack, Hercules, Iolaus, and their prisoner escape through a secret passage, leaving the enemy to attack an empty fortress.

OBSERVATIONS: While Hercules has the strength of, say, ten men, this doesn't mean that he can take on an army by himself. In this episode he and Iolaus have to keep an army from attacking them while they hide out in an abandoned fortress.

The fact that they could have escaped any time ("Now you tell me!") when they're told about the secret passage at the end of the episode, comes close to nullifying the entire story and rendering it pointless because everything beforehand was just time-filler leading up to the, "Oh, didn't you know about the secret passage?" climax.

TRIVIA: In the Hercules blooper reel there surely must be included a shot that shows members of the camera crew joining the soldiers as they pour over the fortress wall.

# H-18: OUTCAST

CREDITS: Teleplay by Robert Bielak; directed by Bruce Seth Green

GUEST STARS: Lucy Lawless (Lyla), Peter Muller (Deric), Neil Holt (Merkus)

SUPPORTING CAST: Jon Brazier (Jakar), Rose Dube (Leuriphone), James Croft (Kefor), Chris Bailey (Cletis), Norman Forsey (Tersius), Kelson Henderson (Demicles), Andrew Kovacevich (Sepsus)

MYTHOLOGICAL BASIS: This is what might be called an *issues* episode in that it chooses Centaurs as the focus of an object lesson on intolerance. In Greek mythology, Centaurs are depicted as half man, half horse and known for their drunken revels, brawling, and debauchery. In this particular episode however, they are portrayed as sympathetic and oppressed.

STORY LINE: Lyla (Lucy Lawless) is taunted because she's married to the Centaur Deric who witnesses the event and then humiliates the ringleader of the bigots. In revenge the bigots set their house on fire killing Lyla. Hercules finds that the troublemakers are Cretans who believe in preserving Athenian purity. Hercules vows that these killers will be brought to justice.

Eventually, the full truth is revealed: Deric the Centaur and his son survived, and Zeus brings Lyla back to life.

OBSERVATIONS: Lucy Lawless returns to *Hercules* in a role different from, though contemporary to, Xena. This is a sequel to "As Darkness Falls" (H-6) although Lyla is not as strong a character as she was initially portrayed in that previous storyline, but then we don't get to see much of her here since she dies at the beginning of the story.

The bigotry angle of this story is well-handled with Centaurs despised for their differences and Lyla hated because she's involved in a mixed marriage. Athenian purity is clearly a parallel to white supremacy as it applies to race mixing. However, having a human marry a centaur and bear his child is about as extreme an example as one could imagine.

HIGHLIGHTS: The reunion between Deric and the revived Lyla is very touching.

TRIVIA: This segment was filmed *after* it had been decided that Lucy Lawless would officially be Xena in future installments. To get around the fact that the same actress was playing two diverse roles on the series, Hercules remarks about the resemblance between Lyla and Xena.

## H-19: UNDER THE BROKEN SKY

CREDITS: Teleplay by John Schulian; directed by Jim Contner

GUEST STARS: Bruce Phillips (Atticus), Carl Bland (Pilot), Maria Rangel (Lucina)

SUPPORTING CAST: Julie Collis (Heliotrope), Katherine Ransom (Mica), John Mellor (Crossbow), Crawford Thorson (Thug), Jim Ngaata (Guard), Jean Hyland (Mother), Christine Bartlett (First Villager), Veronica Aalhurst (Second Villager), Daniel Batten (Weasel), Grant Boccher (Customer)

STORY LINE: The plot of this episode owes as much to events in Chicago in the 1920s as it does to ancient Greek mythology. Hercules helps a man who has been robbed and left for dead by bandits working for the Grecian equivalent of a gangster mob boss. The gangster hires mercenaries to eliminate the bothersome Hercules.

The central plot revolves around thugs collecting protection money; a young woman who has left her husband and is forced to make ends meet by working as a dancer in a pleasure palace; a jealous husband; and a crime boss who makes unwanted advances toward the girl. Naturally, Hercules helps the young couple, and they find themselves trying to hide out from the bad guys until Hercules is forced into a final confrontation.

OBSERVATIONS: This is a by-the-numbers storyline. Hercules encounters people who are in trouble and he sets out to help them. Throw in a crime lord who is extorting protection money from people and you've pretty much seen it all before. They can't all be gems. On the other hand this shows that Hercules is willing to help people whose problems are more down to earth. They aren't menaced by monsters, nor has anyone been spirited off to the Underworld. There isn't even an Olympian god running amuck. It's just plain old ordinary, every-day Grecian crime in the streets. The back story of the couple having lost their two young sons to fever does throw a melancholy air over the proceedings, however. After all, even with the other problems solved, these two people are still trying to put their lives together after suffering a grievous loss, the kind of loss Hercules understands all too well.

Unlike prior episodes, Zeus does not intervene here to bring Lucina's sons back to life. (That's the problem with miracles: when you've seen one, you expect to see more on a regular basis.)

Salmoneus is once again a scene-stealer and his escapades in the pleasure palace are amusing.

HIGHLIGHTS: The final fight scene is exciting as, one by one, Hercules picks off Pilot's thugs.

# H-20: THE MOTHER OF ALL MONSTERS

CREDITS: Teleplay by John Schulian; directed by Bruce Seth
   Green

GUEST STARS: Bridget Hoffman (Echidna), Martin Kove
   (Demetrius), Graham Smith (Leukos)

SUPPORTING CAST: Rebecca Clark (Archer #1), Katrina Misa
   (Archer #2), Ian Miller (Chief Highwayman), Don Linden
   (Master of Ceremonies), Jack Dacey (Trapper), Peter Mason
   (Owner), Colin Francis (Second Thief)

MYTHOLOGICAL BASIS: This episode is a return to a story line that is grounded in Greek mythology. Echidne (spelled *Echidna* in the television credits) was the wife of Typhon. She had the torso of a beautiful woman and the lower half of a speckled serpent and was the mother of the Hydra, Cerberus, the Chimera, and the Sphinx to name but a few of her monstrous offspring.

STORY LINE: Echidna, the mother of all monsters, plots revenge against Hercules because he's killed a number of her monster children. Enlisting the aid of a warrior, the devious creature instructs him to woo Alcmene, the mother of Hercules.

When Hercules returns to his mother's home, the warrior's archers attack him. Thinking Hercules is now dead, the warrior reveals his true nature, kidnaps Alcmene, and takes her to Echidna's cave where she's to be killed. Hercules and Iolaus arrive in time to rescue his mother. Rather than kill Echidna, however, the duo creates a rockslide that seals her in the cave.

OBSERVATIONS: This turns out to be a key episode in the order of things. While initially we view Echidna as yet another creepy crawly that Hercules must battle, her character is later broadened and expanded into much more.

Oddly enough, in future episodes Hercules and Echidna will become friends. It turns out that her children aren't born bad but rather they are kidnapped while still babies and raised to be killers by the humans who steal them. Sometimes the baby monsters are sold to warlords who used them as deadly weapons in their arsenals.

HIGHLIGHT: This first appearance of Echidna, the mother of all monsters, is visually quite stunning, and Hercules' confrontation with Echidna is filled with intriguing special effects.

# H-21: THE OTHER SIDE

CREDITS: Teleplay by Robert Bielak; directed by George
    Mendeluk

GUEST STARS: Tawny Kitaen (Deianeira), Andrea Croton
    (Persephone), Erik Thompson (Hades)

SUPPORTING CAST: Sarah Wilson (Demeter), David Banter

(Tartalus), Simon Lewthwaite (Klonus), Paul McIver (Aeson),
Rose McIver (Ilea), Geoff Allen (Farmer)

MYTHOLOGICAL BASIS: In the original Greek myth Zeus' carnal
desire knows no bounds including incest with his sister Demeter, which
results in the birth of a daughter, Core. Hades, god of the Underworld,
who was brother to both Zeus and Demeter, abducts their daughter, Core,
with the intention of making her his wife. When Demeter finds out where
her daughter is being held, she pleads with Zeus to get her back. Zeus
devises a plan whereby the girl spends three months of the year as the
wife of Hades and is known as Persephone, and the other nine months
with her mother where she continues to use her original name, Core.

STORY LINE: Hades kidnaps Persephone, the daughter of the goddess
Demeter. In this version Demeter goes to Hercules who refuses to help,
claiming that he cannot get involved in a dispute between deities. Demeter uses her power over the elements to create devastating storms. Finally,
Hercules gets the message and agrees to help.
    There is an echo of the events in Hercules' Twelfth Labor, the capture
of Cerberus, when, in crossing the River Styx, Hercules sees his deceased
wife and children in the Elysian Fields. They have a reunion of sorts, which
is marred when his wife finally realizes that she and the children are dead.
    Whereas in the original myth Zeus is the mediating force, in this tele-
vision version Hercules confronts Hades and finds that Persephone rather
likes Hades and isn't in any hurry to return to the upper world. Hades
opposes her return to earth and Hercules must fight his way out. Eventually, Hades and Demeter reach a compromise that allows Persephone to be
with her mother for six months of the year and with Hades for the other
six months.

OBSERVATIONS: This is certainly one of the more ambitious episodes
as it involves not only a return to the Underworld (the first since the telefilm *Hercules in the Underworld* [HM-4], prior to the first season) but also a
confrontation between gods. Ordinarily Hercules is involved with mortals
whom he has to protect from the gods, but here we have a dispute
between the gods themselves. Again, where is Zeus when all this is going
on? Rather than appeal for help to the son of Zeus, why not go right to the
top?

The reunion between Hercules and his family is touching and high-lights this infrequently seen human side of his character that was more pronounced in the original two-hour movies in which he met and wed Deianeira. Thankfully the concept of Hercules wife and children not real-izing that they're dead was not continued very long as it makes it very sad to imagine them wondering why Hercules doesn't return home.

HIGHLIGHTS: The reuniting of Hercules and his family is as senti-mental as the fight between Hercules and Cerberus, the vicious three-headed dog, is exciting.

TRIVIA: Michael Hurst (Iolaus) reprises his heavily costumed role of Charon from *Hercules in the Underworld* (HM-4).

## H-22: THE FIRE DOWN BELOW

CREDITS: Teleplay by Scott Smith Miller and John Schulian; directed by Timothy Bond

GUEST STARS: Stephanie Wilkin (Ayora), Stephen Hall (Purces), Teresa Hill (Nemesis), Andy Anderson (Zandar)

SUPPORTING CAST: Emma Menzies (Syreeta), Daniel Batten (Pyro), Geoff Clendon (Vormann), Roger Goodburn (Promoter), Mark Nua (Wrestler), Jon Brazier (Slave Trader), Jeff Gane (Peddler), Mary Henderson (Kundin), James Marcum (Barkeeper)

MYTHOLOGICAL BASIS: In the pantheon of Greek goddesses, only Nemesis is as beautiful as Aphrodite. Nemesis is the goddess who pun-ishes those who take good fortune but do not thank the gods nor share their fortune with others. Her method of punishment is often humiliation though she has the power to do greater physical harm.

STORY LINE: In this episode Salmoneus strikes it rich when he finds a wealth of treasure in a sealed cave. But Salmoneus' luck suddenly starts to change when his partner is killed. Hercules recognizes the riches as a gift protected by the gods, which means that Salmoneus is next. Hercules convinces Nemesis, the goddess of divine retribution, that Salmoneus is just a pawn being used by the real culprit.

The real villain petitions Hera to give him a fire monster to use against Hercules. Naturally, Hercules prevails, and Nemesis and Hercules part as friends. Nemesis turns into a bird and flies away.

MYTHOLOGICAL BASIS: Having Nemesis turn into a bird makes for intriguing symbology because it was in the form of a swan that Zeus seduced Nemesis. The result of their union was an egg, which was then hatched by Leda, from which Helen of Troy was born.

OBSERVATIONS: Gods and monsters. We have Nemesis on one side and the fire monster on the other. Nemesis, you'll recall, previously appeared in the episode, "Pride Comes Before a Brawl" (H-7). Last time she menaced Iolaus and this time it's Salmoneus.

It is becoming common on the series that all of Salmoneus' schemes eventually sour. Here he's led to a treasure protected by the gods. In "Mummy Dearest" (H-41), he puts an ancient mummy on display that has a dangerous curse attached to it.

The intervention of Hera has been absent for a number of episodes, but she's back in full force making trouble in this episode.

HIGHLIGHTS: The battle with Pyro, the fire monster, is an excellent example of great special effects.

TRIVIA: Nemesis becomes a recurring character, having made her debut previously in "Pride Comes Before a Brawl" (H-7).

# H-23: CAST A GIANT SHADOW

CREDITS: Teleplay by John Schulian; directed by John T. Kretchmer

GUEST STARS: Bridget Hoffman (Echidna), Glenn Shadix (Typhon), Stig Eldred (Maceus)

SUPPORTING CAST: Fiona Mogridge (Breanna), Bruce Hopkins (Pylon), Bruce Allpress (Septus), Bernard Moodi (Proprietor), Steve Hall (Warrior)

MYTHOLOGICAL BASIS: Once again, this is an episode rooted in classic mythological characters. Typhon was born from the mating of Mother Earth and Tartarus. He is the most dangerous of all giant monstrosities with the head of an ass, serpentine legs, and immense arms with serpent heads instead of hands. Typhon and Zeus engage in a mighty battle where they lift huge mountains and throw them at each other. Zeus finally traps Typhon under an enormous rock now known as Mount Aetna. Typhon was also the father of the monster children born to Echidne (spelled *Echidna* in the credits).

STORY LINE: In this episode the details of the myths are altered so that Typhon is now a gentle giant, the rock that holds him is now of conventional size, and it is Hera's evil curse that has trapped him. Hercules, pursuing his quest to undermine Hera, frees Typhon from the rock only to find that Typhon is the husband of Echidna, the mother of all monsters.

In a parallel plot a warrior who seeks revenge on Hercules, locates Iolaus and tortures him to learn of Hercules' whereabouts. With Hera's help, the warrior frees Echidna from her cave and informs Typhon that it was Hercules who trapped Echidna and murdered his children.

Hercules must fight Echidna and Maceus, but in doing so, Hercules undoes Hera's wicked schemes and wins himself a new ally in the person of the mother of all monsters.

OBSERVATIONS: It is an interesting plot twist when a character like Echidna, who had previously been a mortal enemy, becomes a friend to Hercules and Iolaus. When Echidna and Typhon are reunited, she embraces him with her tentacles. Strange stuff!

In the course of this adventure Iolaus gets badly beaten and battered by Maceus, which lends a hard edge to what is essentially a lighthearted episode.

While Hercules encounters and frees Typhon, the friendly giant (and a bit of a clumsy oaf), he has no idea that Iolaus has been kidnapped and is being tortured. There's a good scene when Iolaus escapes and hides in a bog, covering himself with mud in order to blend in to the surroundings while soldiers are searching for him several feet away. By the time he catches up with Hercules he's a real wreck.

This is the episode in which Echidna is freed from the cave Hercules had imprisoned her in, and becomes good when Hercules reunites her with her husband, Typhon. Seeing the monstrous Echidna smiling and laughing is a pretty bizarre sight.

HIGHLIGHTS: Typhon reveals the gentle side of his children including the fact that the Hydra could knit! Later, the kindhearted Typhon accidentally falls on one of Maceus' soldiers.

TRIVIA: Typhon is seen later in "Monster Child in the Promised Land" (H-43).

# H-24: HIGHWAY TO HADES

CREDITS: Teleplay by Robert Bielak; directed by T. J. Scott

GUEST STARS: Erik Thomson (Hades), Leslie Wing (Celeste), Ray Henwood (King Sisyphus), Craig Hall (Timeron), Angela Gribben (Daphne)

SUPPORTING CAST: Michael Hurst (Charon), Tony Wood (Eluvius), Ronald Hendricks (Epicurus), Barry Te Hora (Chief), Jane Cresswell (Maid), Megan Edwards (Servant), Tim Raby (Soldier), David Mackie (Guard)

MYTHOLOGICAL BASIS: In Greek mythology Sisyphus, the ruler of Corinth, is best known for the way in which Zeus punished him: he was condemned to push a giant rock to the top of a hill only to have it roll back down again whereupon he would have to start all over. Less well known is the reason for this punishment. Sisyphus was a cunning businessman, a thief, and a murderer who tricked Hades and escaped Tartarus on two occasions before he was caught by Hermes and returned to the Underworld once and for all.

This episode is loosely based on Sisyphus' wily avoidance of his original death sentence and gives Hercules the task performed by Hermes in the original myth.

STORY LINE: Hades asks Hercules for help. It seems that King Sisyphus of Corinth avoided his death by tricking another man into going in his place to the Underworld. Hercules must bring Sisyphus to Hades within three days.

The man who replaced Sisyphus wants to return with Hercules to earth so he can see his wife to whom he was married for only four hours at the time of his unexpected death.

When Sisyphus is finally taken down to Tartarus, Hercules talks Hades into letting the man have his wedding night. However, the only body available for the task is that of Hercules.

OBSERVATIONS: One would think that death would not be quite so easy to sidestep as King Sisyphus of Corinth makes it seem. This is the same ruler who captures Death in a *Xena* episode, "Death in Chains" (X-9). Sisyphus also tries to escape Hades in "Ten Little Warlords" (X-32). So this *Hercules* episode falls somewhere between those two *Xena* chapters in the story continuity.

The two parallel storylines in this one are quite interesting. While the Sisyphus story is the more dramatic of the two, the Timeron story is quite poignant as his disembodied soul is still very much in love with his bride of four hours, and that story proves the more interesting of the two. Well written, emotionally satisfying stories can actually be much more interesting than your typical hero-villain confrontations. After all, there are really no issues to resolve when you have Hercules in one corner and Sisyphus (who is trying to condemn an innocent man to the Underworld) in the other corner. Reuniting, however briefly, two long-lost lovers is clearly the richer of the two story lines.

This would appear to be the first time that Hercules has made love to a woman since he lost his family in "The Wrong Path" (H-1).

HIGHLIGHTS: Hercules combats the assorted magic tricks of King Sisyphus.

TRIVIA: In a later episode we learn that Jason has become the new king of Corinth, a throne he relinquishes to Iphicles in "The Wedding of Alcmene" (H-34).

## H-25: THE SWORD OF VERACITY

CREDITS: Teleplay by Steven Baum; directed by Garth Maxwell

GUEST STARS: Kim Michaels (Leah), Brad Carpenter (Amphion), Paul Minifie (Trachis)

SUPPORTING CAST: Danny Lineham (Lycus), Kelly Greene (Epius), Brendolan Lovegrove (Man), Anton Bentley (Head Guard), Amanda Rees (Mina), Michael Saccente (Talius), Anthony Ray Parker (Minotaur), Shane Dawson (Assistant Minotaur)

MYTHOLOGICAL BASIS: In this episode two allusions are made to mythological personalities—Amphion and Hestia—but there is little significance to the use of the name Amphion or the reference to the Hestian virgin.

Amphion is yet another of Zeus' sons, this time by Antiope. He is married to Niobe, and because Niobe insults Leto, her children, Apollo and Artemis, slaughter Niobe's children. Amphion takes out his anger on the Delphic priests and is killed by Apollo and tortured in Tartarus.

Hestia is the goddess of hearth and home who is known as the most mild-tempered of the Olympians. She remains chaste and unmarried.

STORY LINE: Amphion, as he appears in this episode, is a former warrior who now preaches peace. When he is arrested for murder, Amphion offers no defense and is sentenced to death.

Hercules and Iolaus meet a Hestian virgin who helps them seek out the sword of veracity, which will prove the innocence of Amphion. In the course of their quest Hercules must fight a Minotaur sent by Hera while Iolaus and the girl search for the right sword.

OBSERVATIONS: This is another instance in which Hercules arrives just as a crisis erupts and feels honor bound to remedy the situation. Isn't it convenient that something exists (the Sword of Veracity) that is exactly what is needed to solve the present dilemma? That's a little too pat, almost as pat as the *Xena* episode "The Execution" (X-41) wherein she arrives just as an old friend is going to be executed and not only saves him from the hangman in a clever way, but shows how it was really she who killed the man her friend was accused of killing! Sometimes events can be a little bit *too* convenient and contrived.

Hera is back, this time creating Minotaurs out of stone to fight Hercules, which is, of course, another opportunity for some wild special effects.

HIGHLIGHTS: The scene in which the battling heroes find a cave full of look-alike swords with only one being the true blade of veracity is quite amusing.

# H-26: THE ENFORCER

CREDITS: Teleplay by Nelson Costello; directed by T. J. Scott

GUEST STARS: Teresa Hill (Nemesis), Karen Sheperd (Enforcer), Jed Brophy (Gnatius)

SUPPORTING CAST: Andrew Kovacevich (Proprietor), Grant Bochner (Hunter), Geoff Snell (Clytus), Paula Keenan (Drunkard), Toni Marsch (First Maid), Asa Lindh (Second Maid), Jeff Gane (Gang Boss), Adrian Keeling (First Man), Ross Harper (Second Man)

MYTHOLOGICAL BASIS: Nemesis, the goddess responsible for punishing those who did not thank the gods for good fortune nor share that fortune with others, has been introduced in a prior episode.

STORY LINE: When Nemesis refuses to carry out a particularly hateful order issued by Hera, the queen of the gods changes her into a powerless mortal. Hercules agrees to help Nemesis, which leads Hera to send the

Enforcer who appears in the guise of a female but is actually made of water and has no soul.

Meanwhile, Hercules and Nemesis have a pleasant roll in the hay (literally), unaware that the sinister Enforcer is tracking him. Nemesis lures the Enforcer into a trap, and Hercules fights the unworldly creature.

OBSERVATIONS: This is a fascinating episode, dealing with the concept of "how the mighty have fallen" and how even a god can gain knowledge by learning what it is like to be a mere mortal. After Nemesis and Hercules make love—a rewarding and revealing experience for her—she decides she must go and find her destiny alone.

Basically this is a long action episode with romantic side intervals. While Nemesis seemed pretty cold in her previous outings (H-7 and H-22), here her fall from Olympus has rendered her warm and human in more ways than one.

The Enforcer is clearly this TV series' answer to the acclaimed film *Terminator 2: Judgment Day* (1991). Since the Enforcer isn't human and is only donning the disguise of a woman, it's fair play for Hercules to beat her up. She is actually more interesting when she is seen again in the season three Hercules episode "Not Fade Away" (H-42). This time out she's just a non-human threat who keeps coming and coming whereas in the sequel she has an actual personality. It's also interesting in the sequel how Hades wants her out of Tartarus because she bothers him.

## H-27: ONCE A HERO

CREDITS: Teleplay by Robert Bielak and John Schulian; directed by Robert Tapert

GUEST STARS: Jeffrey Thomas (Jason), Peter Feeney (Castor), Edward Campbell (Artemus)

SUPPORTING CAST: Anthony Ray Parker (Valerus), Tim Raby (Archivus), Willa O'Neill (Phoebe), John Sumner (Domesticles), Mark Nua (Otus), Latham Gaines (Marcus), Belinda Todd (Princess), Campbell Rousselle (Robber), Paul Norell (Falafel)

MYTHOLOGICAL BASIS: The myth of Jason encompasses much more than his quest for the Golden Fleece. After returning from his famous voyage, he marries Medea and rules Corinth for ten years until he lusts after King Creon's daughter and loses favor with the gods. Thereafter, he becomes a homeless wanderer until he seeks out the remains of his ship, the *Argo*, and attempts to hang himself from the prow. A falling timber from the crumbling wreck strikes him on the head and kills him.

STORY LINE: This episode would appear to take place during Jason's vagabond years. Hercules meets up with Jason who claims that he has been seeing visions of a pursuing demonic warrior.

The warrior appears, steals the Golden Fleece, and Hercules and Jason's old crew embark on a sea chase to recover it. The evil warrior is part of a Hera cult and, in order to retrieve the Golden Fleece, the crew must battle an army of living skeletons. In the end Jason becomes his old self, holds onto the throne, and the Golden Fleece is restored.

OBSERVATIONS: The action movie *Jason and the Argonauts* (1963)— with its great special effects by Ray Harryhausen and its magical tale of the search for the Golden Fleece—is today very much a cult favorite. Since the character of Hercules (played by Nigel Green) appeared so prominently in that 1963 fantasy feature, which starred Todd Armstrong and Gary Raymond, it was both fitting and inevitable that this episode of the Hercules legend would eventually be explored by the 1990s TV series, and the show handles this famous story line with great respect. Rather than attempt to re-create the original voyage and thereby be compared to the classic British-made movie, the *Hercules* producers wisely chose to make their new plot a sequel. As a tribute to the original film, the climax offers a new, state-of-the-art skeleton fight. The results are wonderful to behold.

Although Hercules and Iolaus are central figures in this episode, it is just as much the story of Jason. What results is one of the great episodes of the second season.

Jason is seen for the first time in this episode but we'll see him again in the later key episode "The Wedding of Alcmene" (H-34) when Jason becomes the new stepfather of Hercules. And if you think Jason had a hard time in this episode, in "The Wedding of Alcmene" he and Hercules both get swallowed by a sea monster!

HIGHLIGHTS: Superior special effects include the crafty warrior who haunts Jason's mind as well as a very tricky skeleton.

# H-28: HEEDLESS HEARTS

CREDITS: Teleplay by Robert Bielak; directed by Peter Ellis

GUEST STARS: Audie England (Rheanna), Michael Keir-Morrisey (Melkos), Michael Saccente (Grovelus), Nigel Godfrey (Syrus)

SUPPORTING CAST: Bruce Hopkins (Jordis), Grant Triplow (Clarion), Robert Hogwood (Vericles), Sara Wiseman (Hephates), Doug McCallan (Guard)

STORY LINE: This is an intriguing story premise with surprising twists and turns, but little in the way of mythological underpinning. At the opening of the episode, the reputation of Hercules' compassion is so widely known that it is inevitable someone would try to take advantage of his willingness to help the downtrodden.

A lovely revolutionary leader asks Hercules' help against an increasingly despotic king. While Hercules is coping with the brewing revolution, Iolaus is struck by lightning and can now foresee particular future events. He reveals to Hercules that the girl will betray him. Because Hercules cares for her, he is slow to accept the possibility that she's capable of such a disloyal act. Unfortunately, time reveals the truth of Iolaus' visions.

OBSERVATIONS: This time Hercules is called upon to lead a revolution, but why not if the cause is just? Of course, complications could follow, such as insuring that the successor is a just ruler and keeping in place the mechanisms by which the society functioned smoothly while also insuring that the treasury isn't being looted when no one is looking. Being a hero can be a bigger job than breaking up bar fights and reuniting estranged lovers. It would be interesting to see an episode in which Hercules does lead a revolution, and even though he's in the right ,we could see the realistic difficulties that follow in the wake of such a full scale uprising. But not this time . . . .

Once again Hercules' friendship with Iolaus is tested, just as it was back in "The Warrior Princess" (H-9).

# H-29: LET THE GAMES BEGIN

CREDITS: Teleplay by John Schulian; directed by Gus Trikonis

GUEST STARS: Cory Everson (Atalanta), Matthew Humphrey (Damon), Paul Glover (Brontus), Chris Bailey (Tarkon), John Watson (Taphius)

SUPPORTING CAST: Jason Honte (Lieutenant), Marcus Ponton (Soldier), Chris McKibbin (Chief), Norman Palacid (Salesman), Brenda Kendall (Customer), Morgan Palmer-Hubbard (First Boy), Timothy Dale (Second Boy)

MYTHOLOGICAL BASIS: In Greek mythology Hercules is often associated with the first Olympic games. Usually it is related to the city of Elis and King Augeias, who had refused to pay Hercules for cleaning his stables (the Fifth Labor of Hercules). In most versions Hercules conquers the city and kills the king, then participates in an Olympiad. Eurystheus (Hercules' master, who assigned the tasks to be performed as the Labors of Hercules), fearing that the mighty Hercules will win all the events, declares that the winner shall receive no payment, thus establishing a tradition still in practice.

STORY LINE: The Eleans and the Spartans are determined to fight a bloody war to prove which side is superior. Hercules comes up with a nonviolent alternative to war, which he calls "The Olympics." Meanwhile, crafty Salmoneus develops a fast-buck scheme to take advantage of the pending competition and almost ruins Hercules' plan. However, at the end of the contests, it is the honest victors who emerge as the true champions.

OBSERVATIONS: Actually, didn't we see Hercules in something called the Olympics in the movie *Jason and the Argonauts*? There were also Olympic-style events in the first Steve Reeves *Hercules* movie. But this time the issues are larger and the end result is more far-reaching. Hercules knows that with his super human abilities he could win all the events, so the trick is to come up with an event which is both fair as well as satisfying to the participants and the viewers (in ancient Greece) alike. This is a fun episode and a memorable one.

Salmoneus is back and as usual has a new scheme to try. While his schemes tend to be mostly legitimate, they also have a nasty habit of unraveling to his detriment.

Both *Hercules* and *Xena* have featured episodes that reveal the so-called *true* historical background of well-known traditions. In this case, it's the Olympics. On *Xena,* the origins of both Christmas and the Miss Universe Pageant have been *revealed* to our wondering eyes in "A Solstice Carol" (X-33) and "Here She Comes...Miss Amphipolis" (X-35).

# H-30: THE APPLE

CREDITS: Teleplay by Steven Baum; directed by Kevin Sorbo

GUEST STARS: Alexandra Tydings (Aphrodite), Rhonda McHardy (Artemis), Amanda Lister (Athena)

SUPPORTING CAST: Claire Yarlett (Thera), Jonathan Black (Epius), Ian Mune (King Sidon), Stephen Tozer (Diadorus), John Smith (Socrates), Peter Needham (Plato), Sam Williams (Comrade), Vicky Barrett (Old Woman)

MYTHOLOGICAL BASIS: This episode is based on one of the many myths surrounding Aphrodite, the goddess of desire. According to the legend, Aphrodite was conceived when Cronus cut off Uranus' private parts and threw them into the sea. Aphrodite emerged from the water, naked and so beautiful that flowers bloomed wherever she walked. She is frivolous and flirtatious with only one thought in mind: to make love.

Eris, Ares sister, causes an argument between Aphrodite, Hera, and Athene over who is the most beautiful. (In this television version Artemis replaces Hera who would be inappropriate because of her role as the prime evil antagonist to Hercules).

Paris is chosen to be the judge, and all three try to bribe him. It is Aphrodite's promise to make Helen fall in love with him that persuades Paris to select Aphrodite as the most beautiful.

STORY LINE: While fishing, Iolaus hooks something big, but it is *not* a fish. It is a giant seashell being used as a vessel for wind-surfing by Aphrodite— a goddess who chooses to speak in a jargon similar to that of a 1980s California valley girl. She is soon joined by two other goddesses, Artemis and Athena, and Iolaus is pressed into service to judge who is the most beautiful of the three.

In an echo of the original myth, Aphrodite complicates matters when she casts a spell on Iolaus that makes him irresistible to a certain princess. Naturally, Hercules must step in to unravel this latest mess.

OBSERVATIONS: The character of Aphrodite as presented in this episode, is usually played for laughs. Her lines are almost always valley-speak and she comes across as little more than a self-centered airhead.

One wonders why the goddess of love would want to divide lovers? In her appearance in the Xena episode "For Him the Bell Tolls" (X-40), Aphrodite pits one person against another—using a spell designed to break up lovers because she is deliberately competing against her son, Cupid. But this was her first appearance and she acts exactly the same here as she does in later episodes.

TRIVIA: This episode has three first appearances of recurring characters who will show up often on the series—those of the goddesses Aphrodite, Artemis, and Athena.

This segment provides the directorial debut of star Kevin Sorbo, who does an admirable job behind the camera. He has gone on to direct several more episodes in the series.

# H-31: THE PROMISE

CREDITS: Teleplay by Michael Marks; directed by Stewart Main

GUEST STARS: Marton Csokas (Tarlus), Joel Tobeck (King
  Beraeus), Josephine Davison (Ramina)

SUPPORTING CAST: Calvin Tutead (Natras), Michael Robinson
  (Lieutenant), Paul Norell (Falafel), Lee-Jane Foreman (Servant),
  Matthew Sunderland (Sheepherder), Alistair Douglas
  (Landlord), Kenneth Prebble (Priest)

STORY LINE: The future wife of a king has been kidnapped by a long-time acquaintance of the ruler. Hercules and Iolaus set forth on the trail of the kidnapper and when they finally track him down, they find the king's betrothed clearly does not wish to be rescued. In fact she reveals that she is in love with her kidnapper and has no intention of returning. Her wishes place Hercules and Iolaus in a difficult position as they seek to insure that the right thing is done.

HIGHLIGHTS: What starts out as appearing to be a damsel-in-distress episode turns into something more when the damsel turns out not to be in distress. Thus a straightforward plot explored several times before on earlier episodes becomes complicated with plot and counter plot and expands into a very different story wherein Hercules and Iolaus find themselves in the middle of a tricky game.

Fights, of course, are foremost in this action-filled episode. Once again, Hercules and Iolaus prove that their skills at fisticuffs obviate any need for swords or other pointy weapons.

## H-32: KING FOR A DAY

CREDITS: Teleplay by Patricia Manney; directed by Anson
    Williams

GUEST STARS: Lisa Ann Hadley (Niobe), Robert Polock (Minos),
    Will Kempe (Archias)

SUPPORTING CAST: Brendan Lovegrove (Pylon), Derek Payne
    (Hector), Ross McKellar (Lisos), Max Cryer (Priest), Zo Hart-
    ley (Tenant), Tim Hosking (Host), Brendan Perkins (Attica
    Guard), Tony Williams (Farmer), Matthew Jeffs (First Guard),
    John Ron Kempt (Second Guard), Tim Biggs (Farmer),
    Michael Bajko (Husband), Johanna Elms (Daughter), Matt
    Elliott (Whimpering Lackey)

MYTHOLOGICAL BASIS: Once again, two names of prominent mythological characters are used but with no discernible connection to the original myths.

Orestes, the son of Agamemnon and brother of Electra, is best known for avenging the murder of his father by his mother and her lover. In his later life he became king of Sparta.

Niobe is an arrogant woman whose children are slaughtered by Apollo and Artemis when Niobe mocks their mother, Leto.

Rather than being based on either of these mythological characters, the story line of this episode would seem to be based on the plot of the classic story by Anthony Hope, *The Prisoner of Zenda*.

STORY LINE: Iolaus and his cousin Prince Orestes are look-alikes. When Orestes is drugged by his brother, Iolaus steps in as a substitute prince who must carry out his royal duties and insure that the royal wedding to Niobe takes place as planned.

Iolaus, acting as king, is a more just monarch than Orestes had been, and Niobe finds herself falling in love with the man she thinks is Orestes. Eventually, Iolaus rescues and reinstates Orestes who has come to realize the error of his ways.

OBSERVATIONS: The wit and depth of Iolaus' character comes across much more fully here than in most *Hercules* episodes. In spite of the occasional humor, this installment also has sufficient serious moments to make it a substantial adventure.

Iolaus episodes were still rare at this point, but this one is so well written that it remains one of the best of the entire series. Initially when Iolaus meets Orestes, we see that even though they are lookalikes, in temperament they are quite different. It's interesting the way that writing can make us interested in a character who exists only through the benefit of trick photography. Iolaus makes us care about his cousin, and by the time Orestes is seen again in the sequel, we care about him as well.

HIGHLIGHTS: The rescue of Orestes by Iolaus is hair-raising indeed.

TRIVIA: This episode has a follow-up in the third season. In "Long Live the King" (H-48), all the unresolved plot threads from this segment are tied up.

The director of this *Hercules* chapter is Anson Williams, perhaps best known for playing Potsie Weber on the long-running TV sitcom *Happy Days* (1974–83).

## H-33: PROTEAN CHALLENGE

CREDITS: Teleplay by Brian Herskowitz; directed by Oley
    Sassone

GUEST STARS: Ashley Lawrence (Daniella), Jane Cresswell
    (Proteus), Paul Gittins (Thanus), James O'Farrell (Bornus),
    Stephen Papps (Tritos)

SUPPORTING CAST: John O'Leary (Magistrate), Alan Farquhar
    (First Villager), Tamar Howe (Second Villager), Lillian Enting
    (Old Woman), Meredith Chalmers (Girl)

MYTHOLOGICAL BASIS: Proteus is a name that means "first man,"
and it occurs more than once in Greek mythology. The Proteus that is the
inspiration for this episode was an Egyptian king associated with the myth
surrounding Menelaus' voyage home from Troy. Menelaus is told that he
must capture Proteus and force him to provide information. Proteus turns
himself into a snake, a lion, running water, a tree, and even the wind
needed to fill the sails of Menelaus' ship before he finally gives Menelaus
the directions he needs.

STORY LINE: A sculptor is accused of robbery and is sentenced to
have his hands chopped off unless Hercules and Iolaus can exonerate him.
Complicating the situation is the fact that Iolaus has become smitten with
the sculptor's daughter, and when he sees Hercules kissing her, he becomes furious. But Hercules denies that this ever happened.
    At the bottom of all this confusion is Proteus, a god who can assume
the form of any living thing. He was once spurned by Daniella and is now
attempting to punish her. Hercules takes on Proteus, fighting him as the
god assumes different forms including that of Hercules himself.

OBSERVATIONS: This is certainly an unusual *Hercules* episode, which
introduces another character from the Greek pantheon into the TV universe. But how odd that Proteus in his true form is played by a woman.
    Even though the true form of Proteus is apparently female, the signifi-
cance of this is never addressed anywhere in the storyline. The fact that

this revelation occurs in the final scene enables this slippery concept to get by us in a hurry, but afterwards one cannot help but say, hmmm.... After all, Proteus was not only pursuing Daniella, the sculptor's daughter, but was even seen kissing her while in the phony form of Hercules. Did Proteus want the sculptor out of the way because she knew that Daniella's father would never approve of their unorthodox relationship? After all, this isn't an episode of *Xena*!

That Hercules and Iolaus trust each other implicitly is what enables them to keep from being tricked by the god for very long. This is in contrast to the time when hot-headed Iolaus lost his reason in "The Warrior Princess" (H-9) and came after Hercules. Obviously, Iolaus is a far more mature person now.

HIGHLIGHTS: Hercules' fight with the shape-shifting Proteus provides some captivating special effects.

## H-34: THE WEDDING OF ALCMENE

CREDITS: Teleplay by John Schulian; directed by Timothy Bond

GUEST STARS: Jeffrey Thomas (Jason), Liddy Holloway (Alcmene), Sabina Karsenti (Sera), Nathaniel Lees (Blue Priest), Simon Prast (Patronius), Simone Kessell (Rena), Kevin Smith (Iphicles)

SUPPORTING CAST: Willa O'Neill (Phoebe), Lisa Chappell (Dirce), Peter Muller (Deric), Paul Norell (Falafel), Brad Carpenter (Amphius), Ken Nochalis (Leah), Tim Raby (Archimus), John Sumner (Domesticles), Nancy Schroder (Older Sister), Katherine Ransom (Mica), Julie Collis (Heliotrope), Peter Morgan (Spiro)

MYTHOLOGICAL BASIS: As noted in the previous Jason episode, the Greek myth records that Jason ruled Corinth for ten years. The end of his rule comes when he seeks to divorce Medea and marry King Creon's daughter Glauce (or sometimes, Creusa). Medea kills her rival, Jason flees and becomes a vagabond, Medea travels to Asia, and Corinth falls into the hands of Perses until Medea returns and restores her father to the throne.

STORY LINE: This episode offers an alternative history to both Jason and Corinth in which Hercules' mother, Alcmene, intends to wed Jason.

Hera promises a challenger to the throne that she will make him ruler if he kills Hercules. In addition to the killers sent by the pretender to the throne, a giant serpent is dispatched by Hera. The monster swallows Jason and Hercules, but they defeat it from the inside out. The episode resolves with the marriage of Jason and Alcmene. To settle the royal succession issue, Jason names Iphicles (the brother of Hercules) as Corinth's new ruler.

OBSERVATIONS: This humorous adventure offers the reappearance of a number of characters from past episodes. This includes the daughters of King Thespius who all relish the idea of bearing Hercules' children. Also present are a few of the Argonauts as well as Deric the Centaur.

Kevin Smith as Iphicles looks very different without facial hair and is almost unrecognizable as the same actor who plays Ares.

I can't praise highly enough the special effects of the sea monster swallowing Hercules and Jason (luckily it doesn't chew its food first). In keeping with the continuity of the series (and unlike other shows, this one does follow a continuity), Hercules reveals to Jason that this has happened to him before in *Hercules and the Lost Kingdom* (HM-2). In some ways I think that both of the sequences with Hercules being swallowed by a sea monster are throwbacks or homages to a 1960s episode of the TV show *Voyage to the Bottom of the Sea* in which a diving bell is swallowed by a whale and the men inside it have to walk through the whale's guts and find their way to the outside.

The sequence with Hercules and Jason trapped inside the sea serpent is easily one of the weirdest in the entire series. The special effects of the sea serpent's exterior are excellent and the fantastic sets used to represent the monster's guts are wild.

HIGHLIGHTS: Hercules and Jason are attacked by assassins but defeat them even though the odds are six to one.

When the giant sea serpent gobbles down Jason, quick-acting Hercules jumps down its throat after him. The scenes set inside the monster's stomach are grotesquely memorable.

# H-35: THE POWER

CREDITS: Teleplay by Nelson Costello; directed by Charlie
    Haskell

GUEST STARS:Greer Robson (Siren), David Drew Gallagher
    (Dion), Bruce Phillips (Jucobus), Grant Bridger (Caris)

SUPPORTING CAST: Patrick Wilson (Old Titus), Liam Vincent
    (Young Titus), Greg Johnson (First Bandit), Christian Hodge
    (Second Bandit), Lulu Alach (Delia), Mark Sinclair (Fisher-
    man), Greg Norman (Fishmonger), William Lose (Tavern
    Owner), Elaine Bracey (Villager)

MYTHOLOGICAL BASIS: In Greek mythology Aphrodite is the wife
of Hephaestus, but her favorite lover is Ares who is the father of three of
her children—Phobus, Deimus, and Harmonia—while Paris is the father of
Hermaphroditus, Anchises is the father of Aeneas, and Adonis is the father
of Golgos, Beroe, and perhaps Priapus. With all of her lovers, it is entirely
possible that Aphrodite may indeed have had an unrecorded son named
Dion around whom this episode revolves.
    Sirens are mythological creatures with bird-like bodies and beautiful,
human, female faces. They have voices that are so beautiful and enchanting that sailors passing their island hear their singing and become so distracted they lose course and crash on the rocky coast.

STORY LINE: Dion, the son of the goddess Aphrodite, has the ability
to use his enchanted voice to make people do whatever he wants. His evil
uncle wants his nephew to utilize his special powers to help his criminal
gang. Hercules steps in and attempts to set Dion on the right path.
    Only when the boy sees his uncle try to kill his own brother (Dion's
father), does Dion believe Hercules' claims about the sinister man. Sadder
but wiser, Dion insists he'll learn how to use his power for good, and he
plans to marry Siren.

OBSERVATIONS: Salmoneus' presence in this episode provides for a
minor subplot, but the character is not really vital to the story line.
    The gods mixing it up in the lives of humans again. Just as Hercules is the

Right: Kevin Sorbo's senior year picture as it appears in the Mound-Westonka High School yearbook, 1977.
Photo courtesy Seth Poppel Yearbook Archives.

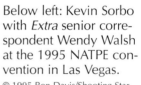

Below: Kevin Sorbo with his parents, Lynn and Ardis Sorbo, in 1996 at the opening of a casino in New Zealand.
Photo courtesy New Zealand Magazines Archive.

Below left: Kevin Sorbo with *Extra* senior correspondent Wendy Walsh at the 1995 NATPE convention in Las Vegas.
© 1995 Ron Davis/Shooting Star.

Below right: Kevin Sorbo with his girlfriend, Sam Jenkins, in 1996 at Planet Hollywood in New York.
© 1996 Albert Ferreira/Globe Photos, Inc.

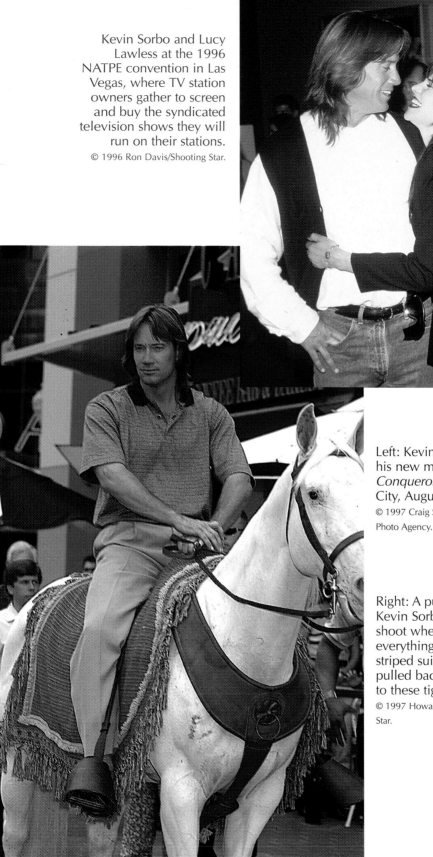

Kevin Sorbo and Lucy Lawless at the 1996 NATPE convention in Las Vegas, where TV station owners gather to screen and buy the syndicated television shows they will run on their stations.
© 1996 Ron Davis/Shooting Star.

Left: Kevin Sorbo promotes his new movie, *Kull the Conqueror,* at Universal City, August 16, 1997.
© 1997 Craig Skinner/Celebrity Photo Agency.

Right: A publicity still of Kevin Sorbo from a photo shoot where he modeled everything from a pin-striped suit with his hair pulled back and hidden, to these tight leather pants.
© 1997 Howard Rosenberg/Shooting Star.

Left: Kevin and Lucy clowning around at the 1997 VSDA convention in Las Vegas, where videostore owners screen and buy the programs they will rent and sell in their stores.

Above: Lucy Lawless,
crowned Mrs. New
Zealand, 1989.
Photo courtesy New Zealand
Magazines Archive.

Right: Lucy Lawless with
her then-husband, Garth
Lawless, and their daughter,
Caitlin, eight months, 1989.
Photo courtesy New Zealand
Magazines Archive.

Left: Kevin Sorbo discusses
the next shot while on
location in New Zealand,
shooting *Hercules.* Photo courtesy New Zealand Magazines Archive.

Above: Lucy Lawless on her opening night as Rizzo in the Broadway revival of the musical *Grease* at the Eugene O'Neill Theatre in New York. © 1997 Henry McGee/ Globe Photos, Inc.

Left: A publicity still of Lucy Lawless from a photo shoot where she took the tapestry prop off the wall, wrapped it around herself, and ended up looking like a high fashion model. © 1997 Tranz/Shooting Star.

Right: Lucy Lawless' parents, Julie and Frank, at home in Auckland, New Zealand. Photo courtesy New Zealand Magazines Archive.

Right: Poking fun at her horse riding accident, Lucy Lawless is carried onto the set of *The Tonight Show.*
Photo courtesy Archive Photos.

Below: Lucy talks with host Jay Leno about the last time she was booked as a guest but couldn't appear because she had been injured while shooting a comedy sketch they were going to use on that show. Photo courtesy Archive Photos.

half-mortal son of a mortal mother and an immortal father, Dion is the half-mortal son of an immortal mother and a mortal father. Where Aphrodite is while all of this plotting and mayhem is going on is unknown. Complicating matters is Siren, but she turns out to be a stabilizing influence in the life of Dion.

One would think that Hercules, who also has Olympian parentage, would be welcomed by Dion as someone who could help him deal with his unique situation (although it is odd that it is not until Hercules shows up that Dion's father tells him who his real mother is). I believe that's called plot manipulation as Hercules should have no bearing on when and where Dion is told the truth about his mother.

In spite of the unusual mix of elements, it turns into a fairly routine telling of the tale.

## H-36: CENTAUR MENTOR JOURNEY

CREDITS: Teleplay by Robert Bielak; directed by Stephen L. Posey

GUEST STARS: Tony Blackett (Ceridian), Julian Arahanga (Cassius), James Townshend (Theseus), Marcia Cameron (Myrra), Mark Clare (Gnoxius)

SUPPORTING CAST: Edward Newborn (Perdiclis), John McKee (Gredor), Robert McMullen (Locus), Mark Clare (Grosius), Jonathan Bell-Booth (First Centaur), Ray Bishop (Second Centaur), John Freeman (Blacksmith), Lance Phillips (Rigis), Fred Craig (Moog)

MYTHOLOGICAL BASIS: As noted previously, although there is no particular mythological basis to the premise, in this series the half man–half horse Centaurs are often used in story lines that symbolically speak to the issues of intolerance and racial equality.

STORY LINE: The leader of the Centaurs is dying and wants the Centaurs and humans to mend fences, but his hard work is threatened by another Centaur who is fed up with Centaurs being treated like second-class citizens. The Centaurs have been secretly training for war at a nearby castle, and they are determined to enter the town and drink from the "humans only" fountain.

Hercules persuades both the Centaur forces and the humans to lay down their arms when he demonstrates that both sides have been cruelly manipulated by a greedy land owner. In a symbolic act Cassius goes to the fountain to drink.

OBSERVATIONS: The opening credits of *Hercules* state that his strength is matched only by the power of his heart, which is why Hercules keeps getting drawn into all these (mis)adventures.

The parallels between the civil rights movement and the Centaurs' equality movement are common plot devices on both this series and *Xena.*

Once again Hercules is asked to get involved with a revolution. While this isn't a revolution to overthrow a government, its effects will nonetheless be far-reaching. In this mythological age Centaurs are outcasts because they are only half human. Amazons hate Centaurs as well and in some *Xena* episodes they are actually at war against each other until Xena intervenes. But the Centaurs themselves are always portrayed as a peaceful race except in this one episode of Hercules. While there are episodes where an individual Centaur will be shown to be violent and threatening, as a race they are portrayed as benevolent. This episode of Hercules is the only one showing an entire group of Centaurs threatening war, a revolution that Hercules manages to avert. The only other storyline that comes to mind that has this many Centaurs in it is the *Xena* episode "Orphan of War" (X-25) in which only a small band of evil Centaurs are seen fighting against a much larger band of peaceful Centaurs.

It is worth noting that although black actors do not appear very frequently on these two series, when they do—as with the main Centaur here—it is almost always in major featured roles.

# H-37: CAVE OF ECHOES

CREDITS: Teleplay by John Schulian and Robert Bielak; directed
    by Gus Trikonis

GUEST STARS: Owen Black (Parenthesis), Mandy Gilette
    (Melina)

SUPPORTING CAST: Mark Perry (Elopius), Grant McFarland (First Ruffian)

STORY LINE: The journalist Parenthesis (an amusing pun on the word) manages to convince our heroes to let him tag along with them as they seek out a young woman lost inside the mysterious Cave of Echoes.

To fill the hours until they locate the lost maiden, Hercules and Iolaus recount some of their past adventures. In the process we are treated to flashbacks of fights with various monsters. The duo suggest to Parenthesis that he can become a hero as well if he'll only try, and when they do find the young woman, it is Parenthesis who saves her.

OBSERVATIONS: Phew, talk about a template! This is a template for what is called a bottle show—a show that takes place on standing sets. Here we have the cave sets dragged out once again for Hercules and company to wander around in while they search for a plot. They never do find one.

One can imagine that after the spectacle of "The Wedding of Alcmene" (H-34) that some belt-tightening was required to bring the season in on time and under budget. The result was apparently the not too memorable "Cave of Echoes." This plot is a pretty thin concept around which to spin an episode using clips from previous shows. It made for a rather weak conclusion to the second season of *Hercules*.

But this is more than made up for with the season-three premiere, "Mercenary" (H-38), an episode that represents the *Hercules* series at the top of its form.

# CHAPTER EIGHT

# HERCULES: THE LEGENDARY JOURNEYS

## SEASON THREE (1996–97)

The episodes created for the television series are all sixty minutes long, the standard length for a drama-adventure series.

## PRODUCTION CREDITS

Created by Christian Williams; co-producer: David Eick; co-producer: Liz Friedman; co-executive producer: Eric Gruendemann; co-executive producer: Robert Bielak; co-executive producer: Jerry Patrick Brown; executive producer: Sam Raimi; co-executive producer: Robert Tapert; coordinating producer: Bernadette Joyce; New Zealand producer: Chloe Smith; story editor: Chris Manheim; unit production manager: Chloe Smith; first assistant director: Paul Grinder; second assistant director: Neal James; director of photography: Donald Duncan; editor: Jim Pryor; visual effects: Kevin O'Neill; production designer: Robert Gillies; costume designer: Nigla Dickson; New Zealand casting: Diana Rowan; stunt coordinator: Peter Bell; additional visual effects: Flat Earth Productions, Inc.; music: Joseph LoDuca

## REGULARS

Kevin Sorbo (Hercules), Michael Hurst (Iolaus/Charon)

## RECURRING

Robert Trebor (Salmoneus), Bruce Campbell (Autolycus), Kevin Smith (Ares), Liddy Holloway (Alcmene)

# H-38: MERCENARY

CREDITS: Teleplay by Robert Bielak; directed by Michael Hurst

GUEST STARS: Jeremy Roberts (Dirkus Patronicus the Mercenary)

SUPPORTING CAST: Neil Duncan (Serfin), Phil Jones (Trayan)

STORY LINE: Hercules is transporting a prisoner to Sparta to answer charges that he killed a man. When the ship begins to sink, Hercules cuts the prisoner loose so he'll have a fighting chance to survive. Hercules awakens on an island and begins a cat-and-mouse pursuit of the prisoner.

When a boatload of pirates come ashore, Hercules and the mercenary realize they must join forces or they'll both die. Together, they survive various perils, which include encounters with vicious desert-dwelling creatures, before they ultimately escape the island.

OBSERVATIONS: Not only is this a rare solo Hercules episode—with no Iolaus on hand—but it's a serious adventure, in contrast to the light-hearted tone of most of the episodes.

It is interesting to note that Hercules, who upholds justice and fairness, will himself break the law to help someone he thinks is being treated unfairly. And in this case he helps someone who is a murderer! Herc is only half-god, but loves that feeling of being in control so things will go his way, a trait no doubt inherited from his father. This is a thinking man's episode, surely, because not only does Hercules let the mercenary go, but the man's word that he will no longer be a mercenary is good enough for Hercules. Trusting the promise of a murderer is a definite risk.

HIGHLIGHTS: The desert-dwelling sandrays are definitely some of the more interesting monsters this series has showcased. There's a clever scene in which Hercules and Dirkus throw a seashell on the sand to distract a sandray. It swallows the shell at first, then spits it back out at them and Dirkus catches it.

Hercules bravely yanks a spike of wood from his arm. Also outstanding is the sequence in which Hercules and the mercenary come across the corpse of a man who's missing his legs. And, of course, the ultimate defeat of the sandrays is spectacular.

TRIVIA: Iolaus may not have been visible in this episode because actor Michael Hurst directed it.

# H-39: DOOMSDAY

CREDITS: Teleplay by Robert Bielak; directed by Michael Lange

GUEST STARS: Derek Payne (Daedalus), Franke Stevens (King
   Nikolas), Fiona Mogridge (Moria)

MYTHOLOGICAL BASIS: Once again the series combines a Greek myth with a new story line. In this case the original tale is that of Icarus and his father Daedalus. To escape from King Minos, Daedalus fashioned artificial wings for himself and his son made from feathers and hardened wax. As they flew away from the island making good their escape, Daedalus warned Icarus not to fly too high because the hot sun would impair the artificial wings. Icarus, however, did not heed his father and flew too close to the sun. The wax in his artificial wings melted and he plummeted to his death. In this version Icarus had been just a young boy, hence his youthful inexperience and fearlessness.

STORY LINE: Bitter over the death of his son, Icarus, Daedalus is freely selling his talents to create the ultimate weapon, which even the mighty Hercules won't be able to withstand.
   Hercules, accompanied by a young girl who fancies herself a reporter, seeks out Daedalus to reason with him. Daedalus' battle-suit invention is used against Hercules and almost succeeds, until our hero figures out a clever way to defeat it. Only then does Daedalus realize that this is not what Icarus would have wanted, and he agrees to stop creating implements of war.

OBSERVATIONS: This is a fairly dramatic episode with the exception of the *reporter* Moria, who acts like a nosy Lois Lane, complete with the usual annoying clichés. Thankfully, her character is softened somewhat—to make her more realistic—in her later appearance with Iolaus in "The Lost City" (H-53).
   This episode shows how destructive grief can be. Daedalus learns a

hard lesson, and it's interesting to note that he almost dies in the same way his son did, by burning as a result of "getting too close to the fire." Mistakes can be made, and accidents happen, but people do still have choices, and the construction of an ultimate weapon by a hardened, bitter man is still a choice, not an accident. Here, the real evil is that in bitterness we can cut off the most valuable commodities we have, compassion and heart. Who says *Hercules* isn't deep?

HIGHLIGHTS: Of particular note is the battle between Hercules and the gargantuan flame-throwing warrior who looks like a walking tank.

# H-40: LOVE TAKES A HOLIDAY

CREDITS: Teleplay by Gene O'Neill and Noreen Tobin; directed by Charlie Haskell

GUEST STARS: Alexandra Tydings (Aphrodite), Sarah Smuts-Kennedy (Leandra), Julian Garner (Hephaestus), Mervyn Smith (Iagos), Fiona Mogridge (Evanthea)

SUPPORTING CAST: Damien Wood (Male Servant), Adam Jackson (Male Villager), Gilbert Gocdoe (Village Elder)

MYTHOLOGICAL BASIS: In the original myth Hephaestus is the son of Hera and either Zeus or Talos. He is a sickly child whom Hera literally throws off Mount Olympus. Hephaestus, though lame and disfigured, survives and goes on to become a master craftsman, which is why he is associated with fire and the forge. His skill at working metals prompts Hera to recognize her son and arrange for his marriage to Aphrodite. Throughout their marriage Aphrodite carries on an affair with Ares, which leads Hephaestus to petition the gods to punish the lovers. The gods deny his request and, out of gratitude, Aphrodite sleeps with Hermes and Poseidon.

STORY LINE: In this episode Hephaestus is pining for a mortal woman. As a further complication, Aphrodite has quit as the goddess of love and women start turning away from their men.

As the plot develops, it is revealed that because the mortal woman rejected Hephaestus, her village has been suspended in time for fifty years, and Iolaus learns that she is actually his grandmother! It is up to Iolaus to deal with this revelation, get Aphrodite back in the love business, and contend with Hephaestus' metallic panther guardian.

OBSERVATIONS: Though the series is entitled *Hercules*, and Kevin Sorbo is the star, it is often interesting to see the other characters get time on screen and add history to their characters. Michael Hurst, along with the writers, has accomplished a major breakthrough in bringing life and interest to his character. Iolaus is sweet, tough, funny, charismatic, the perfect Hercules sidekick as well as a hero in his own right. He really does deserve his own episodes, and the charisma of the character and actor make these "Iolaus" episodes work on their own.

HIGHLIGHTS: Iolaus fights an agent of Hephaestus that turns out to be just a living suit of armor. Later, he challenges three of the armored warriors and defeats them with his wits.

TRIVIA: A title that was considered but discarded before the air-date for this episode about a beautiful woman and a disfigured man, was "Beauty and the Beast."

In this installment we learn that the father of Iolaus was a warrior named Skouros who was killed in battle. Skouros appears later in "Not Fade Away" (H-42).

# H-41: MUMMY DEAREST

CREDITS: Teleplay by Melissa Rosenberg; directed by Anson Williams

GUEST STARS: Galyn Gorg (Anuket), John Watson (Sokar), Henry Vaeoso (Keb), Mark Newham (Mummy), Alan De Malmanche (Phineus)

SUPPORTING CAST: David Stott (Thief #1), Derek Ward (Thief #2)

MYTHOLOGICAL BASIS: Although there is some relationship between Greek and Egyptian mythology, this episode does not draw upon either to any great degree. It seems more likely that its inspiration came from Hollywood and the various movies made about the curses attached to mummified remains.

STORY LINE: In this episode Hercules meets the daughter of Ramses who wants Hercules to locate a treasured missing mummy. Meanwhile, Salmoneus plans to use the mummy as the centerpiece in his projected house of horrors.

A villain is also looking for the mummy, which he plans to use to gain the throne of Egypt. Naturally, the princess must be rescued and Hercules must do battle with both the villain and the mummy.

OBSERVATIONS: This was a Halloween episode in which Salmoneus invents not only a House of Horrors but also a House of Wax. It's a fun, fast-paced episode combining Greek myth, Egyptian culture, and plots from old horror movies.

These spoofs on contemporary life happen often in *Hercules*, one of the reasons, many believe, the show is a success. The series doesn't have to take itself so seriously to be good, and yet the spoofs do not detract from the show's serious or more dramatic moments. This episode, however, is obviously all fun. It's a nice break from more dramatic or tragic story lines. It is a tribute to the writers that they can intersperse their campy stories at just the right times, without going too far and losing their audience to outright silliness.

HIGHLIGHTS: Hercules fights the minions of Princess Anuket using a human skeleton as a weapon.

# H-42: NOT FADE AWAY

CREDITS: Teleplay by John Schulian; directed by T. J. Scott

GUEST STARS: Cynthia Rothrock (Enforcer II), Karen Sheperd (Enforcer I)

SUPPORTING CAST: Jeffrey Thomas (Jason), Bruce Allpress (Skouros), Erik Thomson (Hades), Andrea Croton (Persephone), Gordon Hatfield (Freedom Fighter), Geoff Clendon (Witness)

MYTHOLOGICAL BASIS: This episode picks up threads of two previous stories: the myth of Hades and Persephone (in which Hercules took the role of Zeus and arranged for Persephone to spend part of the year as the wife of Hades) and the story based on Hera's soulless monster, the Enforcer.

STORY LINE: In this episode Enforcer II, a soulless entity created by Hera from the element of fire, in the likeness of a woman, kills Iolaus. Hercules calls on Hades to restore Iolaus' life as repayment of the debt owed him for helping Hades marry Persephone. Hades agrees on the condition that Hercules defeat Enforcer II by sunset.

Hercules needs the help of the first Enforcer (introduced in "The Enforcer" [H-26]), and when the two Enforcers meet, it is a battle royal until Enforcer II causes Enforcer I to burst from the heat, leaving it up to Hercules' strength and ingenuity to defeat her.

OBSERVATIONS: The Enforcer is the *Hercules* series' variation on the Terminator featured in the film *Terminator 2: Judgment Day* (1991). Having the original Enforcer return so that she can acquire a soul and become human is an imaginative creative touch.

Once again, Iolaus is severely beaten by one of Hercules' enemies, but this time he dies, which provides the opportunity for an encounter between Iolaus and his deceased father, Skoura. Ultimately, they clear up some issues and reconcile.

This episode is another example of Hercules demanding fairness and control in a major way and getting it! The scene where Iolaus dies in Hercules' arms is no minor drama. This is a major upset in a series where the two heroes often fight impossible-to-win battles and get no more than scrapes or minor bruises. So it is a huge surprise when Iolaus actually dies! The loyalty between the two characters in this episode is unquestionable. But the fairness Hercules seeks comes with strings attached. He has to work hard to gain back his friend's life from Hades.

We also see that Hercules does not always win. In this episode we are reminded that Hercules' wife and three children remain dead, despite Hercules' efforts to protect them.

The established fact that there is another world where the dead live—and proof of it exists since Hercules has actually been there—does seem to make death somehow softened or less tragic in this series. So if you see people die in *Hercules*, it does not necessarily mean you've seen the last of them.

HIGHLIGHTS: Hercules visits the graves of his family. He is joined in this touching and somber reunion by his mother and Jason.

Enforcer I is a water-based entity with the ability to re-form its shape. Enforcer II is made from the element of fire, and it is intriguing to see the embodiment of these two elements do battle.


# H-43: MONSTER CHILD IN THE PROMISED LAND

CREDITS: Teleplay by John Schulian; directed by John T. Kretchmer

GUEST STARS: Bridget Hoffman (Echidna), Glenn Shadix (Typhon), Grant Heslov (Klepto)

SUPPORTING CAST: Tony Wood (Bluth), Rebecca Clark (Head Archer), Bernard Woody (Messenger), Jane Bishop (Elderly Woman)

MYTHOLOGICAL BASIS: This episode brings back the mythological characters Echidne (spelled *Echidna* in the credits) and Typhon in a story that elaborates on the idea that, contrary to the original myth that portrays them as vicious monsters, they are, in fact, misunderstood victims.

STORY LINE: In this episode a small-time thief goes to the cave of Echidna, the mother of all monsters, and claiming to be a friend of Hercules, convinces Echidna and Typhon to trust him. Echidna leaves the cave, Typhon falls asleep, and the thief steals a baby monster to sell to a warlord. The crux of the story is that the thief bonds with the baby creature and regrets parting with it.

OBSERVATIONS: Echidna began as a villain back in the second season. In fact in her debut appearance in "The Mother of All Monsters" (H-20), she even kidnaps Alcmene (Hercules' mother) and plans to kill her in revenge for Hercules having killed all of her children. In "Cast a Giant Shadow" (H-23), Echidna has a decided change of heart toward Hercules when he reunites her with her husband, Typhon (who had been unjustly imprisoned by Hera).

Leave it to *Hercules'* excellent scriptwriters to show, in fairness, the villain's perspective. At first a character such as Echidna appears only evil and empty, merely a monster without a heart. Later we are shown her as a wronged being who has been forced to do evil. It is much more challenging when story lines do not rely on a definite demarcation of good and evil with no shades of grey.

Also, it is an ingenious touch to show Echidna's child, though perhaps odd-looking to us because of its green scales and many tentacles, as a very normal kid who enjoys playing games and who can laugh at funny things. It hurts when it is tortured. It can appreciate love.

This story is as much about the thief Klepto and the kidnapped baby as it is about Hercules, and it's odd how we are actually manipulated into liking the little tentacled creature.

# H-44: THE GREEN-EYED MONSTER

CREDITS: Teleplay by Steven Baum; directed by Chuck
    Braverman

GUEST STARS: Alexandra Tydings (Aphrodite), Karl Urban
    (Cupid), Susan Ward (Psyche)

SUPPORTING CAST: Patrick Brenton (Satyr #1), Mike Howell
    (Pelops), Simon Gomez (Saltar)

MYTHOLOGICAL BASIS: This episode is very loosely based on the story of Eros and Psyche. Cupid is the Roman name given to the Greek god Eros who is Aphrodite's son and is known to be wild and capricious, recklessly shooting his arrows that stir up sexual passion in whomever they hit.

Psyche is the young maiden in a myth very similar to the story of

Beauty and the Beast. The significant difference in the Greek myth is that Aphrodite, jealous of Psyche's beauty, commands her son Eros to make Psyche become infatuated with the ugliest creature he can find. When Eros sees Psyche, he immediately falls in love with her and devises a way to have her while still obeying Aphrodite's command.

It is always dark night when Psyche is ravished by her supposedly monstrous captor. One night she lights a lamp and discovers that her lover is not a monster but the handsome youth Eros. But because she has seen his true nature, Eros' deception is unveiled and they can no longer be lovers in the night.

Psyche surrenders herself to Aphrodite who tortures her and sets impossible tasks for her to accomplish. Finally Eros appeals to Zeus for permission to marry Psyche. Zeus agrees, and Psyche and Aphrodite are reconciled.

STORY LINE: Cupid is associating with a bad crowd of satyrs and Aphrodite wants Hercules to straighten him out. But Cupid's real problem is that he loves Psyche. Hercules has known Psyche since she was a child, so he goes to her too, but he's accidentally shot with Cupid's arrow. Cupid is so angry over this mistake he throws his bow away and kidnaps Psyche for himself.

When Aphrodite attempts to prove that Cupid only loves Psyche for her beauty by making her look old, Cupid wants to marry her regardless. As in the original myth, Aphrodite relents and reconciles with Psyche, resulting in the marriage of Eros (Cupid) and Psyche.

OBSERVATIONS: Cupid is an interesting character and that, along with his mother Aphrodite, make the episode a fun one. Their twentieth century euphemisms add a touch of good humor, coupled with the fact that the gods, for all their superior powers and ability to control humans, have the same petty problems we have. They may be superior in magical ability but are not any more psychologically evolved than mere mortals.

There is a recurring bit with Cupid's arrows accidentally striking a man who then becomes infatuated with another man nearby.

Salmoneus is thrown into the mix for potential humor but doesn't really affect the story. Even when he finds Cupid's bow, he doesn't do any damage with it.

HIGHLIGHTS: Cupid turns into the green-eyed monster courtesy of computer graphics imaging (CGI).

TRIVIA: A sequel of sorts to this episode is the *Xena* episode "A Comedy of Eros" (X-46) in which we meet the baby that Cupid and Psyche have together.

# H-45: PRINCE HERCULES

CREDITS: Teleplay by Robert Bielak; story by Brad Carpenter; directed by Charles Siebert

GUEST STARS: Jane Thomas (Queen Parnassa), Paul Gittins (Lonius), Sam Jenkins (Kirin)

SUPPORTING CAST: David Press (Garas), Nicko Vella (Marcareus), Tom Agee (Styros), Vanessa Valentine (Mountain Maiden), Steven Wright (Scarred Man)

STORY LINE: In this episode Hercules loses his memory after being struck by lightning (courtesy of Hera), and is convinced that he is a prince. Because he believes that he is this prince, Hercules intends to pledge his loyalty to Hera on Equinox Day and thus, at long last, become enslaved to her forever.

In a subplot Iolaus joins with the prince's wife to help Hercules remember the truth. They trash the Equinox ceremony, which results in the death of a wicked queen who does Hera's bidding and the elevation of the princess to the throne.

OBSERVATIONS: The fight sequences offered on this series are very elaborate and are some of the most aggressive combat scenes created for any TV series since the 1960s. This is a solid episode in which the Hercules sequences are real action scenes while the Iolaus sections provide the amusing highlights to the story.

The chemistry between Hercules and Kirin is so credible that the scene in which Hercules bids goodbye to Kirin and the children is particularly touching. In the scene it is apparent that Hercules is turning away from a family that parallels the one he lost thanks to Hera.

It is true that Zeus, were he to know of and interfere with every problem Hercules gets into, would cause the demise of the series. He must be out of the picture or no story. But it is curious that Hera can continue to be such an adversary without Zeus knowing.

HIGHLIGHTS: The depiction of an armored war machine here is quite imaginative and engrossing.

TRIVIA: Sam Jenkins (Kevin Sorbo's real-life girlfriend) plays Kirin, the wife of Prince Milius. She returns to play another character, Serena, in "Encounter" (H-50) and its sequels. It was rumored that Sorbo wanted Jenkins to become a semi-regular on the series.

# H-46: A STAR TO GUIDE THEM

CREDITS: Teleplay by John Schulian and Brian Herskowitz; story by John Schulian; directed by Michael Levine

GUEST STARS: Denise O'Connell (Queen Maliphone), Edward Newborn (King Polonius)

SUPPORTING CAST: Jon Brazier (Trinculos), Kirstie O'Sullivan (Loralie), Sam Williams (Comrade), Vickie Bennet (Old Woman)

MYTHOLOGICAL BASIS: This episode mixes mythology with elements of both Old and New Testament biblical stories to create a suitably Christmas-like episode.

STORY LINE: Iolaus has a vision that tells him he has to go north on a quest. Hercules decides to accompany his troubled friend.

Meanwhile, the Oracle at Delphi has decreed that a newborn child will succeed a king, so his queen orders that all babies be rounded up. Hercules and Iolaus end up in that kingdom, and in the inevitable battle, Hercules destroys the king and Hera's super-soldiers, the queen is exiled, the babies are saved, and Iolaus and two fellow dreamers, like the three wise men, follow a star summoning them to a nearby stable.

OBSERVATIONS: It's fascinating to watch Hercules as he first indulges the baffled Iolaus, then realizes that there is something powerful and real happening when they meet the two other travelers.

An interesting event at the end of this story is that Hercules will not go with Iolaus to the stable. Is it that he can't? Would two "gods" from two different universes or myths clash if they met? Does Herc feel threatened?

If events in *Hercules* are happening roughly 2000 years ago, there are many other gods that could become part of this series. The Tao Te Ching existed at that time and there are many ancient gods from the tribes in Africa. The Chinese creator, Nu-gua, the Great Mother, could also make for an interesting encounter as would the many Hindu gods and goddesses, not to mention Lord Shiva.

HIGHLIGHTS: Of note here is the final battle between Hercules and Hera's nonhuman soldiers.

## H-47: THE LADY AND THE DRAGON

CREDITS: Teleplay by Eric Estrin and Michael Berlin; directed by
    Oley Sassone

GUEST STARS: Catherine Bell (Cynea), Rene Naufahu (Adamis),
    Alexander Gandar (Gyger)

SUPPORTING CAST: Charles Pierard (Lemnos), Phaedra Hurst
    (Leandra), Grant Tilly (Toth), Bryce Berfield (Bartender),
    Graham Smith (Marcius)

MYTHOLOGICAL BASIS: Although dragons and serpentine creatures appear throughout mythology, this episode would not appear to be based on a particular myth.

STORY LINE: Hercules learns that a villain has returned from exile and is looting the countryside with the help of a vicious dragon known as Braxis. However, in the course of the story, it is revealed that the beast is actually very young (it speaks with the voice of an adolescent boy) and just wants a friend.

When Iolaus and Hercules set out to vanquish the dragon, they discover that the dragon is being used by the villain and some villagers that he is in league with.

OBSERVATIONS: This is one of the rare episodes in which Hercules fights with a sword, and when the warriors see him masterfully swinging two swords at once, they decide to be somewhere else.

This is another great example of an episode where appearances are not what they seem. The dragon isn't evil, it's just put into a position of evil by a bad circumstance and a bad man. One wonders, though, if the dragon were not young and kind of cute, would it have met a worse fate? It is an easy decision to save a monster that has a heart. It is more difficult when the monster is so alien that we cannot judge if it has a heart, and if its nature is a threat to humankind, its future would be pretty much decided on that one count.

The talking dragon has obvious similarities to the creature (with the voice of Sean Connery) in the film *Dragonheart* (1996).

HIGHLIGHTS: In a great special-effects scene, Iolaus is picked up by the dragon. When a boy falls from a cliff and the dragon saves his life, Braxis flies around with him in a way reminiscent of *The NeverEnding Story* (1984).

## H-48: LONG LIVE THE KING

CREDITS: Teleplay by Sonny Gordon; story by Patricia Manney; directed by Timothy Bond

GUEST STARS: Roger Oakley (King), Lisa Ann Hadley (Queen Niobe), Derek Payne (King Xenon)

SUPPORTING CAST: Walter Brown (King Phaedron), Peter Ford (Borea), Ronald Hendricks (Colius), David Downs (Cletus)

MYTHOLOGICAL BASIS: As noted in the previous episodes featuring Orestes and Niobe, the personalities of these two characters as they appear in the television stories bear no particular resemblance to their mythological counterparts.

STORY LINE: King Orestes is killed by an assassin's arrow because he had agreed to sign a peace pact with a neighboring king. Iolaus, the cousin of Orestes (and his identical look-alike), masquerades as Orestes in order to unmask the killer.

The last time Iolaus masqueraded as Orestes (in "King for a Day, [H-32)" Iolaus and Queen Niobe had fallen in love. Fate has drawn them together once again and this time they consummate their love. But in the end Iolaus must fake his own death and leave, knowing that he can never return.

OBSERVATIONS: This is a sequel to "King for a Day" (H-32). One might ask why Iolaus wouldn't want to continue on as King Orestes. However, it is clear from past episodes that he has an identity crisis from living in the shadow of the mighty Hercules. Were he to live his life as King Orestes, then the name Iolaus would surely vanish and his existence would be a lie in spite of the good he might do.

The fact that Iolaus can support an entire episode on his own demonstrates how well his character has been developed.

HIGHLIGHTS: One especially memorable moment occurs when Iolaus swings down into the conference room and exposes Xenon as a traitor.

# H-49: SURPRISE

CREDITS: Written by Alex Kurtzman; directed by Oley Sassone

GUEST STARS: Hudson Leick (Callisto)

SUPPORTING CAST: Liddy Holloway (Alcmene), Jeffrey
    Thomas (Jason), Kevin Smith (Iphicles), Paul Norell (Falafel)

MYTHOLOGICAL BASIS: The Tree of Life and similar images are common to many mythologies and are most often related to genesis or creation stories.

STORY LINE: Hercules crosses paths with Callisto when he finds that with Hera's help she has poisoned a number of his friends at a celebration. An apple from the Tree of Life is the only thing that can save them.

After evading numerous deadly traps, Hercules is confronted with the sight of Callisto setting fire to the Tree of Life as she eats its fruit, which will give her immortality. Hercules retrieves one apple and, leaving Callisto trapped once again, he escapes to bring the antidote to his friends.

OBSERVATIONS: Callisto appears several times in the *Xena* series. This episode is not the only time she's released from Tartarus, but it's the first occasion in which she crosses paths with Hercules.

The subplot of the party guests experiencing hallucinations is not particularly imaginative and does not serve to advance the plot. It merely fills up screen time.

The humor in this episode is great. And the philosophical debate between Herc and Callisto contains some good stuff. But when Callisto gets the apple from the Tree of Life, she certainly takes her time in eating it, which is her downfall. It's a wonder, however, how tempting immortality is in a world where it is proven that the dead live on, either in Tartarus or the Elysian Fields. The only temptation for Callisto would be that through immortality she would be in control of her life and not subject to the torments of Tartarus, which is controlled by Hades.

TRIVIA: Kevin Smith (without a beard) returns as Iphicles for the first time since "The Wedding of Alcmene" (H-34). Smith is more commonly seen as Ares, the god of war.

# H-50: ENCOUNTER

CREDITS: Teleplay by Jerry Patrick Brown; directed by Charlie
Haskell

GUEST STARS:  Sam Jenkins (Serena), Joel Tobeck (Strife)

SUPPORTING CAST: David Mackie (Hemnor), Steve Hall (Prince Nestor)

MYTHOLOGICAL BASIS: The Third Labor of Hercules was the capture of the Ceryneian Hind, a beast that is also known in mythology as the Golden Hind. The Hind was sacred to Artemis, the goddess of the hunt, and is most often described as a female red deer, enormous in size, with brazen hooves and golden horns.

Although the Prince Nestor who appears in this episode is a villain, there is a mythological Nestor who was, in fact, a friend to Hercules. He first appears as one of the hunting party who helps Hercules track the Calydonian Boar. Later, Nestor is the only one who will help Hercules get purified after killing Iphitus for which Hercules made Nestor the King of Messenia.

STORY LINE: In this episode Prince Nestor intends to kill the Golden Hind because its blood can slay a god. Ares' nephew, Strife, has told him that if he eliminates the Hind, Ares will help him kill Hercules.

Hercules first encounters the Golden Hind in the form of a beautiful woman named Serena whom he believes to be a healer. Iolaus first sees her in the form of a hind. She thinks he is hunting her and shoots him with an arrow, which results in great confusion. As Serena the woman, she can heal Iolaus; as Serena the Golden Hind, she and Hercules are in great danger from Nestor and Ares.

OBSERVATIONS: The scenes where the Hind is being hunted are well-done in that they are horrifying. They show how it feels to be hunted, to be chased for no reason other than your hide or your head or your blood. The Hind is a magical being, yet she is not revered. She is a healer, yet ignorance keeps people from learning this fact. This episode shows that at this point in the time of Hercules and the world, people are turning away from mystery and magic. It is a sad fact that magic is dying. Amidst all the silliness and camp of the series, this tragedy is occurring. "Encounter" embodies that tragedy.

Strife, the nephew of Ares, is somewhat like Aphrodite in that he speaks in various twentieth-century clichés. He even uses the phrase "I could've been a contender" from the 1954 Marlon Brando movie *On the Waterfront*—not exactly ancient Greek parlance.

HIGHLIGHTS: A particularly good action sequence occurs when Hercules, on horseback, fights the army of Prince Nestor.

TRIVIA: Once again Kevin Sorbo's girlfriend, Sam Jenkins, makes a guest appearance.

## H-51: WHEN A MAN LOVES A WOMAN

CREDITS: Teleplay by Gene O'Neill and Noreen Tobin; directed by Charlie Haskell

GUEST STARS: Sam Jenkins (Serena), Joel Tobeck (Strife), Tawny Kitaen (Deianeira), Ted Raimi (Joxer), Kevin Smith (Ares)

SUPPORTING CAST: Paul McIver (Aeson), Rose McIver (Ilea)

MYTHOLOGICAL BASIS: This episode is a continuation of the previous story, featuring the same basic characters.

STORY LINE: The main thrust of the story is the confirmation of the love between Hercules and Serena, which is formalized by his proposal of marriage. Iolaus' bad feelings about the pending marriage prompt Hercules to visit the Elysian Fields and tell Deianeira, his late first wife, that he's going to remarry.
When Hercules returns, Ares informs him that because of the kind of offspring such a union could produce, Hercules must relinquish his god-given special powers and Serena must give up being the Golden Hind. At tale's end the couple wed and the spirits of Hercules' dead family appear to him.

OBSERVATIONS: This is a milestone episode because it has been pretty much established that Herc is a confirmed bachelor. He believes himself to be faithful to Deianeira though she is dead. Her existence in the Elysian Fields is supposedly eternal. Events in the mortal world are fleeting. Why tell her of something that is but a blink of an eye to the eternal world? But then, it might be rather awkward should Herc ever find himself a resident of the Elysian Fields, to be confronted by two wives!

Iolaus' feeling of abandonment in this episode is quite understandable, and a good subplot to add to the depth of the character. It is touching when he does show up for the wedding. And the wedding itself is lovely, taking place in the best church of all, the natural world.

The scene when Hercules informs Deianeira that he's going to remarry is quite touching as is the tender scene in which Hercules is reunited with his ageless children.

Ares is pretty nasty in this episode, which makes it odd to see him later portrayed in a sympathetic light in the *Xena* episode "Ten Little Warlords" (X-32).

# H-52: JUDGMENT DAY

CREDITS: Teleplay by Robert Bielak; directed by Gus Trikonis

GUEST STARS: Sam Jenkins (Serena), Lucy Lawless (Xena), Renee O'Connor (Gabrielle), Kevin Smith (Ares), Joel Tobeck (Strife)

SUPPORTING CAST: Peter Vere-Jones (Zeus)

MYTHOLOGICAL BASIS: This episode is a continuation of the prior episode's story line.

STORY LINE: This episode in the trilogy hinges around the fact that Hercules is now mortal. The major turning point in the plot occurs when Hercules awakens to find blood on his hands and Serena lying next to him, dead. When the townspeople gather to lynch Hercules, Xena and her sidekick, Gabrielle, rescue him, but in the process Hercules is badly hurt.

Hercules is convinced he's guilty of Serena's murder and plans to surrender. Iolaus tries to stop him and, in the struggle, stabs Hercules. Xena attacks Iolaus. Ares shows up, gloating, and Strife admits to killing Serena. Zeus finally appears and restores Hercules' special powers and our hero thoroughly trounces the dastardly Strife.

OBSERVATIONS: This is another very serious episode, which makes three such solemn installments in a row, something of a record (even though Joxer, as the series' resident embodiment of humor, appears in two of them).

Here we finally have some interference by Zeus. It is pretty obvious that Ares and Strife have overstepped even their muddy boundaries as meddling gods. It is interesting that Zeus only steps in to stop the gods and aid Hercules. He appears to have no regard for the Hind or for other mortals and non-family members.

The inclusion of Xena and Gabrielle in this episode is a nice surprise. But to see Xena, Gabrielle, Hercules, and Iolaus all together is almost too much. Each actor has so much charisma that in order not to steal scenes from one another, it appears sometimes they are holding back, waiting for the others to get equal time. Each one deserves to be the star, but four stars in one scene gets chaotic.

HIGHLIGHTS: Xena comes to the rescue of Hercules in a big fight scene. Later, Xena sings the dirge at Serena's graveside.

Hercules is guilt-ridden about Serena's death—she was killed only because he fell in love with her. At her graveside a still-grieving Hercules pounds her marriage bracelet into her headstone.

TRIVIA: With Lucy Lawless so popular with TV viewers in her hit spin-off series *Xena: Warrior Princess*, having her and Gabrielle reappear as guest stars on *Hercules* was a definite ratings booster.

## H-53: THE LOST CITY

CREDITS: Teleplay by Robert Bielak; story by Robert Bielak and
    Liz Friedman; directed by Charlie Haskell

GUEST STARS: Fiona Mogridge (Moria)

SUPPORTING CAST: Amber Sainsbury (Regina), Marama
    Jackson (Aurora)

STORY LINE: This episode concerns itself with the very contemporary issue of cults and cult leaders. In this instance, the cult entice Salmoneus, Iolaus, and his friend Moria into its clutches.

The members are all in a hypnotic-like state, living in a commune that worships a child goddess. Through the efforts of Iolaus and his party, the child goddess reveals that she is not a deity. The real cult leader fights with Iolaus and the false prophet is crushed in a huge, spinning, hypnotic wheel, which brings his empire crashing down.

OBSERVATIONS: In this episode the ancient Greek cult members look an awful lot like they came from San Francisco in 1967. There is free love and a lot of pretty, young, drugged people who are happy because they no longer have to think.

This solo Iolaus episode once again demonstrates how engaging this character can be on his own. In fact unlike other Iolaus episodes, Hercules doesn't even appear in the teaser or the tag of the show.

HIGHLIGHTS: The most effective moments in this segment are the brainwashing of Iolaus and the sword battle between Iolaus and Karkis, which occurs in the Re-education Room with its wheel of spinning light. The scenes where Iolaus is tortured and brainwashed are chilling. Aren't we tired of torture scenes where the hero is a stoic, standup commander? Don't we love to see real people just let loose and scream and then beat the tar out of the oppressor? In these instances, *Hercules* is a refreshing change.

## H-54: LES CONTEMPTIBLES

CREDITS: Teleplay by Brian Herskowitz; directed by Charlie Haskell

GUEST STARS: Robert Trebor (Francois), Danielle Cormack (Chartreuse Fox)

SUPPORTING CAST: Patrick Nelson (Captain Gerard), Phil Sorrell (Criminal), Mark Perrett (Executioner), Robert Lee (Guy)

MYTHOLOGICAL BASIS: This episode is largely a wrap-around for a collection of clips from previous episodes. Rather than having a mythological basis, its antecedents are more likely, *The Three Musketeers* or *The Scarlet Pimpernel*.

STORY LINE: In 1789 during the French Revolution, Francois (Robert

Trebor) informs his female companion that he is really the Chartreuse Fox, a masked revolutionary. He claims that in every man's heart there is a hero. The lady wagers that he cannot make heroes out of two bumbling thieves, Robert (Kevin Sorbo) and Pierre (Michael Hurst). To inspire the thieves, he tells them stories about Hercules.

In the end it turns out that the lady is the real Chartreuse Fox. When she is captured by the gendarmes she is rescued by Robert, Pierre, and a most reluctant Francois.

OBSERVATIONS: This is a show intended to highlight clips from previous episodes, along the lines of "The Xena Scrolls" (X-34). However, while that *Xena* segment had a story that was interesting even without the flashback clips, "Les Contemptibles" is quite silly, which may account for the fact that this installment contained even more flashback clips than "The Xena Scrolls."

Despite its silliness, the fact that the characters (and actors) get tangled up in their fake French accents and often resort to repeating their lines in flat American accents to make themselves understood to each other is hilarious. And in what other episode in all the series do you get to see Hercules (who is actually not Hercules but a bumbling thief) picking his nose? It is fun to see these actors get to do something entirely different from their normal, heroic deeds.

## H-55: REIGN OF TERROR

CREDITS: Teleplay by John Kirk; directed by Rodney Charters

GUEST STARS: Rainer Grant (Penelope), Alexandra Tydings (Aphrodite)

SUPPORTING CAST: Grant Bridger (King Augeus), Bruce Phillips (Palamedes), Les Durant (Soldier #1)

MYTHOLOGICAL BASIS: Palamedes, in Greek mythology, was known for his great wisdom and inventions including the alphabet and the first pair of dice. He also plays a significant role in the war against Troy. The action that surrounds the Palamedes in the television story is not reliant upon these well-known attributes, so it is difficult to know whether this character was inspired by his mythological namesake.

STORY LINE: King Augeus has gone mad and, believing he is Zeus, has a temple of Aphrodite turned into a temple devoted to Hera. Hera uses her powers to transform King Augeus, giving him the powers of a god and arming him with explosive glowing globes.

Augeus accidentally kills his old friend Palamedes. Hercules devises a plan to save Palamedes' life. He tricks Augeus into hurling a power globe that strikes the body of Palamedes and revives him. Then, when Augeus is hit with one of his own bolts, it seems to knock some sense into him and he no longer thinks he's Zeus. But now he thinks he's Ulysses!

OBSERVATIONS: This is a rare episode featuring Aphrodite that is not played entirely for laughs, but which actually has serious scenes. Even Hercules ends up respecting her.

As usual, when the destructive Hera appears, all we ever see are her eyes

# H-56: THE END OF THE BEGINNING

CREDITS: Written by Paul Robert Coyle; directed by James
   Whitmore, Jr.

GUEST STARS: Bruce Campbell (Autolycus), Kevin Smith (Ares),
   Kara Zediker (Serena)

SUPPORTING CAST: Joel Tobeck (Strife), Ian Watkin (Quallus)

MYTHOLOGICAL BASIS: Autolycus is the son of Hermes and Chione, and is known to be a thief most famous for his ability to steal cattle and horses and disguise them so their owners can't recognize them. Autolycus is also known as the man who taught Hercules to box and was with Hercules in his exploits with the Amazons.

Ares, the god of war, and the Golden Hind, both explained and introduced in previous episodes, also figure in this story.

STORY LINE: Autolycus steals a crystal that can control time. Hercules catches him and while they're struggling, they are thrown back in time. In this past, Ares has killed all of the other Golden Hinds, but when Serena is shot with an arrow and is dying, Hercules forces Ares to make Serena human so she may live.

To escape from the past Autolycus joins with his past self to again steal the crystal. Hercules and Autolycus return to their own time where Hercules sees that Serena is still human and is married with children. Thus, her marriage to Hercules and her death never happened.

OBSERVATIONS: Bruce Campbell is amusing in the dual role of Autolycus from the present and Autolycus from the past. The temporal paradox created by the fact that the older Autolycus has no memory of meeting his younger self (and therefore no recollection of what happened then) is explained by the device of having the memories of the past participants in these events be wiped clean once the time travelers return to their own time.

However, another anomaly not taken into account is that with all the lovers, marriages, and infidelities that went on among the Olympians, such an act would probably have repercussions throughout the entire population of gods and mortals, not to mention a surprising number of animals, serpents, and sea creatures.

TRIVIA: The role of Serena the Golden Hind, formerly played by Sam Jenkins, is played in this episode by Kara Zediker.

## H-57: War Bride

CREDITS: Written by Adam Armus and Nora Kay Foster; directed by Kevin Sorbo

GUEST STARS: Lisa Chappel (Princess Melissa), Josephine Davison (Alexa), Ross McKellar (Prince Gordius)

SUPPORTING CAST: Mark Rafferty (Acteon), Marcel Kalma (Hargus), Chic Littlewood (Tolas)

MYTHOLOGICAL BASIS: Although mythology abounds with threatened kingdoms, arranged marriages, and children challenging parents for control, there is no particular myth upon which this story is based.

STORY LINE: In this episode a petulant princess wants no part of the marriage that has been arranged for her. She is kidnapped and is about to be sold as a slave when Hercules recognizes and rescues her. Naturally, the spoiled-brat princess, makes life difficult for her rescuers, Hercules and Iolaus, as they escort her home.

Meanwhile, the princess' younger sister murders her father, usurps the throne, and declares war on the adjacent country, which puts her on a collision course with Hercules.

OBSERVATIONS: There are several grossly violent scenes including the king being smothered with a pillow and the scene in which Hercules comes upon bodies impaled on deadly spiked balls hurled by a war machine.

The horror in this episode is offset somewhat by the humorous scenes of the spoiled *valley-girl* princess. It seems the more tongue in cheek the spoiled princess gets, the more evil her sister becomes. For someone as ignorant as princess Melissa, it stands to reason from a writer's point of view that it would take a major trauma or horror to knock her to her senses. That's probably why there is so much violence and terror, otherwise the change in Melissa would seem too quick or too easy. She has to see the worst of the world and her sister in order to learn.

Since this segment was directed by Kevin Sorbo, it would appear that he prefers episodes with a balanced mixture of humor and action.

## H-58: A ROCK AND A HARD PLACE

CREDITS: Teleplay by Roberto Orci and Alex Kurtzman;
    directed by Robert Trebor

GUEST STARS: Lindsey Ginter (Cassus)

SUPPORTING CAST: Tony Ward (Perius), Caleb Ross (Nico),
    Lee-Jane Foreman (Lyna), Sterling Cathman (Geryon)

STORY LINE: Hercules attempts to capture an accused killer. As they fight in a cave, the roof collapses, trapping the two inside, shutting out Iolaus and the townspeople.

Hercules eventually works his way to freedom, but the killer is still trapped and mortally wounded. Iolaus finds the man's estranged son who confronts his dying father. The man confesses to the crime before he dies and apologizes for having abandoned the boy.

OBSERVATIONS: This is a well-structured, serious episode, much more downbeat than almost any episode of the series to date. Hercules recalls how he was found standing over Serena's body with a knife, depicted in "Judgment Day" (H-52), which is why he has doubts about the guilt of Cassus who insists he is innocent.

It seems, though, that this episode has one weak spot. It is that Hercules, in his ever fair and just desire to control events, thinks he can change things if he can just reunite this bad man with his embittered, teenage son. It is sort of like the *Oprah* hour where we will try to solve the problem in the time allotted. It doesn't work that way. Hercules cannot undo the damage this man has done in his life and in the life of his son. Perhaps that is the message, but it does seem that the dying man's apology to his son is not really worth much after years of giving people only misery.

It is also interesting to note there is very little humor in this episode to offset the grim melodrama.

# H-59: ATLANTIS

CREDITS: Teleplay by Alex Kurtzman and Roberto Orci; directed by Gus Trikonis

GUEST STARS: Claudia Black (Cassandra), James Beaumont (King Pantheus)

SUPPORTING CAST: William Davis (Skirner), Ross Harper (Demitrius), Norman Fairley (Aurelius)

MYTHOLOGICAL BASIS: In Greek mythology Cassandra has the gift of prophesy, but it is her fate that her prophesies are never believed. This episode combines the character of Cassandra with the legend that has developed around the mythical island of Atlantis.

Although not technically a part of classic Greek mythology, the story of Atlantis was included in Platos' *Dialogues* as he described his conception of a perfect society. *The Dialogues* date from around 500 B.C., and in these writings Plato claims to be describing a society that existed almost one thousand years before. It is unknown if his tale of Atlantis was based on folk legends or if he simply made up the story to illustrate his philosophical point.

STORY LINE: Hercules is aboard a ship that is destroyed by lightning. He is the sole survivor, and when he washes up on the shore of Atlantis, he is found by Cassandra who explains that she's been having visions of the destruction of Atlantis.

Hercules urges her to reveal what she's seen, but as in the myth, Cassandra is not believed. Hercules is condemned as an outsider who is disrupting their society and put in a deathtrap. He escapes and rescues Cassandra just as earthquakes start to destroy the city.

OBSERVATIONS: It is interesting to note that in many ways the very technologically advanced civilization of Atlantis mirrors the Western ideal of a world where reason and science are the religions of the day and magic or unexplained phenomena are ignored or attacked.

This episode makes for an interesting bookend to the season because Hercules is washed up on an island after a shipwreck, which is what happens to him in the first episode of this season, "Mercenary" (H-38).

HIGHLIGHTS: Hercules fights to escape from a deathtrap cell with crystals that fire deadly beams.

TRIVIA: The capital of Atlantis has crystals that power airplanes and other devices. These clever special effects hearken back to the George Pal film *Atlantis, The Lost Continent* (1961) in which Atlantis was a scientifically advanced civilization. In that movie the monarch also had a deadly crystal that shot bolts of power.

Hercules is seen bare-chested, not a common sight on this show anymore.

# XENA:

# WARRIOR

# PRINCESS

# WHO IS XENA?

"I, personally, do not derive any great joy from violence inflicted upon other human beings, but the show sure is fun, isn't it?"          Lucy Lawless from *America Online*

Look in the index of any book of mythology and you will find multiple entries for the name Hercules. Look under the *X*s and there's not a Xena to be found. When the producers of *Hercules* created the television series, they had a wealth of stories and characters around which to write scripts. In addition to the famous Twelve Labors of Hercules, there was literally a pantheon of bickering gods and goddesses in his family tree and a bestiary of neighborhood monsters, mermaids, half-men, centaurs, satyrs, and serpents that the writers could contrive to threaten their star, Kevin Sorbo, on a weekly basis.

The character of Xena does not exist in ancient Greek or any other ancient mythology. When the producers and writers created *Xena*, all they had to draw on was their fertile imaginations. The legend of the warrior princess is pure twentieth-century, Hollywood fabrication. The character of Xena was created out of whole cloth. (Or, the way she's played by Lucy Lawless, whole leather might be more to the point.)

## XENA'S STORY

Xena rises to prominence following the sacking of her village, Amphipolis, by the outlaw warlord Cortese. The people of Amphipolis are not warriors and they live in fear that if they attempt to defend themselves when the raiders attack again, the retribution at the hand of Cortese will be devastating. But Xena, along with her brother Lyceus, convinces the villagers to join with them in assembling an army to defend the village against Cortese and any other brigands who threaten it.

And so it is, that when the next attack comes, it is Xena's army that triumphs. It is a bitter victory, however, because Lyceus and many of the villagers have been killed. In the aftermath of the battle, dissension arises among the townspeople. Many feel that the victory has come at too great a price and they blame Xena for what they consider to be many needless deaths. Ostracized, Xena sets out to recruit an even greater fighting force to conquer the lands surrounding Amphipolis to create a protective buffer zone around her homeland.

It is most unusual for any woman of the time to be a leader of men and even more unusual to find such a fierce warrior spirit in the guise of a lowly innkeeper's daughter. But her prowess in battle and the victories won under her leadership are undeniable proof of her bravery and abilities. Her reputation among the troops grows to mythic proportions; they speak of her as almost the equal of Ares himself. Although no specific ceremony is depicted in the series, it is acknowledged that it is Xena's troops who conferred upon her the title of Warrior Princess.

Still despondent over the death of her brother, Xena's hunger for control of the surrounding lands is not yet sated, and the adulation of her army only serves to further increase her desire for bloody revenge. Xena's purity of purpose begins to falter. Instead of fighting to protect her homeland, Xena becomes corrupted by power and, like her sworn enemy, Cortese, she fights merely for the thrill of battle.

Because she spares women and children, Xena is able to delude herself into believing that she is better than her enemies, not realizing that she is becoming as feared by the people as her enemies before her.

Though her early victories prove Xena a born warrior, her mentor in the more magical arts of warfare is a woman named M'Lila. Xena first encounters M'Lila when she is discovered as a stowaway aboard a ship commanded by the warrior princess. When Xena learns that her prisoner possesses magical fighting skills, she offers to spare the woman's life in exchange for her arcane knowledge. M'Lila agrees to teach her secret fighting techniques to Xena, not so much because she fears for her own life, but because she sees the possibilities for good that are still at the core of Xena's being.

Not long after this encounter, Xena manages to capture the Roman leader Julius Caesar. During the time that Caesar is being held hostage, a romance develops between the warrior princess and her captive. But when Rome pays the ransom demand, she is obliged to grant him his release. Caesar repays her love by returning with an army, capturing Xena, and crucifying her on a cross. To ensure that Xena is rendered helpless, Caesar instructs one of his soldiers to break both of her legs with a large wooden mallet.

But M'Lila returns and rescues the warrior princess from the cross. M'Lila takes Xena to a cave on Mount Nessus where a person named the Healer lives. The Healer uses his skills to hold the pain at bay while he resets the broken bones. Before Xena can heal completely, however, Roman soldiers track them to the cave and attack. M'Lila perishes using her body to shield Xena from an arrow. Enraged over the death of her friend and rescuer, Xena kills all of the soldiers, telling the last to die to warn Hades that more dead will follow saying, "A new Xena is born tonight with a new purpose in life—death."

This *new* Xena believes that only with complete conquest will her homeland be safe. In her single-minded obsession she even sees Hercules as an obstacle to that goal. Employing all her feminine wiles, she seeks to turn Hercules' close friend, Iolaus, against him. Though Iolaus is sorely tempted, his bond of friendship with Hercules ultimately proves to be stronger than his attraction to the beautiful warrior princess.

Xena's army, corrupted by the spoils of war, becomes even more vicious in battle than she. When she prevents her forces from harming an infant, they take it as a sign of weaknesss and in a coup lead by her lieutenant, Darphus, her troops turn against her. To win her freedom, Xena is forced to pass through a gauntlet of warriors who beat her brutally and leave her to die alone.

Xena survives the beating and seeks out Hercules to ask his assistance in defeating the army she once commanded. Though reluctant at first to help a woman who has conspired against him, Hercules finally does join forces with Xena to rid the land of the marauding hoard. Through their alliance for good, Hercules is also able to make Xena see herself for the monster she has become. Xena vows that in the future she will follow a different path in life, one that will atone for the death and destruction she has caused in the past.

## XENA THE SERIES

Some of these events are depicted in the three *Hercules* episodes that pre-date the debut of the regular weekly *Xena* series while others are revealed in key flashback sequences in later *Xena* episodes. As the series progresses, we learn more about Xena's past. We learn that she comes from a humble family of innkeepers. Her mother is Cyrene and is seen in the episode "Sins of the Past" (X-1). Her father is a mysterious figure who walked out of Xena's life when she was a child. The circumstances surrounding his desertion remain unexplained. In "Ties That Bind" (X-20), frequent Xena adversary Ares, the god of war, impersonates Xena's father.

Xena has two brothers. Her older brother, Toris, appears in the episode "Death Mask" (X-23). Her younger brother, Lyceus, can be seen in the segment "Remember Nothing" (X-26).

We also learn that Xena's greatest secret is that she has a son, Solon. The boy's father is Barias who dies about the time the boy was born. Although Xena harbors tremendous guilt over the death of Barias, her obsession with conquest is even greater. It becomes apparent to Xena that to properly raise her child she will have to abandon her self-proclaimed mission, something she will not do. Her solution is to give her infant son into the care of a tribe of Centaurs. She does not see the boy again until he is twelve, and even then she does not tell him that she is his mother. These events are depicted in "Orphans of War" (X-25), in which Xena convinces the boy that she is not at fault in the death of his father, Barias.

Xena continues to pursue her quest to right wrongs in the hope that these acts of contrition will absolve her of some of her guilt. Accompanied by Gabrielle, a young bard who once came to her aid and who has now become her closest friend, she travels the countryside battling injustice, armed with her chakram (a sharp, circular weapon that she can throw and retrieve like a boomerang) and her extraordinary agility and fighting skills.

## WEAPONS AND FIGHTING TECHNIQUE

The chakram (also known as a chaka) is not a fanciful device created by the writers of the series. It is an actual weapon with origins in historic India. A flattened, ring-shaped piece of iron (called a *quoit* weapon), the chakram varies from twelve to thirty centimeters in diameter with a blade that is two to four centimeters in width. It has a sharp outer edge and a rounded inner edge to allow it to be caught without injury. Historically, it was not used strictly like a boomerang (the way Xena uses it), but rather the ring was whirled around the forefinger to give it velocity before it was thrown and it was hurled more in the manner that an Olympic athlete hurls a discus.

Xena's fighting technique is perhaps the single most fantastical aspect of the show. She uses a sort of ancient Grecian aerobics-workout-bionic-karate-street-fighting method. The episode "Destiny" (X-36) explains how she learned these fantastic athletic skills, which include being able to make extraordinary leaps that seem to verge on flight. In fact in "Lost Mariner" (X-45), she outdoes herself by leaping from a tree to a ship that is at least a hundred feet offshore! According to the producers, this aspect of the show was actually inspired by the style of filmmaking employed in Japanese Kung-fu action films. However, the similarity to both *Wonder Woman* (1976–79) and *The Bionic Woman* (1976–78) obviously can't be ignored.

## Spin-off to Success

Although *Xena* began as a spin-off of *Hercules*, it has turned into a much different show. The dramatic *Xena* episodes can be very dark. Xena was, after all, a ruthless warlord whose past deeds often come back to haunt her. In "Callisto" (X-22), for example, she meets a young woman whose entire family was killed nine years before when Xena's army raided her village. Callisto now lives only to exact vengeance on Xena. In "The Return of Callisto" (X-29), she tries to kill the newly wed Gabrielle, but when Xena prevents this, Callisto kills Gabrielle's husband instead. Unlike most contemporary television drama, Xena often features story lines that involve blatant cruelty, wanton destruction, and the most base forms of human behavior. The saving grace in all this mayhem is, of course, that good—the *new* Xena—triumphs over evil.

Both Xena and the recurring characters that appear on the show have grown and changed throughout the first two seasons on the air. Even her sidekick, Gabrielle, has matured from an annoying little tagalong into the voice of Xena's conscience.

# THE CAST

A t the center of all the action, of course, is Lucy Lawless, a compelling screen presence with striking beauty, athleticism, and talent.

## LUCY LAWLESS (Xena)

On March 29, 1968, Lucy Ryan (later Lawless) was born in Mt. Albert, Auckland, New Zealand. The fifth of seven children, she has four older brothers and one younger sister. Her father was elected Mayor of Mt. Albert the year that Lawless was born and more recently became the Chairman of Finance for Auckland City. As a child Lawless was known as a bit of a tomboy, being highly influenced by her older brothers. Today, at six feel tall and 140 pounds, she is a remarkably beautiful young woman with piercing blue eyes. Her natural brown hair is dyed raven-black for the TV series.

Although she went to public school for two years, her early youth was spent attending convent schools. Her interest in the performing arts first manifested itself in school plays, particularly musicals. She even studied opera for a few years, but her real musical love is jazz.

At the age of seventeen after a short stint as a student at Auckland University, she left New Zealand to visit Europe. She described what she saw in the Players' Park in Prague, Czechoslovakia, to Erik Knutzen of *Cleo* magazine: "I'd go to see free plays there—just rubbish. The worst was by a group of Canadian students whacking each other over the head with big mutton chops and screaming about the plague. I sat there, watched it a while, and decided that I wasn't as miserable as I thought."

## MINING AND MARRIAGE

While Lucy Ryan was "doing the continent," back in New Zealand, her boyfriend from her high school days, Garth Lawless, was still thinking about her. Garth packed his bags, caught up with Lucy, and the two of them went bumming around Europe together.

When their money ran out, Lucy and Garth decided that they would head to Australia together and get jobs in the gold-mining camps. They worked in a camp in Kalgoorlie, a small town in the Australian outback, some five hundred miles from Perth. Later, they moved to another camp situated a little closer to civilization.

Although women miners were not particularly common, she worked alongside the men, driving trucks, digging ore, and pushing core samples through a diamond-cutting saw. She told *USA Today,* "People seem to have some romantic notion of what gold mining is. Like you're down there with the seven dwarfs with little lamps on their heads chipping bits of gold out of rock. Reality is drilling a deep hole and pouring in explosives. It's like a bloody atomic blast that lays waste to the landscape, leaving enormous pits about two miles wide."

Lucy and Garth worked there for eleven months, but when she discovered she was pregnant, she and Garth left the mining camps and moved back to Auckland, New Zealand. Lucy was three months pregnant when she and Garth were married in a registry office, foregoing the traditional church wedding. A few months later Lucy gave birth to their daughter, Daisy.

Unfortunately the marriage didn't last. Lawless had already begun to play Xena when she and Garth divorced in 1995. The parting has apparently been amicable. When asked about rumors that the production of *Xena* would relocate to Hollywood, Lawless told *Cleo* magazine that she would find this personally disruptive. "For my needs, the show should stay in New Zealand, because my daughter adores her dad, who lives not very far from me. I would hate to make her choose between the two of us. This is as together as a separated family can be, and it works very well."

## THE ROAD TO XENA

For Lucy Lawless the road to Xena was a long one filled with small parts and roles in TV commercials. When she was twenty, she appeared on a comedy show called *Funny Business*. In 1992 she went to Canada where she studied for eight months at the William Davis Center for Actors Study in Vancouver, British Columbia. Lawless told *Cleo* magazine, "I felt like I had received some very fine training that will always sustain me. It's stuff that works and I don't hesitate passing it on to others. I'll always be grateful to them."

Lawless considers her Vancouver drama teacher, Bill Davis, to have had a profound influence on her. Today, TV audiences know Bill Davis as the "Smoking Man" on television's popular *The X-Files* (1993– ).

When she returned to New Zealand, she won the job of co-host on a morning TV show called *Air New Zealand Holiday*. It was a travel magazine show that was broadcast not only in New Zealand but in Asia as well. She traveled a lot in her capacity as co-host on the show and did a second year on the travel show before she landed the role of Lysia the Amazon in the first *Hercules* telefilm.

In an interview in the January 1997 issue of *Cleo* magazine, Lawless explained the ups and downs of hosting a travel show and the restrictions it presented. "It paid okay, was fun, and took me to some thrilling locations—particularly Israel—but you often couldn't tell the whole truth. You'd really want to say, 'Wow! Don't go here. It's crappy!' But I knew in my heart that it wasn't what I was meant to do. I was either going to become a big fish in a small pond or risk it all. So I gave it up, even though there was nothing in sight. When a part in the two-hour television film *Hercules and the Amazon Women* came along, I knew that I had made absolutely the right decision. Going on as a presenter would have made me heartsick."

## HERCULES AND OTHER TELEVISION SHOWS

In the interim between the first *Hercules* movies and the launch of *Xena,* Lawless appeared on various TV shows including a part in the episode "Fe, Fi, Fo, Fum" on the American syndicated series *Ray Bradbury Theater.* A feature film entitled *Women from Down Under* featured Lucy Lawless in a short segment entitled "Peach." Then she appeared with Jon Voight in the 1992 docudrama *Rainbow Warrior* about the controversial environmental organization Greenpeace. This was followed by more TV work including two episodes of the series *High Tide* in 1994 in which the character she played got to kiss Rick Springfield. Those *High Tide* episodes were "Shanghaied" and "Dead in the Water." She was also in an episode of the syndicated series *The New Adventures of the Black Stallion.*

During that same period she found work on *Hercules.* The *Hercules* series presented Lawless in two very different parts prior to her being cast in the fateful role of Xena. In 1994 in the very first Hercules TV movie, *Hercules and the Amazon Women* (HM-1), Lawless played Lysia, the Amazon enforcer, a character similar in toughness to Xena. Then in 1995 in the episode "As Darkness Falls" (H-6), she appeared as Lyla, bride of Deric the Centaur and mother to Kefor. She repeated this role in the *Hercules* episode "Outcast" (H-18) after she'd already begun playing Xena.

Needless to say, it was her appearance as Xena on the *Hercules* episode "The Warrior Princess" (H-9) that set the stage for everything that followed. Her character looked very different in that initial outing. She wore a black costume with claw-like epaulets and a cape. The costume was made more "viewer friendly" in the subsequent two-part *Hercules* episodes "The Gauntlet" (H-12) and "Unchained Heart" (H-13), which groomed the character for her own series. Although Lawless's hair is naturally reddish brown, it was she who decided that it should be dyed black for the role. The producers had been thinking that Xena should be blond, but Lawless felt that a dark-haired Xena would go against type and might be more effective. (She also believed that her hair could not take the frequent bleaching it would take to keep her hair blond and that she'd end up bald by the end of the first season.) It was also Lawless who suggested that Xena's skin should have a Mediterranean look—her tan is painted on with a sponge before shooting.

## LAST ON THE LIST

Although Lucy Lawless and Xena have become synonymous, she was not the producer's first choice for the role. She told *Cleo* magazine, "When the producers of *Hercules* decided on the spin-off series, the actress originally cast as Xena pulled out. They had a list of five other actresses for the part and they all turned it down—God bless 'em. So they got down to Lucy Lawless, who was in country and available."

They did have to track her down, however, because she was on a camping trip with her daughter. The producers kept calling various relatives until they found the one who knew where she was. The camping trip was cut short, her hair was dyed black, her tan was applied, her costume was fitted, and Lawless emerged as the warrior princess.

The character of Xena registered an instant positive audience reaction. *Newsweek* magazine described her character on *Hercules* as a "formidable natural resource." Lucy Lawless describes Xena as "a woman as strong as any man or woman has ever been who lives by her wits but is also a fighter. She's a very human hero who knows all about the darker side of human nature since she must battle it within herself every day."

In an interview in the February 17, 1996, *New York Times,* Lawless remarked, "I love playing Xena because she is not little Miss Perfect, not solely good. In fact, Xena's life prior to where we are in the series had been quite malevolent, and she's looking not exactly to redeem herself, but for a more worthy path. She's far from a moral character, but she's an individual who unwittingly finds herself a hero. And as this unapologetic, unselfconscious woman, she appeals to young women in a big way. And of course there are a lot of 50-year-old men who are in love with her."

She also says that Xena is "a woman with a devil on her shoulder, or that's how I first imagined her." The actress would like to see Xena get a bit darker, a taste of which was given to viewers in the late second-season episode "The Price" (X-44). But neither she nor her co-star, Renee O'Connor, have any input in the writing of the scripts. In fact Lawless admits that she doesn't even read a script until four days before it is scheduled to begin filming.

## TALENT AND TRAINING

Regarding her martial arts abilities, a press release from Universal revealed, "Though she had practiced yoga for some time, Lawless had no special training in martial arts, sword play, or stunt work when she landed the role of Xena." She had ridden horses as a child, however, and this ability came in handy as one less skill she had to perfect for the role. Lawless learned swordplay and martial arts techniques from Douglas Wong, a martial arts teacher, during a 1995 visit to Los Angeles. Wong may be best known as the martial arts advisor on the much acclaimed *Dragon: The Bruce Lee Story* (1993). She is surprised by the speed and accuracy with which she performs martial arts given that in high school her nickname was Unco, which is an abbreviation of *uncoordinated.*

Lawless has a knack for languages and accents and must hide her New Zealand accent when playing Xena. While working on a U.S. series she was able to perfect a standard midwestern American accent, which created the impression for American audiences that she had no accent at all. Something that must have come as a shock to many the first time they saw her on a talk show.

When *Xena* was first offered to TV stations in 1995, there was some initial reluctance because the action show was regarded as something of a long shot. There had not been a female superhero TV show since *Wonder Woman,* and that series had been only a marginal success. Some stations that decided to take the show ignored the *Wonder Woman* parallel and looked to more recent history and the success of the muscular women on *American Gladiators.*

## SHOOTING TAKES ITS TOLL

Asked what it is like working on a TV series shot largely outdoors in Auckland, New Zealand, Lawless mentioned that, even though she is a native, she is not immune to climatic privations. She told *Cleo* magazine, "Although the North Island is subtropical, the winters can be bloody miserable—especially when you're wearing nothing but a corset and a whip. It's no fun to walk around in a frost-bitten mini-leather outfit. It doesn't fill me with enthusiasm." "Chariots of War" (X-2), for instance, was filmed in the bitter cold in the worst New Zealand winter she'd ever experienced. In 1996 during an interview conducted by America Online, she recalled that episode: "I was wearing wet leather; it was sleeting. We were driving chariots on a beach in the wind, and I would cower down in the chariot in between takes and just repeat the mantra, 'This too shall pass. This too shall pass!' The bleakest day of my life."

The fight scenes can also take their toll on the performers. "Well, we all take cuts and bruises. I have a marvelous stunt double, but there are action scenes calling for the star's face and I'm on. I got a beautiful black eye once, turning my head the wrong way just as an actor took a swing at me. But I've been a lot luckier than Kevin Sorbo who took a nasty cut on the head with a metal sword and had to have ten stitches." In describing how the fight scenes are done, she explained, "Fighting is like doing a dance. You do it to an extent, a double comes in, then they try to clip as much of you into the fight as possible."

## THE HORSEBACK RIDING ACCIDENT

Oddly enough, when Lawless was hurt in October 1996 in a horseback riding accident, she wasn't on the set of *Xena*. She was halfway around the world in California in the parking lot of the NBC Studios in Burbank rehearsing a skit for her scheduled appearance on *The Tonight Show with Jay Leno*. The horse slipped on the asphalt and fell on her. She had to be taken by ambulance to the hospital where she spent four weeks recovering from the four fractures she received in the accident. The two-part story line in which Xena winds up in the body of Callisto was incorrectly rumored to have been written to deal with the downtime resulting from her injuries. "Intimate Stranger" (X-31) and "Ten Little Warlords" (X-32) had both been filmed in July and August 1996, several weeks prior to the accident.

Regarding the accident, Lawless told the February 7, 1997, *TV Guide* that she looks back on it as a "bad dream—I don't care to remember it." The one positive outcome of the accident was that it brought Lawless and her daughter, Daisy, closer together. "She's more proud of her mum now that the show is such a success," Lawless said. "Originally she hated it. She blamed *Xena* for the breakup of my marriage. But not any more."

The accident seems to have had an additional silver lining in that it was reported so widely in the press that it focused increased attention on the TV series. "Falling off that horse really put me on the map," explained Lawless. "Before it happened, there were a lot of people out there who had never heard of me or Xena. The publicity all over the world about my accident changed all that and now a lot more people are watching the show. So, in a way, it was a blessing in disguise." That doesn't mean she'd ever want to go through such a painful ordeal again. "No way! It was much too painful and too frightening to repeat. It may have been the best thing that happened to Xena, but not to Lucy Lawless." In fact the accident spooked her so badly that when she was well enough to return to work, she initially refused to do any horseback riding scenes. "I'm not going to be pushed into it. I want to recover fully," she told the New Zealand *TV Guide*.

Although her hips were fractured, not broken, she admitted in a March 26, 1997, interview with the *Los Angeles Times*, "It just took me a long time to learn to walk again." At the time of the interview she explained that while she was doing her own fights again, she was toning down the kicks. But running wasn't something she was up to yet. By the time she said she was ready to get back to horseback riding, she would be thinking of Christopher Reeve and his near-fatal accident. "I won't ski for that reason. I don't want to hurt myself and let people down, but I can't not do everything, so I'm going to get back on that horse. It's important for me to give myself that challenge. Otherwise, I'm forever going to be frightened." Her physical therapy included swimming while using flotation devices that create resistance to work against, and taking brisk walks carrying hand weights.

## RECOVERY

By January 1997 Lawless had recovered from the accident sufficiently to go back to Los Angeles to make a guest appearance on a TV series and appear at the first-ever Xena fan convention. She then flew on to New Orleans where she met with loyal television station managers at the National Association of Television Program Executives convention who had been carrying her TV series in the United States.

On April 24, 1997, an interview with Lucy Lawless was broadcast on *Entertainment Tonight* about her guest appearance on the sitcom *Something So Right* where she played herself. She turns up to confront a character who is an actress starring on a show that is a supposed rip-off of *Xena*. "There's no fighting," she explained. "But you do get to see me go a little bananas." The episode aired on April 29, 1997, but it featured Lawless only in the pre-title sequence, which was a disappointment, particularly to fans who tuned in too late. Had the producers been more judicious in using the actress in that episode, it might have produced enough of a peak in the ratings to save the sitcom, which was canceled a few weeks later.

It was Lawless's first performance in front of a live television audience, not including talk show appearances. The sitcom appearance also helped to quell rumors that her accident had caused lasting effects. (These rumors started when she was carried out on stage for her return to *The Tonight*

*Show* a few months earlier.) Lawless is clearly well on her way to a complete recovery.

## NOT INTERESTED

Lawless sifted through movie offers in 1997 but turned all of them down because she wanted to relax during the three month production hiatus. "This is the show that made me famous," she explained. "If I spent my hiatus making a movie I'd be exhausted by the time it came to filming *Xena* again. And that wouldn't be fair to the show. Sure, one day I'd like to make movies . . . and maybe even move to America for a while. But for the moment, I'm content to stay in New Zealand and concentrate on *Xena.*"

She also wanted to be able to spend more time with her daughter, whom she sees a lot less than she'd like. "My daughter is the most important person in the world to me," Lawless told the February 10, 1997, *New Zealand Women's Weekly,* "and, with the long hours I have to work on *Xena,* I don't get as much time with her as I'd like. So when I get a hiatus from the show I want to spend it with her, being a mum."

Having time off can prove to be an absolute necessity to renewing her energy and enthusiasm, particularly when the show is especially strenuous or has to shoot in bad weather. "Sometimes I go into my camper in the morning, see that bloody thing waiting for me and say, 'Oh God, not today!' There's rain and hail coming down and you're on the side of a cliff, about to jump onto your horse and trying to look good at the same time." But Lawless admits that at least the job isn't boring.

## CHARACTER EVOLUTION

The producers are also concerned that the audiences not become bored with the series. That is why the character of Xena has continued to grow and change since the show premiered in 1995. "It constantly evolves," the actress said. "We're always throwing twists on some line or some plot, so the writers feel free now to write what they want to. We don't aim to be politically correct. Just as the audience gets comfortable, we turn it around on them." But sometimes they can push it a little too close to the edge. The final episode of the first season, "Is There a Doctor in the House?" (X-24), proved to be a prime example. Instead of being scheduled as the resounding finale before the summer reruns began, it was broadcast in the midst of the summer reruns. Nevertheless, Lucy Lawless considers it one of the best shows they've done.

"It was a five-day shoot and one of the most intense five days of my entire life. We had to cut a lot out of that because it was too bloody and intense for the sponsors. Fortunately, the composer, Joe LoDuca, managed to glue everything together with music so that it had all this poignancy and suspense and drama. He filled in the gaps and helped make the episode stunning." It remains one of the most talked about episodes to date and is a paradigm for other studios to try to imitate. The imitations of *Xena* they've already tried, however, have all fallen flat because of a little thing called creativity and because of a lead actress who presents a stunning interpretation of the material she's given.

"Is There a Doctor in the House" (X-24) and "Warrior...Princess... Tramp" (X-30) are two of Lawless's favorite episodes because they were so demanding and because she was active in every scene. She dislikes episodes where she's not as physically active.

In the fall of 1997 Lawless will appear on Broadway for a few weeks in the long running revival of the musical *Grease*, playing the roll of Betty Rizzo (played previously in the New York revival by Rosie O'Donnell and Brooke Shields, among others).

## UNLOOKED-FOR EXPOSURE

Lawless continues to have an exciting life beyond *Xena*. On May 6, 1997, she was singing the Star Spangled Banner in front of a live audience before a Mighty Ducks–Detroit Red Wings hockey game in Anaheim when everyone in the arena saw the top of her outfit come loose, revealing for almost a minute that which she normally keeps plated with armor. The story made the news all around the country, and anyone who was taping the game has the *unedited* version of Xena, which you don't see on the show. The funny part of all this is that Lucy Lawless once said, "The only thing I really want to sing is the national anthem at a Red Wings game. That would give me immense pleasure, as long as I'm good at it! As long as I don't crap out! That would be a real highlight in my entire life." It was certainly a highlight for a lot of people in the audience that night.

However, there may be more to this incident than, if you'll pardon the pun, meets the eye. An examination of a videotape of the incident cannot help but lead to the suspicion that this event may have been staged! Lawless is wearing a blue coat for most of the number. When she removes it near the end of the anthem, she raises her left arm, and the left side of her costume slips down. It is clear on the tape that after it slips she looks down out of the corner of her eye, but she does nothing to rectify the situation for nearly a minute!

Afterward she was quoted as saying, "Obviously I was mortified. I actually didn't even realize what happened until it was over. Let's just say it was quite a bit more exposure than I wanted." While that may be true, the incident occurred at the beginning of the television ratings sweeps month, and the fallout from her *fallout* created exactly the kind of publicity that gets viewers to tune into a show.

# RENEE O'CONNOR (Gabrielle)

Renee O'Connor was born on February 15, 1971, in Katy, Texas, and has an older brother, Christopher. O'Connor's mother and stepfather are the owners of the Austin, Texas, restaurant Threadgills, which just happened to be the location chosen for the first Xena-fest held in Texas. The 5' 4" actress is clearly in good shape but prefers not to reveal her weight.

She began to study acting at the age of twelve in Houston's Alley Theater and also attended Houston's High School of the Performing and Visual Arts. Her first professional acting job was in a McDonald's commercial when she was sixteen. Her favorite actresses include Holly Hunter, Sally Field, and Jessica Lange.

She really enjoys jazz, just like Lucy Lawless. She is also a sports enthusiast and horsewoman. She's fond of dancing, which helps keep her limber for the fight scenes and her trademark somersaults. She says she does all of her stunts that don't involve jumping over crates. To help in all of this, O'Connor practices with Sam Williams, the stunt double for Kevin Sorbo.

Although O'Connor is not native to New Zealand, she lives there during the nine-month shooting schedule. She calls Los Angeles her home during the hiatus but also visits her family in Texas during that period.

## FILM AND TELEVISION ROLES

Like Lucy Lawless, she first appeared on *Hercules* in a completely different role. In one of the early two-hour movies, O'Connor played Deianeira in *Hercules and the Lost Kingdom* (HM-2). In addition she's appeared in other films including *Follow the River* (1995), *Darkman II* (1995), and the TV movie *Danielle Steele's Changes* (1991). Her other film credits include two Disney Channel Mickey Mouse Club serials from 1989, *Teen Angel* (which marked her professional acting debut) and *Match Point.* Other TV movies in which she is seen are *The Adventures of Huck Finn* (1993), *Flood: Who Will Save Our Children?* (1993), *Sworn to Vengeance* (1993), *Follow The River* (1995) and *The Rockford Files: A Blessing in Disguise* (1995). Television appearances include an episode of *Tales From the Crypt* (1994– ), which was directed by Arnold Schwarzenegger, and *NYPD Blue* (1993– ).

The fact that her character is both tough *and* emotionally responsive is important to her. O'Connor said, "I love the fact that the writers keep Gabrielle sensitive to the world around her even though she is faced with such adversity." To date her favorite episode is "A Day in the Life" (X-39) because she and Lawless have more scenes and bantering with each other than usual.

## SHOULDERING THE WORK

In spite of the many action roles she had prior to being cast as Gabrielle, nothing prepared her for the demands of a weekly series. In the December 1996 issue of *SFX* magazine she explained, "The hours were surprising. I'd never worked on a one-hour action television series before, so I had no idea of the number of setups we would try to accomplish in one day, much less the physical action that comes with it. That took a long time to get used to. The other thing for me is that I didn't know any martial arts or have any type of fighting skills, so I sort of learned as Gabrielle did. I think that's really inspired me to become more physical."

When Lucy Lawless was hurt, the scripts had to be tailored to feature O'Connor more fully such as in "For Him the Bell Tolls" (X-40). "I finally had a taste of the long hours that Lucy puts in. She puts in these hours day in and day out," O'Connor told America Online early in 1997. On a normal basis she receives a script two weeks before filming starts. While she's reading and memorizing her lines for that script, she's also performing another script in front of the cameras.

"In the beginning, it was hard for me to play someone a great deal younger than myself, because Gabrielle is so naive and enthusiastic about experiencing life. But I love her verve. The more spirited and comical she is, the better for me because that's how I like to see life. The more she grows up—as you'll see especially in the next season—the closer to me she becomes. I've definitely developed more of a dry wit from being over here in New Zealand, and I have to hold that back a bit because Gabrielle is much more optimistic and her humor is much more obvious."

As to whether or not the young actress feels that *Xena* will prove to be a stepping stone to major feature films or her own series, O'Connor expresses cautious optimism. "Perhaps, but that's still in the future. I think the potential is there, that the show is still growing in visibility, so it will be interesting to see what doors it might open next year. But right now I'm still growing as an actress, so I'm quite content to be working on *Xena*, learning as much as I can, really."

## GABRIELLE'S STORY

Gabrielle was introduced in the first regular *Xena* episode, "Sins of the Past" (X-1). When Xena saves the village of Poteidaia from the forces of the warlord Draco, she wins the undying admiration of young Gabrielle. Although Gabrielle is betrothed to Perdicus at the time, she decides she's not yet ready for marriage and chooses to leave Poteidaia when Xena does. Xena isn't interested in having a sidekick and rejects Gabrielle's offer. Gabrielle follows Xena to her home village of Amphipolis, and when Xena finds herself unwelcome and surrounded by men who want to do her harm, Gabrielle manages to talk them out of attacking her. While this places Xena in Gabrielle's debt and gives a reason for Gabrielle to stick around, in later episodes we see Xena take on more men than threateaned her in this scene and beat them all. So maybe she did want Gabrielle to stay after all.

Gabrielle is not a warrior like Xena and in fact does not know how to fight with a sword. Xena is opposed to teaching someone how to kill and refuses to teach Gabrielle. Gabrielle then learns how to fight with a wooden staff, which she acquires in "Hooves and Harlots" (X-10), from the Amazons who later make her one of their tribe. Gabrielle can return to the Amazons whenever she wants and does so in "The Quest" (X-37) when she believes that Xena has died. But unlike Xena, Gabrielle has vowed never to kill, and she gets upset whenever Xena seems to kill unnecessarily. They have a spirited debate over this issue in "The Price" (X-44). Gabrielle tends to be an optimist while Xena is often a pessimist. The only time Gabrielle's personal code is challenged is in "Return of Callisto" (X-29) when she marries her childhood sweetheart, Perdicus, and the next day he is killed by Callisto.

Gabrielle's true skill is as a bard or, more specifically, as a talker. She talks a lot, but usually she has something to say. When she attends the Academy for Performing Bards, she even bests Euripides but loses out to Homer at the audition.

Although Gabrielle started out in the series as something of an innocent, she has grown over the first two seasons and has become not only more mature, but now often acts as Xena's conscience. Despite their close friendship, Gabrielle is willing to challenge Xena's decisions. When her friend Meleager is accused of murder in "The Execution" (X-41) and Gabrielle helps him to escape from prison, Xena goes after him even though Gabrielle protests stridently. A fight between the two women is prevented only when Meleager admits that he's guilty of the crime for which he was tried. Their friendship is sorely tested in that moment and most likely will be tested again in the future.

# SUPPORTING CHARACTERS

These characters are not seen in every episode of *Xena*, but they form a basic part of the continuity of the series in that they return from time to time in different stories. Their new stories may be unrelated to previous appearances or may be follow-ups to ideas and plots explored in previous episodes.

ARES (Kevin Smith)

Ares, the god of war, thinks that war is a great idea and dislikes the fact that Xena has turned her back on her warlike past. He is determined to lure her back to his side and has tried a number of ways to accomplish this. He frames her for murdering a group of villagers in "The Reckoning" (X-6), believing that he can convince her to join him as his representative on earth. In "Ties That Bind" (X-20), Ares impersonates Xena's long lost father in an attempt to lure her back to her old ways. In "Intimate Stranger" (X-31), Ares punishes Xena by switching her body with that of Callisto. But Callisto in Xena's body proves to be even more troublesome than the real Xena. Ares gets his comeuppance in "Ten Little Warlords" (X-32) when his sword of power is stolen by Sisyphus, and Ares becomes mortal. Ironically only Xena (still in Callisto's body) can help him. When she succeeds in regaining his sword for him, as well as saving his life, Ares proves he does have some honor after all by restoring Xena to her rightful body. Even though the gods of ancient Greece are only legend by the time of the twentieth century, Ares still exists and he and Xena are still antagonists as is shown in "The Xena Scrolls" (X-34).

## AUTOLYCUS (Bruce Campbell)

First introduced in the *Hercules* episode "King of Thieves" (H-14), Autolycus has made many more appearances on *Xena,* becoming a greater part of her continuity than he ever was on *Hercules.* He is the self-proclaimed King of Thieves, which is no idle boast. Xena first meets him in "A Royal Couple of Thieves" (X-17) when she uses his unorthodox skills to track down a chest that has been stolen from a nomad band to whom Xena feels she owed a great obligation. Autolycus has no choice but to help Xena in "The Quest" (X-37) when her wandering soul enters his body and insists that he steal her body before it can be cremated by Gabrielle and the Amazons who believe that Xena has died.

## CALLISTO (Hudson Leick)

In the days when Xena was the evil warrior princess, a raid on a village by Xena and her army resulted in an accidental fire that destroyed the village and took many innocent lives. Callisto was one of the few survivors and she swore vengeance on Xena and vowed to destroy everything that Xena loves, just as Xena caused the death of Callisto's mother and sisters. She is more brutal than Xena ever was and feels compassion for no one. Xena first encounters her in "Callisto" (X-22) when Callisto masquerades as Xena and destroys villages in order to draw Xena to her for a final confrontation. But Callisto is exposed and captured by Xena. In "Return of Callisto" (X-29), she escapes her captors and returns to plague Xena. When Callisto fails in her attempt to kill Gabrielle, she takes second best and kills Perdicus, whom Gabrielle had just married. Now Gabrielle wants nothing more than to kill Callisto. Xena doesn't want her friend to follow through with her threat, however. Instead Xena tracks down Callisto and in their final duel Callisto falls into a pool of quicksand and drowns while Xena stands by and does nothing. But death is not the end for Callisto. In "Intimate Stranger" (X-31), Callisto switches bodies with Xena, thanks to the help of Ares. Ares discovers that Callisto is more trouble than she's worth and returns Xena to her rightful form in "Ten Little Warlords" (X-32). Callisto becomes immortal in the Hercules episode "Surprise" (H-49), and Xena even has to team up with her in "A Necessary Evil" (X-38), but they remain enemies.

## CUPID (Karl Urban)

The son of Aphrodite, the goddess of love, Cupid and his mother don't always see eye to eye on the course true love should take. He has appeared in such episodes as "For Him the Bell Tolls" (X-40), "A Comedy of Eros" (X-46), and the *Hercules* segment "The Green-Eyed Monster" (H-44).

## PRINCESS DIANA (Lucy Lawless)

Diana is inexplicably Xena's identical twin (and by no means the only one). She is first seen in "Warrior…Princess" (X-15) where Xena is hired by King Lias to protect his daughter, Princess Diana, who is betrothed to wed Minius even though she really loves Philemon, Minius's brother. Xena masquerades as Diana but alienates Minius when he sees her get into a brawl on their wedding day. Diana returns in the second-season episode "Warrior…Princess…Tramp" (X-30) where yet another double named Meg is introduced. This time King Lias is dying and fears that there are plans to usurp the throne from his family now that Diana has married Philemon.

## EPHINY (Danielle Cormack)

This Amazon appears in "Hooves and Harlots" (X-10) the episode in which Gabrielle is granted the right of caste in the Amazon tribe. When the Centaur Terreis is killed, Ephiny must put aside her resentment of Gabrielle to help her and Xena uncover the killer and head off a potential war between the Amazons and the Centaurs. Ultimately Ephiny weds Phantes, the son of the Centaur chieftain. Ephiny returns in "Is There a Doctor in the House" (X-24) when Phantes is killed and Gabrielle and Xena find the wounded and pregnant Ephiny. Ephiny gives birth to a male Centaur. Ephiny and Xena meet again in "The Quest" (X-37) and "A Necessary Evil" (X-38).

## HADES (Eric Thomson)

Hades is the Greek god of the Underworld and his sister is Death. He appears in the episodes "Death in Chains" (X-9), "Mortal Beloved" (X-16), and "Intimate Stranger" (X-31). In "Ten Little Warlords" (X-32), he makes a pact with Sisyphus to free him if he can deliver ten souls in his place. When Sisyphus can only come up with eight before his plot is exposed, Hades puts Sisyphus back to work trying to push a boulder up a hill. Every time he nears the top, the boulder rolls back down and he must start all over.

## HERCULES (Kevin Sorbo)

This legendary hero is the illegitimate son of the god Zeus and the mortal woman Alcmene. Because he is the offspring of Zeus's illicit affair, he has super-human strength, which he uses to help mankind. When Xena first encounters Hercules in the *Hercules* episode "The Warrior Princess" (H-9), she is the evil Xena. When she is defeated by Hercules, Xena vows vengeance upon him. But it is Hercules who helps turn Xena to the path of justice in "The Gauntlet" (H-12) and "Unchained Heart" (H-13) where they briefly become lovers. That they continue to have feelings for each other is made apparent in the *Xena* episode "Prometheus" (X-8) where Xena tries to prevent Hercules from sacrificing his life, and Hercules tries to prevent Xena from sacrificing her life, to save the imprisoned god Prometheus. Xena concedes her admiration for him when she states that it is only the existence of Hercules, her mother, and Gabrielle that gives her the strength to stay on the righteous path in life.

## IOLAUS (Michael Hurst)

He is the best friend of Hercules. In the episode "The Warrior Princess" (H-9), the still evil Xena seduces Iolaus and tries to turn him against Hercules. In "Prometheus" (X-8), the reformed Xena encounters Iolaus once again and apologizes for her earlier misdeeds. Gabrielle is clearly attracted to Iolaus in "Prometheus," and in "The Greater Good" (X-21), she turns to him when she thinks that Xena is dead. Gabrielle encounters him again briefly in "The Quest" (X-37) when she's taking Xena's body back to Amphipolos.

JOXER (Ted Raimi)

Joxer is a well-meaning but inept pseudo-warrior. Seen first in "Callisto" (X-22), Joxer tries to make a name for himself by capturing Xena and Gabrielle for Callisto. When Callisto captures Gabrielle on her own, she orders Joxer to kill the girl, but Joxer starts babbling and can't bring himself to do it. He turns up with great frequency and usually when least expected as in "Girls Just Wanna Have Fun" (X-28), "Return of Callisto" (X-29), "Warrior...Princess...Tramp" (X-30), "Intimate Strangers" (X-31), "Ten Little Warlords" (X-32), and, most significantly, in "For Him the Bell Tolls" (X-40). In this last episode Joxer is the victim of a spell cast by Aphrodite that turns him into a skilled warrior. At the sound of a bell the spell is broken and he doesn't remember that while under the spell he has been everything that the inept Joxer ever dreamed of being. Joxer has his own personal theme song: "Joxer the Mighty, He's Very Tidy." Ted Raimi, who plays Joxer, is the brother of series co-producer Sam Raimi. Ted was a regular on *Seaquest DSV* as well as making appearances on other shows including *Twin Peaks*.

MARCUS (Bobby Hosea)

Marcus was Xena's lover back when she was an evil warlord. They meet again in "The Path Not Taken" (X-5) where Xena is hired to rescue a woman who has been kidnapped. Marcus thinks Xena is there to steal weapons but comes to realize that she now follows a different path. Because of Xena's transformation he begins to examine his own life. Although he turns Xena over to the authorities when he discovers her trying to rescue the kidnapped woman, he has a change of heart when Xena is about to be executed. Marcus saves her life at the cost of his own. It must be remembered, however, that death is just another place to visit on *Xena*. In the episode "Mortal Beloved" (X-16), Marcus is freed by Hades for forty-eight hours to help Xena find the helmet of invisibility which belongs to the god of the Underworld. During those two days they re-ignite their love affair.

Xena convinces Hades to release Marcus from Tartarus (the place of torment and punishment in the Underworld). However, it is only by killing Marcus that Xena may free him from the torments of Tartarus and enable him to enter the utopian Elysian Fields.

## MELEAGER (Tim Thomerson)

Meleager is actually a friend of Gabrielle's whom she meets when she returns home in "The Prodigal" (X-18). He is a former warlord who froze up in the midst of a battle and is so ashamed of his cowardice that he has become a drunkard and a wandering sword for hire. Employed by Gabrielle's village to fend off a warlord, only Gabrielle's friendship and belief in his abilities enables him to rise to the occasion and help save the village. Meleager returns in "The Execution" (X-41) where he is sentenced to hang for the apparent murder of a man. Although Meleager claims that he'd given up the bottle, he had briefly fallen off the wagon on the night of the murder, and he remembers little of what happened. Xena not only cleverly saves Meleager when he is hanged, but she proves that he is innocent of the crime as well.

## M'LILA (Ebonie Smith)

Seen only in the episode "Destiny" (X-36), she is a woman who was a stowaway on Xena's ship when the warrior princess still commanded her army. Xena agrees to spare M'Lila's life if the woman will teach Xena the strange secrets of her fighting skills and knowledge of pressure points that will paralyze someone with just a touch. These techniques come to be Xena's greatest weapons. M'Lila is a strange woman who has an inner awareness of who Xena is and how important she will be to the future of Greece. Xena hides M'Lila from Julius Caesar when he captures Xena's ship. In return M'Lila rescues Xena from the cross on which Caesar orders her crucified. M'Lila then takes Xena to a healer who mends her broken legs. When three Roman soldiers track Xena down and try to kill her, M'Lila throws herself across Xena and is mortally wounded with the arrow intended for the warrior princess. Xena kills the soldiers and vows vengeance for the death of M'Lila.

## PERDICUS (Anton Bentley, Scott Garrison)

Played by two actors—Anton Bentley in "Sins of the Past" (X-1) and

Scott Garrison in "Beware Greeks Bearing Gifts" (X-12) and "Return of Callisto" (X-29)—Perdicus is Gabrielle's betrothed. However, Gabrielle decides not to marry him and leaves to follow Xena. She and Perdicus cross paths again in "Beware Greeks Bearing Gifts," and their love is consummated when they get married in "Return of Callisto." But Callisto returns and plans to kill Gabrielle to avenge herself on Xena. When Callisto is stymied, she chooses to kill Perdicus instead, knowing that this will hurt both Xena and Gabrielle. So Perdicus now resides in the Underworld, awaiting resurrection on some future episode.

## SALMONEUS (Robert Trebor)

A semi-regular on *Hercules,* Salmoneus first encounters Xena in the *Hercules* episode "The Gauntlet" (H-12), her second appearance in the series and the one in which Salmoneus stands up for her, stating his belief that she has changed for the better. He is also with Xena in the *Hercules* installment "Unchained Hearts" (H-13). Usually he's a fast-talking salesman with a get-rich quick scheme in which he tends to embroil his friends. Although well meaning, he has poor business judgment. He helps Xena again in "The Black Wolf" (X-11) by organizing prisoners to fight on her behalf. In "The Greater Good" (X-21), he actually offers himself in exchange for villagers threatened by the evil warlord Talmadeus. Because a little of Salmoneus goes a long way, he has been restricted to appearing just on *Hercules* while Joxer has become the recurring comedic presence on *Xena.* The only *Xena* episode in which Salmoneus has appeared during the second season is "Here She Comes...Miss Amphipolis" (X-35).

## SISYPHUS (Ray Henwood, Charles Siebert)

Played by two actors—-Ray Henwood in "Death in Chains" (X-9) and Charles Siebert in "Ten Little Warlords" (X-32)—Sisyphus is the famous mythological figure who must spend eternity rolling a huge rock up a hill, only to have it roll back down whereupon he must start all over again. In the series he is a magician who condemns himself to Tartarus for eternity when he imprisons Death (the sister of Hades) in "Death in Chains" because he mistakenly believes that she is coming to take his life. Sisyphus returns in "Ten Little Warlords" when he makes a deal with Hades to deliver ten souls in exchange for his release from the Underworld. Thanks to Xena he fails in his ignoble task and is confined once again to Tartarus.

SOLON (David Taylor)

Xena's ten-year-old son, Solon, is introduced in "Orphan of War" (X-25). His existence is a closely guarded secret and even the boy doesn't know that Xena is his mother. Shortly after his birth Xena gave her baby to Kaleipus, the Centaur leader, to raise. In exchange she promised to withdraw her army and never return. The boy had been conceived by Xena and Borias, but after Borias died under mysterious circumstances Xena chose to give the boy to the Centaurs to be raised so he could never be harmed by her enemies. Xena wants her son to grow up without learning those things that would make him a warrior.

# CHAPTER ELEVEN

# ARE XENA AND GABRIELLE MORE THAN JUST FRIENDS?

I n the atmosphere of heightened awareness created in April 1997 by
the much discussed *coming out* episode of the TV sitcom *Ellen,* it is surprising that the media has not made more of the relationship between
Xena and Gabrielle. Right from the beginning the fact that *Xena* features
two female leads attracted a loyal following of lesbian viewers. When the
friendship of the two characters seemed to take on greater depth, in particular in the second-season episode "The Quest" (X-37), this following
became more vociferous. The question remains, however, whether some
of these viewers are merely projecting their own agenda on the show.

## HINTS AND SUBTEXT

In an interview with Lucy Lawless published in the *Denver Post* in
November 1996, she stated, "We are aware and we're not afraid of [the lesbian element]. This is a love story between two people. What they do in
their own time is none of our business." (More recently, in a July 1997
interview in *People,* Xena co-star Renee O'Connor said, "But the more lesbians started watching, and the more feedback we received from them,
our characters started to develop a little more intimately. We have to keep
it a family show, but the subtext is there.")

That the writers on the show insert bits of business to play to the
expectation of that segment of the audience is clear. The first time this subtle characterization went beyond innuendo was in "The Quest" (X-37)
when Gabrielle enters the dream plane to converse with Xena. Xena's

spirit, or soul, was at that moment housed in the body of Autolycus (much against his will), but on the dream plane Gabrielle finally sees Xena again after believing her friend has died. In her joy to see her again, Xena and Gabrielle kiss, but at the moment their lips touch, the action cuts to Gabrielle kissing Autolycus, whose hand is on her buttocks.

In "A Day in the Life" (X-39), when Xena is in a creek fishing with her bare hands, a man named Hower asks Gabrielle if Xena ever thinks about settling down and getting married. Gabrielle happily replies, "No, she likes what I do..." but doesn't get the chance to finish the sentence because Xena hurls a fish from off-camera that hits her in the face—accidentally or on purpose? Later in the same episode Xena and Gabrielle are in a hot tub together. Gabrielle again kisses Xena, but this time on the cheek.

In "Ulysses" (X-43), Xena and Gabrielle are helping Ulysses sail his ship back to his kingdom of Ithaca. When Xena and Ulysses start to make love, thinking Gabrielle is asleep, the camera moves from Xena and Ulysses to show us Gabrielle who clearly looks unhappy.

In *Cleo* magazine (January 1997), Lawless again discussed the on-screen relationship of the pair when interviewer Erik Knutzen pointedly asked, "Feminists often wonder exactly what Xena's relationship is to Gabrielle, her loyal sidekick?" Lawless replied, "Xena is a woman of many skills." But in the February 7, 1997, New Zealand *TV Guide,* she was less flip in her observations when she stated, "There are a lot of people out there who have suffered from some kind of abuse — women, gays, kids—and they all relate to Xena. She's always fighting the good fight."

In New Zealand gay pride is celebrated more openly and with greater acceptance than in the United States, so its inclusion in a TV series produced there is not to be unexpected. In fact in the January 1996 issue of *Femme Fatales,* Lawless was quite candid about this aspect of life in New Zealand.

"We had a sort of gay Mardi Gras recently. The American producer was down here and couldn't believe all the women's breasts around. He said, 'This just wouldn't happen in the States!'" Lawless was observing the parade with her then seven-year-old daughter, but decided it was time to leave when the S&M float came along. "I thought maybe my kid had seen enough then. But she never blinked. It was cool."

## MALE LOVERS

In spite of the laissez-faire approach to the subject taken by the producers, both Xena and Gabrielle have also been shown to have intense male love interests, and Gabrielle was even married (however briefly) in "Return of Callisto" (X-29). Both in "Return of Callisto" and "Ulysses" (X-43) the subject is raised about how the other feels when one of them becomes involved with a man. Xena explains her feelings for Ulysses to Gabrielle and Gabrielle says that whatever makes Xena happy makes her happy, which is exactly what Xena tells Gabrielle before she marries Perdicus in "Return of Callisto" (X-29).

But the only enduring relationship on the series is the one between Xena and Gabrielle. Every time one of them becomes involved with a man, it just doesn't work out—or else he dies. When Xena is reunited with her old lover Marcus in "The Path Not Taken" (X-5), he dies protecting Xena. They are briefly reunited in "Mortal Beloved" (X-16) and even pick up where they left off before he died, but his time on earth is past and he is sent to the Elysian fields where his spirit can have a peaceful afterlife. In the end she goes back to Gabrielle who patiently waits for Xena to return from her mission to the Underworld.

## DEEP FEELINGS

The depth of Xena's feelings for Gabrielle are made evident in the first-season episode "Is There a Doctor in the House?" (X-24) when Gabrielle appears to die. Xena loses it, screaming and frantically working to return her friend to consciousness. It is the first time that the usually stoic Xena is portrayed crying.

But what if Xena had to choose between her family and Gabrielle? What would that reveal? In the second-season episode "Remember Nothing" (X-26), the Three Fates give Xena the opportunity to live her life as though she had never become the warrior princess. Thus, she finds that her beloved younger brother, who died beside her in battle, is alive again. Along the way she encounters Gabrielle who is a slave and has no knowledge of Xena or any other kind of existence. All Xena has to do to maintain this alternate path of reality is to not spill blood in anger. But when

Gabrielle slays her slave master and it becomes clear that unless Xena acts Gabrielle will be killed, Xena picks up a sword and fights, causing time to resume its shape and her brother to return to the Underworld. Clearly, her decision is made because she cannot stand to watch Gabrielle die even though they are not close friends in this reality.

## Reality Check

Does any of this really matter? Unlike the television sitcom *Ellen,* which made an overt issue of the main character's sexuality, *Xena* continues to be ambiguous. The lives of the characters off-camera are hinted at but not made an issue of discussion. Clearly the two characters are portrayed as caring for each other a great deal. How often do we see such deep feelings and intense friendship explored on any television series? It is this portrayal and the positive theme of good struggling against evil that raise *Xena* to the heights of its genre.

# XENA: WARRIOR PRINCESS
## INTRODUCTORY EPISODES (1995)

The introductory episodes of *Xena* were part of the *Hercules: The Legendary Journeys* series, and were all sixty minutes long.

## H-9: THE WARRIOR PRINCESS

CREDITS: Teleplay by John Schulian; directed by Bruce Seth Green

GUEST STARS: Michael Hurst (Iolaus), Lucy Lawless (Xena), Elizabeth Hawthorne (Alcmene)

SUPPORTING CAST: Bill Johnson (Petrakis), Michael Dwyer (Theodorus)

STORY LINE: A power-hungry evil warrior princess sees Hercules as the only obstacle in her path to conquering all she surveys. This fiend is a woman called Xena! Judging Iolaus, Hercules' sidekick, as his weak link, she seduces the gullible Iolaus to drive a wedge between him and his friend Hercules.

In a skirmish between the two former friends, Iolaus inevitably loses to Hercules, but quickly realizes what a fool he has been when Hercules refuses to kill him. Xena can't abide such loyalty and she angrily rides off, threatening to return one day soon to kill Hercules herself.

OBSERVATIONS: In this episode of *Hercules*, Xena is introduced as a typical villainess. There is no indication of the Xena we will come to know and love. Rather, she's just a hissing, spitting vixen who fears nothing. However, some members of the production team must have realized that the character played by statuesque Lucy Lawless could become something more even though this first appearance of Xena is pretty lame stuff. There is no indication of her character's potential (as a heroine) or that Lucy Lawless the actress could transform the part into a charismatic characterization.

# H-12: THE GAUNTLET

CREDITS: Teleplay by Peter Bielak; directed by Jack Perez

GUEST STARS: Lucy Lawless (Xena), Robert Trebor (Salmoneus), Matthew Chamberlain (Darphus)

SUPPORTING CAST: Dean O'Gorman (Iloran), Peter Daube (Spiros)

STORY LINE: Xena's right-hand man, Darphus, challenges Xena's ability to rule her followers. Xena is deposed and forced to run a brutal gauntlet where, unarmed, she is beaten until she collapses and is left for dead. Her soldiers should have known, however, that the warrior princess was made of tougher stuff than that!

Once recovered, Xena searches out Hercules for help. Eventually, Xena manages to confront and kill Darphus. Ares, however, who has been watching these events and has always admired Darphus, returns him to life. Naturally, Darphus is now out for revenge.

OBSERVATIONS: This time around Xena is depicted as not being all bad, showing compassion toward women, children, and those who lay down their arms. Because her barbarian army feels that these rules cramp their warring style, Darphus has the opportunity to supplant Xena as their leader.

The gauntlet Xena is forced to pass through is exceedingly dangerous and, in fact, she's left for dead by Darphus. But Xena is one resilient combatant and revives to fight another day.

# H-13: Unchained Heart

CREDITS: Teleplay by John Schulian; directed by Bruce Seth
Green

GUEST STARS: Michael Hurst (Iolaus), Lucy Lawless (Xena),
Robert Trebor (Salmoneus), Matthew Chamberlain (Darphus)

SUPPORTING CAST: Stephen Papps (Pylendor), Mervyn Smith
(Village Elder), Robert Pollock (Villager), Shane Dawson (First
Warrior), Ian Harrop (Camp Boss), Margo Gada (Quintas),
Bruce Allpress (Eros), David Mercer (Warrior), Gordon Hat-
field (Lieutenant), Campbell Rousselle (Sentry)

STORY LINE: This episode is a continuation of the prior episode, "The
Gauntlet." Ares, the god of war, has brought Darphus back from the land
of the dead. Salmoneus, the character who most often provides comedic
relief on Hercules is introduced into this episode as a captive of Darphus.

Hercules and Xena rescue the bungling Salmoneus and maneuver the
situation so that Darphus and his lieutenant fight over the leadership of the
army so that they are no longer a threat to the peace.

Anxious for redemption, Xena turns over a new leaf. She realizes that
helping people is far more satisfying and rewarding than laying waste to
the countryside.

OBSERVATIONS: In these early segments Xena and Hercules have
good chemistry together (even when their characters are at odds with each
other). Although Xena's personality is still quite abrasive, her character
traits will be softened by the time her own starring TV series (*Xena: Warrior Princess*) is launched. Even by this third appearance, she's no longer the
embodiment of nastiness that she represented when she was first introduced in "The Warrior Princess" (H-9). In fact she officially reforms in this
installment as she comprehends the error of her ways and makes sloppy
apologies all around, even to Iolaus.

In these three episodes we see the rapid evolution of the striking and
physically imposing Xena. Initially she appeared as a sinister version of
Joan of Arc, a calculating woman not above granting sexual favors to her
most useful troops.

In "The Gauntlet" (H-12), however, Xena's more humane facets are revealed, which ironically lead to the mutiny of her troops. Her reformation is complete as she goes off alone to find out whether performing charitable acts will be as rewarding as Hercules has suggested.

Well, this is where it all began! Viewers' enthusiasm for Xena's showy character convinced the producers to capitalize on her growing popularity. As a result, the statuesque Lucy Lawless won her own syndicated TV series—and the rest is history.

# CHAPTER THIRTEEN

# XENA:
# WARRIOR PRINCESS
## SEASON ONE (1995–96)

The episodes created for the television series are all sixty minutes long, the standard length for a drama-adventure series.

## PRODUCTION CREDITS

Created by John Schulian and Robert Tapert; developed by R. J. Stewart; producer: Liz Friedman; producer: Eric Gruendemann; supervising producer: Steven L. Sears; co-executive producer: R. J. Stewart; executive producer: Sam Raimi; executive producer: Robert Tapert; coordinating producer: Bernadette Joyce; New Zealand producer: Chloe Smith; story editor: Chris Manheim; unit production manager: Chloe Smith; first assistant director: Paul Grinder; second assistant director: Neal James; director of photography: Donald Duncan; editor: Jim Pryor; visual effects: Kevin O'Neill; production designer: Robert Gillies; costume designer: Nigla Dickson; New Zealand casting: Diana Rowan; stunt coordinator: Peter Bell; additional visual effects: Flat Earth Productions, Inc.; music: Joseph LoDuca

## REGULARS

Lucy Lawless (Xena), Renee O'Connor (Gabrielle)

### X-1: SINS OF THE PAST

CREDITS: Story by Robert Tapert; teleplay by R. J. Stewart; directed by Doug Lefler

GUEST STARS: Jay Laga'aia (Draco), Darien Takle (Cyrene)

SUPPORTING CAST: Anton Bentley (Perdicus), Huntly Eliott
(First Citizen), Wally Green (Old Man), Stephen Hall (Hector),
Winston Harris (Boy), Linda Jones (Hecuba), Roydon Muir
(Kastor), Willa O'Neill (Lila), David Perrett (Gar), Geoff Snell
(Herodotus), Patrick Wilson (Cyclops)

STORY LINE: This Xena episode introduces Gabrielle whom Xena befriends in a village she protects from a vicious warlord. A grateful Gabrielle
insists on following Xena, choosing the dynamic warrior princess as her
mentor.

When Xena is outnumbered in battle, Gabrielle saves her life. Thus, Xena
is now in Gabrielle's debt and so must accept her. Ironically, the longer the
admiring Gabrielle remains in Xena's company, the more their friendship
grows into solid mutual respect.

OBSERVATIONS: This episode establishes the reformed version of
Xena following her appearances in three episodes of *Hercules*. In the pre-
title sequence in which Xena encounters victims being plagued by bandits,
the action is far more flamboyant than the fighting employed on the *Hercules* series, which immediately establishes one of the distinct differences
between these two linked TV shows. In her own showcase Xena leaps and
kicks and often comes across to viewers as a superhero (which is reminiscent of *Wonder Woman*, 1976–79). In contrast, Hercules' mode of operation
is typically to pick people up and hurl them twenty feet away.

In evaluating these early episodes, we see that originally Gabrielle was
little more than a friendly companion with the knack of constantly getting
into trouble from which Xena had to rescue her. Eventually, however,
Gabrielle's character matures (which is none too soon because even a little
of her personality can get on one's nerves).

HIGHLIGHTS: A solid sequence is Xena's fight with the warlord
Draco on the scaffolding. It is improved upon only in the episode "Callisto" (X-22) with its brawls on balanced ladders. These examples demonstrate that this program has a lot more inventiveness than one would have
ever suspected. It also demonstrates why the imitator TV shows have con-
sistently failed to meet the entertainment standards set by *Xena*.

TRIVIA: This episode introduces Gabrielle who is Xena's co-star. As presented here, Gabrielle is a somewhat naive but enthusiastic young woman who at first has little knowledge of the ways of a fighter. She proves to be a quick study, however.

# X-2: Chariots of War

CREDITS: Story by Josh Becker and Jack Perez; teleplay by Adam Armus and Nora Kay Foster; directed by Harley Cokeliss

GUEST STARS; Nick Kokotakis (Darius), Jeff Thomas (Cycnus), Stuart Turner (Sphaerus)

SUPPORTING CAST: Nigel Godfrey (Tynus), Robert Harte (Ugly Ruffian), Morgan Palmer Hubbard (Argolis), Dane Jerro (Homesteader), Patrick Morrison (Lykus), Ruth Morrison (Sarita)

MYTHOLOGICAL BASIS: This espisode is centered around a group of Trojan pacifists, an interesting choice because in Greek mythology the Trojans were said to be the descendants of Dardanus, the son of Zeus and Electra. It was Dardanus who founded Troy, and four generations later, Hercules killed his descendant, Laomedon, and all of his sons except one. The survivor became known as King Priam with whom Ares, the god of war, sided during the Trojan wars.

STORY LINE: Just as in any good *Xena* episode, this one opens with a battle. It all begins when Xena encounters a colony of peaceful Trojans and has to come to their defense. In the battle she is wounded by an arrow.

In a cross-plot development Gabrielle encounters and befriends the young bowman who shot the fateful arrow. The young man regrets his warrior actions, much to the consternation of his father.

Ultimately, Xena and the young man's father have their moment of truth, and in the battle the man sacrifices himself so that his remaining son can find the peace in his life that was denied his brother.

OBSERVATIONS: This segment establishes a story line structure that would be used in many forthcoming episodes. The formula has Xena and Gabrielle each meeting different members of those involved in a conflict. In this instance it's a demanding father who wants his son to be just as bloodthirsty as he is and who hates what we might call *peaceniks* (i.e., warriors such as Xena and the man's other son who've turned their backs on war.) Ultimately, Xena and this bloodthirsty parent must fight to the finish. The result is that Hades soon has a new guest down below.

The violence quotient is definitely high in this episode as demonstrated when Xena takes an arrow in the side and is forced to remove it herself.

HIGHLIGHTS: There is a chariot race that allows ample opportunity for a great deal of friendly banter between Xena and Gabrielle.

## X-3: DREAMWORKER

CREDITS: Teleplay by Steven L. Sears; directed by Bruce Seth Green

GUEST STARS: Nathaniel Lees (Manus), Desmond Kelly (Elkton)

SUPPORTING CAST: Polly Baigent (Doppelganger), Grant Boucher (2nd Xena Warrior), Michael Daly (Mesmer), Colin Francis (Swordsmith), Bruce Hopkins (Termin), Sydney Jackson (Storekeeper), Matthew Jeffs (Gothos), John Palmer (Baruch), Peter Phillips (1st Xena Warrior), Patrick Smith (Dolas), Lawrence Wharerau (Mystic Warrior)

MYTHOLOGICAL BASIS: In Greek mythology the familial relationship between gods is often apparent as with these three who seem quite logically to be of the same family: Thanatos, who is a personification of death, is the brother of Hypnos, the god of sleep, whose son is Morpheus, the god of dreams. This episode involves priests who seem to have confused Morpheus with his uncle Thanatos.

STORY LINE: In trouble once again, well-meaning Gabrielle is captured by the priests of Morpheus, the god of dreams. In order to prepare her for sacrifice, Gabrielle is given a series of tasks designed to force her to take a human life.

To rescue Gabrielle, Xena must enter the dream realm so that her soul can pass through a trial that focuses on her past self. Soon the evil Xena and the good Xena face off in their tug of war. Although the bad Xena is powerful, the good Xena has something more to fight for—the blood innocence of Gabrielle.

OBSERVATIONS: This odd episode, involving dream scapes and surreal contests of will, presages even more peculiar installments to come. Both Xena and Gabrielle manage to triumph on their own very different terms. In addition the fact that Xena is willing to risk her mortal soul to save both Gabrielle's honor and her life proves that Xena is thinking of her more as a friend than just a temporary sidekick.

This segment demonstrates that Gabrielle has profited from her lessons in self-defense from Xena and has learned how to win a match without killing the opponent. The series returns to this sort of fight situation repeatedly with Gabrielle the focus of the battle. A good example occurs in "Return of Callisto" (X-29) in which Xena, once a wanton killer, must now convince Gabrielle not to take a life—even for just revenge.

This multi-leveled story also re-emphasizes the internal battle Xena must continually fight to maintain her goal of redemption from her evil past. In the dream realm good Xena fights bad Xena and virtue triumphs. Nevertheless, it's always intriguing to encounter the sneering, amoral Xena once again.

While still a bit on the helpless and annoying side in these early episodes, Gabrielle is starting to mature. In fact her personality alters to such a degree that, looking back at these early stories from the hindsight of the second year, Gabrielle's character is barely recognizable. The fact that Gabrielle was originally almost a useless annoyance is mocked in the second-season segment "The Xena Scrolls" (X-34).

HIGHLIGHTS: Seeing the evil Xena again.

# X-4: CRADLE OF HOPE

CREDITS: Teleplay by Terence Winter; directed by Michael Levine

GUEST STARS: Mary Elizabeth McGlynn (Pandora), Edward Newborn (King Gregor), Simon Prast (Nemos)

SUPPORTING CAST: Christine Bartlett (Philana), Tony Bishop (Weasel), Alan De Malmanche (Old Man), Lathan Gains (Kastor), Paul Minifie (Innkeeper), Paul Norell (Street Vendor), Kirstie O'Sullivan (Ophelia), Carl Straker (Young Man), Beryl Te Wiata (Cynara), Susan Winter (Woman)

MYTHOLOGICAL BASIS: This episode seems to draw its inspiration from the Book of Exodus in the Old Testament, a touch of Greek history, and at least one classic myth, the story of Pandora.

Pandora (from two words meaning *all* and *gift*) was a beautiful woman to whom each of the gods gave an attribute. Hermes' gift was to put trickery and deceit in her heart so that when Pandora came to earth she began to snoop and pry into everything. It wasn't long before she came upon a jar or box that contained old age, sickness, vice, and all the other things that would plague mankind. Pandora opened the container and all the spirits escaped except for one. Only hope remained.

STORY LINE: When an oracle predicts to a king that a newborn infant will succeed him as ruler, the monarch fears that the child will one day grow up to kill him. The king's servants try to save the baby by placing it in a basket and putting it on the river. The baby is found by Xena and Gabrielle who decide to find out the story behind this abandoned baby.

In their travels they encounter the granddaughter of the legendary Pandora. She carries around a box that contains the Hope of Humanity. Meanwhile, the box and the baby are both being sought everywhere.

Xena helps the king to see the real truth behind the prophecy, and the king and Pandora embark on a romance.

OBSERVATIONS: This story imitates the Bible narrative of Moses in that to save the baby it is placed in a basket and sent floating down a river. Didn't anybody wonder what the baby would do if the basket overturned? Presumably, infants couldn't swim any better then than now. However, such awful possibilities apparently are not considered in TV plots such as this one.

When Xena and Gabrielle discover the infant, Gabrielle is excited and thinks it's cute while Xena is clearly repelled by the prospect of having to care for a baby on an ongoing basis. Obviously, Xena's maternal instincts are not as pronounced as Gabrielle's.

The granddaughter of Pandora, who is carrying around this mysterious box, turns out to be a red herring. The box is empty because the Hope of Humanity is actually carried in each one of us. The moral here may be fine, but it certainly represents a new twist on the familiar legend of Pandora's box.

Likewise, the Moses-like story of an abandoned baby being found by the water side, and the babe who one day will become king (also featured in the 1963 movie *Jason and the Argonauts*) are examples of how both the *Xena* and *Hercules* TV series rework legends for their own purposes. Another classic example occurs in *Xena's* second-season Christmas episode "A Solstice Carol" (X-33) in which Xena and Gabrielle are supposed to have encountered Mary and Joseph going to Bethlehem, thus mixing Biblical and Greek mythology in a grand manner.

TRIVIA: This episode has an unusual scene where Xena has to both fight and juggle the baby at the same time (including throwing the baby straight up into the air so that she can deal with several attackers at once). This scene led to the first disclaimer ever to appear on the show: "No babies were harmed during the production of this motion picture."

## X-5: THE PATH NOT TAKEN

CREDITS: Teleplay by Julie Sherman; directed by Stephen L. Posey

GUEST STARS: Bobby Hosea (Marcus), Stephen Tozer (Myzantius)

SUPPORTING CAST: Nicola Cliff (Jana), Jimi Liversidge (Agranon), John O'Leary (Antonius), Iain Rea (Brisus), Peter Saena-Brown (Soldier #1), Crawford Thompson (Dictys)

STORY LINE: An arms dealer kidnaps a princess, hoping to instigate a war and stimulate his business. Xena infiltrates the warlord's camp where she is recognized by an old flame, Marcus, and they soon reignite their romance. Gabrielle's story is a subplot involving the young man to whom the princess is betrothed.

When Xena is about to be killed, Marcus uses his body as a shield to protect her and dies in Xena's arms. The full depth of her feelings for Marcus become quite clear when she sings a dirge over his funeral pyre.

OBSERVATION: Marcus was apparently one of the few pre-reformation friends that Xena has ever seen again. This is of some significance as she apparently has few associates remaining from her days as a pillager.

HIGHLIGHTS: Lucy Lawless demonstrates talents beyond her excellent acting capabilities. She actually wrote the dirge she performs at the funeral. She sings the same song in year two of the TV series in "Return of Callisto" (X-29) after Perdicus is slain by Callisto.

TRIVIA: Even though Marcus dies in this installment, he reappears in "Mortal Beloved" (X-16), which further explores the complicated history between Marcus and Xena.

# X-6: THE RECKONING

CREDITS: Teleplay by Peter Allan Fields; directed by Charles
     Siebert

GUEST STARS: Kevin Smith (Ares)

SUPPORTING CAST: Ross Harper (Polinios), Christian Hodge
     (Teracles), Sam Holland (Teen Son), Phaedra Hurst (Teresia),
     Bill Johnson (Benitar), Danny Lineham (Grathios), Meryl
     Main (Areolis' Widow), Christopher Mayer (Peranis)

MYTHOLOGICAL BASIS: In Greek mythology Ares, the only son of Zeus born of Hera, is one of the twelve ruling deities and is known as the god of war. His sole focus is to create chaos, turmoil, and war, and he plays a role in virtually every battle or conflict recorded in mythology. As a warrior, Xena would have most probably worshipped at his shrine. Her reformation would be the perfect motivation for such a god to meddle in her life.

STORY LINE: Xena encounters a group of poor villagers being attacked by a rampaging warrior who clearly possesses mystical powers. Xena is blamed for the carnage.

It turns out that the masked intruder was Ares who visits her in her cell and tries to appeal to the old Xena to form an alliance with him. Ares' offer is enhanced when some of the peasants try to torture Xena. This dire situation brings the dark side of Xena to the fore once again, much to Ares' delight. Only the timely arrival of Gabrielle holds matters in check.

HIGHLIGHTS: Possessed by her corrupt side, Xena gives Gabrielle a good hard sock, which reminds us that the old violent Xena is still just beneath the surface.

TRIVIA: Ares' desire to win Xena back to the side of war and bloodlust is a recurring element in the series. The several rematches with Ares sometimes take on unusual forms, particularly in the second-season episode "The Xena Scrolls" (X-34).

# X-7: THE TITANS

CREDITS: Teleplay by R. J. Stewart; directed by Eric Brevig

GUEST STARS: Andy Anderson (Hesiot), Edward Campbell (Crius), Mark Raffety (Hyperion), Paolo Rotondo (Philius), Amanda Tollemache (Thea)

SUPPORTING CAST: Tania Anderson (First Woman), Simon Cameron (Villager #2), Jack Dacey (Creon), Julianne Evans (Second Woman), Sian Hughes (Young Woman), David Mackie (Rhodos), Syd Mannion (Calchas), Peter Morgan (Barkeep), Maggie Tarver (Villager #1)

MYTHOLOGICAL BASIS: In the chronology of ancient Greek myth, the Titans came into being just after the world began and ruled long before the Olympians. There were twelve Titans and Titanesses who were the early, elemental gods, fathered by Uranus on Mother Earth (their other off-spring included the Cyclopes and the hundred-handed Giants). The Titan Chronus dethroned his father, Uranus, and thereafter, to save himself from the same fate, ate his own children. But his wife, Rhea, saved one child, Zeus, who, when he reached manhood, caused his father to vomit up the other children, whom Zeus then led in a ten-year war against the Titans. With the help of the Cyclopes, Zeus and the Olympians prevailed. At first Zeus condemned the Titans to Tartarus but later killed them with his thunderbolts.

STORY LINE: Xena and Gabrielle come upon a cave full of worshippers who are in the midst of a ceremony designed to return the mighty Titans to life. Gabrielle reads an incantation which releases three of the Titans. The revived ancients revere Gabrielle as a goddess.

When her deception about being a true goddess is revealed, the three gods rebel and plot to release the rest of the Titans, which, if accomplished, would place all of humanity in grave danger.

OBSERVATIONS: This is another installment where Xena has to save Gabrielle's hide although in the future Gabrielle becomes self-sufficient enough to slip out of scrapes on her own.

HIGHLIGHTS: Still a bit immature, Gabrielle finds great pleasure in playing goddess and controlling these gigantic Titans. Obviously, a part of Gabrielle's darker side surfaces here.

# X-8: PROMETHEUS

CREDITS: Teleplay by R. J. Stewart; directed by Stephen L. Posey

GUEST STARS: Michael Hurst (Iolaus), Kevin Sorbo (Hercules)

SUPPORTING CAST: Jodie Dorday (Io), John Freeman (Prometheus), Russell Gowers (Demophon), David Mitchell

(Innkeeper), Paul Norell (Statius), Sara Wiseman (Young Woman)

MYTHOLOGICAL BASIS: The primary myth upon which this episode is based is the story of Prometheus who tricks Zeus into giving him the knowledge of fire, which he then shares with mankind. As punishment, Zeus has Prometheus bound to a rock where a vulture ate his liver each day, and each night it grows back. It is Hercules who kills the vulture, and argues with Zeus for Prometheus's release.

Another mythological thread woven into this plot is an allusion to Hephaestus, the son of Hera and either Zeus or Talos. Hephaestus was a sickly child whom Hera literally threw off Mount Olympus. Though lame and disfigured, he survived and went on to become a master craftsman, which is why he is associated with fire and the forge. Because of Hephaestus' dependence upon fire and his anger at what Prometheus had done, it is Hephaestus who nails Prometheus to the rock.

The Roc, which captures Xena, in Arabian mythology, is a bird of extraordinary size and strength.

STORY LINE: Hercules and Xena go on a quest to find the magic sword of Hephaestus, which is the only thing that can free Prometheus. Whoever uses the sword to free Prometheus, however, will sacrifice his or her own life in the process.

Xena attempts to free Prometheus on her own. When she is captured by a Roc, she throws the magic sword to Hercules who deflects it, causing the sword to shatter the chain. Not exactly the way it happened in the myth, but the end is the same—Prometheus is freed by Hercules.

OBSERVATIONS: During this quest Gabrielle reluctantly remains behind. She confesses to Iolaus, however, that she won't allow that to happen much longer. She is determined to fight side by side with Xena, not be just a follower.

There are monsters galore showcased in this segment, which is more common to *Hercules* than to *Xena*.

HIGHLIGHTS: When Xena believes that she is facing death, she reveals to Hercules that she considers Gabrielle to be her true heir in her fight against evil, but that Gabrielle should attend the Athens Bard Academy!

TRIVIA: If anyone is wondering how tough Xena really is, the scene with the Roc should answer the question. When the rope hanging from the Roc onto which she is clinging slams her into a cliff, the entire mountain shakes!

## X-9: DEATH IN CHAINS

CREDITS: Story by Babs Greyhosky, Adam Armus, and Nora Kay Foster; teleplay by Adam Armus and Nora Kay Foster; directed by Charles Siebert
GUEST STARS: Ray Henwood (Sisyphus), Kate Hodge (Celesta), Kieren Hutchison (Talus), Erik Thomson (Hades), Leslie Wing (Karas)

SUPPORTING CAST: Wayne England (Wounded Man), Chris Graham (Toxeus), Kelly Greene (Guard), Gordon Hatfield (Seerus), Paul McLaren (Streptus), Beryl Te Wiata (Old Woman), Allan Wilkins (Thug)

MYTHOLOGICAL BASIS: In Greek mythology Sisyphus, the ruler of Corinth, is best known for the way in which Zeus punished him: he was condemned to push a giant rock to the top of a hill, only to have it roll back down again whereupon he would have to start all over. Less well-known is the reason for this punishment. Sisyphus was a cunning businessman, a thief, and a murderer, who tricked Hades and escaped Tartarus on two occasions before he was caught by Hermes and returned to the Underworld once and for all.

This episode is loosely based on Sisyphus's wily avoidance of his death sentence, and casts Xena in the role usually assigned to Hermes, that of returning Sisyphus to Tartarus.

STORY LINE: Sisyphus, who turns up later in "Ten Little Warlords" (X-32), is introduced in this episode when he captures Death, the sister of Hades (ruler of the Underworld). In an idea borrowed from the old movie *Death Takes a Holiday* (1934), Sisyphus believes that by imprisoning Death he will insure that he himself cannot die.

When Hades asks Xena to help rescue Death, she reluctantly agrees even though it is well known that anyone who touches Death will die instantly.

OBSERVATIONS: Unlike the typical visualizations of Death, here she is portrayed in a positive light, and the person who imprisons her is the villain. This makes for an intriguing twist.

Several reasons are given to substantiate why Death can be a good thing—Dr. Kevorkian, please take note.

HIGHLIGHTS: At the castle of Sisyphus the trio encounter rats in a tunnel (now immortalized in the *Xena* TV show blooper reel).

## X-10: HOOVES AND HARLOTS

CREDITS: Teleplay by Steven L. Sears; directed by Jace
   Alexander

GUEST STARS: David Aston (Tyldus), Alison Bruce (Melosa),
   Danielle Cormack (Ephiny), Mark Ferguson (Krykus)

SUPPORTING CAST: Chris Bailey (Celano), Tanya Dignan
   (Eponin), Andrew Kovacevich (Tor), Rebekah Mercer (Ter-
   reis), Colin Moy (Phantes), Aurora Philips (Magdelus),
   Antony Starr (Mesas), John Watson (Arben)

MYTHOLOGICAL BASIS: The Amazons, daughters of Ares, worship their war-loving father and Artemis, the goddess of virginity and feminine power. These fearless female warriors kill or maim their male babies and have little regard for decency or justice.

In Greek mythology Centaurs are half man and half stallion, and are known mostly for their unruly, brawling behavior and their numerous rapes of Greek maidens. They are the descendants of Centaurus and a herd of Magnesian mares.

STORY LINE: Because of her efforts to help a wounded Amazon,

Gabrielle is granted the title of Amazon princess. Unfortunately she has become a princess right at the time that an arms dealer engineers a fight between the Amazons and the Centaurs,.

A subplot reveals that the Amazon queen has her own reasons for wanting war. To turn the tide, Gabrielle challenges the queen to battle and names Xena as her champion. When the dust from the fight settles, the arms dealer and his band are no more, and Xena has become the new Queen of the Amazons. Xena explains that she and Gabrielle have places to go and things to do and the duo depart under amiable conditions.

OBSERVATIONS: Centaurs turn up from time to time on both *Hercules* and *Xena*. The producers have found a way of portraying them convincingly onscreen by utilizing a combination of live-action cinematography and computer graphic imaging (CGI), which works beautifully.

Even when accused of mayhem, the Centaurs are generally protagonists who are discriminated against by humans who find the concept of a half-man–half-horse to be grotesque. It's the most commonly held prejudice portrayed on these two TV series.

HIGHLIGHT: The well-trained Amazons teach Gabrielle how to use the staff as a weapon for fighting. Gabrielle's desire to be self-sufficient at any price is a personality trait that continues throughout the series.

TRIVIA: Although Lucy Lawless first appeared as Xena on an episode of *Hercules*, she'd appeared in a previous episode (one of the two-hour movies) as an Amazon in *Hercules and the Amazon Women* (H-1). It was this telefeature that established the character of the Amazons as they are portrayed in this episode.

## X-11: THE BLACK WOLF

CREDITS: Teleplay by Alan Jay Glueckman; directed by Mario
   Di Leo

GUEST STARS: Nigel Harbrow (Koulos), Ian Hughes
   (Diomedes), Robert Trebor (Salmoneus), Emma Turner
   (Flora), Kevin J. Wilson (Xerxes)

SUPPORTING CAST: Jonathan Bell-Booth (Chief Guard), Ross Duncan (Parnassus), John Dybvig (Brigand/Ox), Colin Francis (The Grump), Tim Hosking (Blacksmith), Adam Middleton (Black Wolf Sympathizer), John Pemberton (Arresting Guard), Jimmy Rawdon (Father), Maggie Tarver (Hermia)

MYTHOLOGICAL BASIS: Although there are Greek myths that suggest some of the events in this episode, it would appear to be equally inspired by the Robin Hood legend.

STORY LINE: Black Wolf robs from the rich and gives to the poor. The tax collector believes that many of the young adults of a village are in league with Black Wolf and imprisons all of them for this crime, refusing to release them until somebody confesses who the culprits are.

Xena gets herself imprisoned in order to help her young friend Flora. Later, the comic foil, Salmoneus, is also incarcerated and used to unmask Flora as the Black Wolf.

Just as the headsman's ax is about to fall, Gabrielle tosses Xena her chakram (which she'd hidden in her hat!), precipitating a full scale revolt.

OBSERVATIONS: Although Salmoneus tends to be little more than a good-hearted buffoon when he appears on *Hercules*, on *Xena* his actions are of more consequence, such as organizing prisoners and standing up for Xena's character. This appearance is one of Salmoneus's last on *Xena* as it was decided to restrict him to *Hercules* so the *Xena* series could develop its own separate and original supporting cast. A new recurring comedic character named Joxer is introduced later in this season.

TRIVIA: Robert Trebor (Salmoneus) appeared as a different character in the second two-hour movie *Hercules and the Lost Kingdom* (HM-2), which also happened to have as a guest star the pre-*Xena* Renee O'Connor.

HIGHLIGHTS: The show's unique brand of humor is displayed in the scene where a friend of Flora's asks Xena with some surprise, "You embroider?" To which Xena replies, "I have *many* skills!" This comeback—"I have many skills"—becomes a running joke in the series.

## X-12: BEWARE OF GREEKS BEARING GIFTS

CREDITS: Story by Roy Thomas and Janis Hendler; teleplay by Adam Armus and Nora Kay Foster; directed by T. J. Scott

GUEST STARS: Warren Carl (Paris), Scott Garrison (Perdicus), Galyn Goerg (Helen), Cameron Rhodes (Deiphobus)

SUPPORTING CAST: Ken Blackburn (King Menelaus), Peter Ford (Trojan Soldier #2), Matthew Jeffs (Trojan Soldier #1), Adrian Keeling (Miltiades), Geoffrey Knight (Trojan Guard), John Manning (Greek Scout), Aidan MacBride Stewart (Greek Soldier)

MYTHOLOGICAL BASIS: This episode draws upon the *Iliad* and the myths that surround the Trojan War. The central myth is that Paris, son of King Priam of Troy, has fallen in love with Helen, wife of Menelaus of Sparta. The two lovers flee to Troy where Priam shields them from the Greeks. A war ensues in which Paris would have been killed by Menelaus, but Aphrodite intercedes. Paris is also credited with shooting the arrow that kills Achilles. For these acts, Agamemnon sends three warriors who kill Paris.

Helen is then forced to marry Paris's brother, Deiphobus, which so disgusts her that she provides aid to the Greeks who are still assaulting Troy. Then, for no apparent reason, the Greeks appear to retreat, leaving behind a giant wooden horse, which the Trojans take to be a favorable sign. The Trojans bring the horse inside the walls of Troy, and during the night the Greek soldiers concealed inside the wooden horse emerge from their hiding place and take the city.

Menelaus immediately goes to kill Deiphobus. In some versions of the story Helen assists Menelaus and stabs her husband in the back. In other versions Menelaus is so overcome by the sight of the partially naked Helen that he forgives her infidelities. In both versions Menelaus takes Helen back with him to Sparta.

STORY LINE: Xena goes to visit Helen who is in the besieged city of Troy. While Xena is meeting with Helen, Gabrielle renews old ties with Perdicus who had been her boyfriend before she met Xena.

As in the classic myth, the Greeks abruptly depart, leaving behind the wooden horse. In this version Deiphobus, who is portrayed as Paris's right-hand man, has been bribed by the Greeks. Deiphobus kills Paris and sets the Greeks loose in Troy.

When the Greeks remove the wooden horse from the city, Xena and the others are hiding inside and escape the Greeks the same way that the Greeks invaded the city.

OBSERVATIONS: In this episode Troy falls and Paris is slain—which is as Homer relates—but Helen escapes, a very different ending from the ancient Greek story.

Homer left out of the *Illiad* and the *Odyssey*, however, that it was Xena who killed Deiphobus and that Perdicus had a *thing* with Helen and offered to escort her to safety, leaving Gabrielle behind just as she previously left him behind.

HIGHLIGHTS: There are a higher number of amazing skirmishes and athletic Xena somersaults than usual.

TRIVIA: Perdicus, Gabrielle's ex-fiancé, hasn't been seen since "Sins of the Past" (X-1) and this appearance sets the stage for his inevitable rendezvous with Xena in "Return of Callisto" (X-29) where Perdicus is slain.

## X-13: ATHENS CITY ACADEMY OF THE PERFORMING BARDS

CREDITS: Teleplay by R. J. Stewart and Steven L. Sears; directed by Jace Alexander

GUEST STARS: Grahame Moore (Polonius), Dean O'Gorman (Orion)

SUPPORTING CAST: Patrick Brunton (Stallonus), Alan De Malmanche (Docenius), Lori Dungey (Kellos), Joseph Manning (Euripides), Bernard Moody (Drunk), Andrew Thurtell (Twickenham), David Weatherley (Gastacius)

MYTHOLOGICAL BASIS: Homer was an eighth-century Greek epic poet who wrote the *Iliad* and the *Odyssey*.

STORY LINE: Gabrielle goes to the Bards Academy in Athens, which is having a competition to fill student vacancies.

Gabrielle bluffs her way into the oratory competition. Each of the other competitors take a turn at storytelling, which include flashbacks to one of the Steve Reeves Italian-made sword-and-sandal movie as well as other *Hercules* and *Xena* flashbacks.

Gabrielle loses to a young man who tells the tale of Spartacus, then reveals to Gabrielle that his real name is Homer!

OBSERVATIONS: This is certainly an original approach to the concept of a clip-laden, economy-minded TV show. The concept started back in the 1930s when Saturday morning movie serials would have a seventh-inning stretch in which the main characters sat around trying to figure out who was behind the various nefarious events by discussing past incidents. This paved the way for flashbacks to earlier episodes. *Xena*'s producers would use the gimmick again in an even more unusual manner in the second-season episode "The Xena Scrolls" (X-34).

It should be noted that this is also the first of the all-Gabrielle episodes (just as *Hercules* once in a while will have a strictly Iolaus segment). It makes for a refreshing change of pace. By the end of the first season Gabrielle would be elevated from sidekick to co-star, proving what an interesting character she has become in her own right.

HIGHLIGHTS: The flashbacks to Steve Reeves's Hercules movies and then, most surprisingly, to Stanley Kubrick's *Spartacus* (1960) are a riot.

## X-14: A FISTFUL OF DINARS

CREDITS: Teleplay by Steven L. Sears and R. J. Stewart; directed by Josh Becker

GUEST STARS: Peter Daube Hurst (Petracles), Jeremy Roberts (Thersites)

SUPPORTING CAST: Huntly Eliott (Head Villager), Richard Foulkes Jr. (Calicus), John Smith (Klonig), Merv Smith (Marleus), Lawrence Wharerau (Lycus)

MYTHOLOGICAL BASIS: In Greek mythology, Ambrosia was the food, drink, or perfume of the gods, and there is the suggestion that to ingest it would bring immortality.

STORY LINE: Xena aligns herself with a motley crew who each have vital clues to the location of a secret treasure. The other treasure hunters include Xena's ex-fiancé, Petracles.

Following various trials and tribulations, they all arrive at the cavern that conceals the fabled Titan's key, which will unlock the entrance to the ambrosia horde. One of the assassins finds the key and kidnaps Gabrielle.

If a human eats ambrosia they are given the powers of a god, so Petracles and Xena join forces to prevent the creation of an immortal assassin. In the final confrontation Petracles is mortally wounded and reveals that he's never stopped loving Xena.

OBSERVATIONS: A question arises about this episode. If Petracles turned out to be a decent sort after all, why didn't Xena use the ambrosia to revive him the way Gabrielle gave ambrosia to Xena to revive her in "The Quest" (X-37)? The answer seems to be that nobody had yet thought of this plot twist.

The episode title, of course, is a takeoff on the title of the Clint Eastwood–Sergio Leone Italian western *A Fistful of Dollars* (1964), which was not a quest story but a tale of a lone bounty hunter who ventures into the wrong town. (This classic movie, in turn, was remade in 1996 as the American film *Last Man Standing* starring Bruce Willis.) In actuality "A Fistful of Dinars" is more like an Indiana Jones film than a Sergio Leone western.

HIGHLIGHTS: The interplay between the assassin and Gabrielle is surprising, and Xena's dramatic rescue of Gabrielle from a collapsing bridge provides the exciting climax.

TRIVIA: This segment has an additional importance in that it allows the introduction of ambrosia on *Xena*. This plot device will prove vital in returning Xena to life in the second-season episode "The Quest" (X-37).

# X-15: WARRIOR PRINCESS

CREDITS: Teleplay by Brenda Lilly; directed by Michael Levine

GUEST STARS: Iain Rea (Philemon), Norman Forsey (Lias),
    Latham Gaines (Minius)

SUPPORTING CAST: Jonathan Acorn (Mirus), Chris Bohm
    (Guard), Jason Hoyte (Timus), Michelle Huirama (Tesa), Mia
    Koning (Waif), Ian Miller (Low Life), Patrick Smith (Glauce)

STORY LINE: Twins are recurring themes on both the *Hercules* and
*Xena* series. In this instance Xena encounters her double, Diana, on the eve
of her arranged marriage. As always happens with arranged weddings,
Diana loves the groom's brother.

To further complicate things, slave traders want to prevent the marriage. Since the naive Diana is in no position to defend herself from attack,
Xena agrees to stand in for her until the wedding can take place.

After much swapping of clothes, dodging of assassins, and mistaking
of identities, Xena dressed as Diana totally scandalizes the groom who
calls off the wedding. Thus, when everything is finally sorted out, the
lovers are united.

OBSERVATIONS: This Xena installment is probably the most humorous of the first season.

It demonstrates in particular the range of Lucy Lawless's acting. The
character of Diana couldn't be more different from Xena, and it is clear to
us which character we are watching even though the same actress is playing both roles. Lucy Lawless would play an even more demanding identi-
cal-twin character in the second-season episode "The Xena Scrolls" (X-34).

Also of note is the touching scene in which Diana comes upon a poor
family and realizes that the aid her father had been sending to the indigent
hasn't been reaching them. This sequence demonstrates that the usually
timid Diana has true human depth.

HIGHLIGHTS: Diana dressed as Xena rides out of the city sidesaddle!
Seeing Diana and Xena circling each other and touching each other in a
wide shot is a triumph of modern special effects.

TRIVIA: This first all-out humorous episode of *Xena* will have its sequel in the second-season episode "Warrior...Princess...Tramp" (X-30).

# X-16: MORTAL BELOVED

CREDITS: Teleplay by R. J. Stewart; directed by Garth Maxwell

GUEST STARS: Bobby Hosea (Marcus), Paul Willis (Atyminius)

SUPPORTING CAST: Michelle Armstrong (Young Woman), Chantelle Brownlee (Bride), Geoff Clendon (Bride's Father), Chris Graham (Toxeus), Michael Hurst (Charon), John Palmer (Traveler), Erik Thomson (Hades)

MYTHOLOGICAL BASIS: Hades is one of the children of the Titan Chronus. He and his brothers and sisters are swallowed at birth by their father. Later when Zeus causes Chronus to vomit up his children, Hades joins with Zeus and becomes one of the Olympians who usurps the Titans. The Cyclopes, who also aid Zeus in his war against the Titans, make Hades a helmet of darkness that allows him to see at night so that he can help Zeus and Poseidon kill their father, Chronus.

STORY LINE: Xena receives a visitation from the ghost of Marcus, her former lover. He asks for her help because a murderer condemned to Tartarus has stolen the Helmet of Invisibility from Hades and escaped from the Underworld. Xena agrees to help if Hades will grant Marcus forty-eight hours of life so he can assist her.

When Xena and her former lover have accomplished their task, Xena convinces Hades to allow Marcus to reside in the peaceful Elysian Fields rather than in Tartarus, which is a place of torment and punishment. To do this, however, Xena must kill Marcus to end his mortal existence once again.

OBSERVATIONS: The relationship between Xena and Marcus is interesting for a number of reasons including the fact that Marcus is played by one of the few black actors to have appeared on *Xena*. Another role played by a black actor is M'Lila in "Destiny" (X-36), and, like Marcus, she is killed during her initial appearance.

Gabrielle isn't exactly thrilled at Xena going off with Marcus, especially when it means going to visit Hades. In addition when Xena and Marcus return, with Marcus now being mortal rather than a spirit, Gabrielle must cope with the two of them renewing their physical relationship, which is tough for Gabrielle to endure.

There's a lot going on in this complex narrative, what with people starting out dead, then returning to life, only to be killed again later. There also is the lurking danger of a serial killer on the loose. Slow paced this episode is not!

HIGHLIGHTS: Gabrielle sitting by the lake proves her devotion to Xena by waiting for her, not knowing what tribulation Xena may be facing, which is yet another example of the growing bond that Gabrielle feels she has with Xena.

TRIVIA: Michael Hurst, who plays Iolaus on *Hercules*, performs another of his alternate roles. Here, he is Charon, the boatman on the river Styx.

# X-17: THE ROYAL COUPLE OF THIEVES

CREDITS: Teleplay by Steven L. Sears; directed by John Cameron

GUEST STARS: Bruce Campbell (Autolycus)

SUPPORTING CAST: Grant Bridger (Sinteres), Arch Goodfellow (Kelton), Ian Harrop (Magmar), Patrick Khutze (Belart), Mark Raffety (Arkel), Crawford Thomson (Prognese), David Telford (Malthus)

MYTHOLOGICAL BASIS: This episode incorporates both Greek myth and Old Testament references to the Ark of the Covenant, which was believed to hold the tablets given to Moses. A point that is ignored in this story, but clear in the Bible, is that to touch the Ark, except when it was specially prepared for transporting, meant death.

In Greek mythology Autolycus, the son of Hermes and Chione, is known to be a thief. He is most famous for his ability to steal cattle and horses and disguise them so their owners can't recognize them. Autolycus is also known as the man who taught Hercules to box and who accompanies Hercules during his exploits with the Amazons.

STORY LINE: When a chest containing a secret weapon is stolen, Xena is asked to retrieve it. Xena concludes that she needs the talents of the thief named Autolycus.

Before they can steal back the chest, they find themselves framed for theft and murder, Gabriel is taken prisoner, and they must do battle with an assassin who would sell the weapons chest to the highest bidder.

OBSERVATIONS: When the chest is finally recovered, they look inside and find the tablets inscribed with the Ten Commandments! (Shades of the 1981 film *Raiders of the Lost Ark*!) Xena returns the chest to her friends, one of the lost tribes of Israel.

This is not the only time that Xena will cross paths with biblical elements. In "A Solstice Carol" (X-33), for example, Xena and Gabrielle encounter Mary and Joseph! "Cradle of Hope" (X-4) contains a distinct parallel to the biblical story of the baby Moses being placed in a basket and sent down a river where he is found and raised by others.

The appearence of Autolycus, the king of thieves, is always welcome. He first turns up on *Hercules* in "The King of Thieves" (H-14) at the beginning of the second season. This appearance is his first of many on *Xena*. Somehow he fits with *Xena* better than *Hercules* where he inevitably becomes lost in Herc's enormous shadow.

On *Xena* Autolycus emerges as a major co-star whenever he appears and proves as vital to the plot as Xena and Gabrielle. Bruce Campbell (a long-time friend of series producer Sam Raimi) has a knack for playing characters who are half serious and half comic as demonstrated in the three *Evil Dead* movies and in the 1993–94 TV series *The Adventures of Brisco County, JR.* As Autolycus, Campbell is at the top of his form and seems to be loving every minute of it. He also keeps being called on to do something completely different in each new episode he appears in, which allows the character to remain fresh.

HIGHLIGHTS: Of note is the fight between Xena and the assassin, Sinteres. Because they both know the secret of the lethal pressure point touch, they are evenly matched and equally deadly.

# X-18: The Prodigal

CREDITS: Teleplay by Chris Mannheim; directed by John T.
  Kretchmer
GUEST STARS: Tim Thomerson (Meleager), Willa O'Neill (Lila)

SUPPORTING CAST: Anton Bentley (Athol), Margaret Conquest
  (Villager), Alan Palmer (Pharis), Wally Green (Elderly Driver),
  Kelly Greene (Derq), Steve Hall (Damon), Barry Te Hira
  (Head Highwayman), Ashley Stansfield (Sentry), Stephen
  Walker (Peasant)

MYTHOLOGICAL BASIS: In Greek mythology, Meleager, a son of
Ares and Althaea, is born with the blessing that he will only die when one
of his mother's firebrands is consumed with fire. Meleager's mother heeds
the Fates' warning and hides the torch so her son may become invincible
as a warrior.
  Meleager marries Cleopatra (not the ruler of Egypt), but lusts after Atalanta, a woman warrior he meets when she joins the hunt for the Calydonian Boar. His actions anger his uncles who attack him, but Meleager is
the victor and kills them instead. This in turn angers his mother who
throws the magic torch into the fire, insuring that Meleager will himself be
killed.
  In the Herculean myth when Hercules goes to Tartarus to perform his
last labor, the capture of Cerberus, he encounters the spirit of Meleager
who asks him to go back to the land of the living and marry his sister,
Deianeira.

STORY LINE: This episode focuses on Gabrielle, the first in which she
has returned home since she left to travel with Xena. She arrives home to
discover that her village is in the path of a warlord's army. The villagers'
only protection is a drunken warrior named Meleager the Mighty who
turned to drink after he froze in fear during a battle.
  A little like Lee Marvin's Oscar-winning character, Kid Shaleen, in the
1965 western spoof *Cat Ballou*, Meleager is nowhere to be found when the
battle starts to get near. And, as also happens in that movie, just when it
looks really bleak, Meleager shows up and saves the day.

OBSERVATIONS: Although Gabrielle's reason for abruptly leaving Xena to return home seems contrived, it does enable us to see another story based solely on her. Little did the show's producers know that this developing independence on Gabrielle's (and actor Renee O'Connor's) part would prove important a year later when star Lucy Lawless would have her off-set accident and become temporarily incapacitated.

Interestingly, in this episode's sequel, "The Execution" (X-41), the re-appearance of Meleager would again have Gabrielle uncharacteristically turning away from Xena. What is that all about?

Actually there are several episodes in which Gabrielle takes off on her own including "Is There a Doctor in the House?" (X-24) and "Athens City Academy of the Performing Bards" (X-13). It's a plot contrivance that always seems to come from out of nowhere and then vanish from the story line until the next time the gimmick is required.

Meleager is played by Tim Thomerson, an actor who has been active in many low budget movies including the *Trancers* series (1985, 1991, and 1992) and *Dollman* (1991) in which he appears as a thirteen-inch-tall cop from outer space. Thomerson is a fine performer who easily rises to the material when he's given something good, and Meleager is a solid character in both of his appearances on the series.

HIGHLIGHTS: Gabrielle attempts to make the drunk-out-of-his-mind Meleager appear to be possessed of all his faculties. Also noteworthy is her attempt to apologize to Xena at the story's conclusion.

TRIVIA: This episode is the second of the Gabrielle-runs-off-alone-half-cocked type.

## X-19: ALTARED STATES

CREDITS: Teleplay by Chris Mannheim; directed by Michael Levine

GUEST STARS: David Ackroyd (Anteus), David de Latour (Ikus), Karl Urban (Mael)

SUPPORTING CAST: Sean Ashton-Peach (Zealot #1), Jack Dacey (Brawny Zealot), Peter Ford (Zealot Guard), Graham Smith (Senior Zealot), Teresa Woodham (Zora)

MYTHOLOGICAL BASIS: Not mythologically but biblically inspired, this story is taken from the Old Testament tale of God commanding Abraham to sacrifice his young son, Isaac.

STORY LINE: Anteus, the leader of a group of monotheists, hears a disembodied voice telling him to sacrifice his son, Ikus. Xena and Gabrielle set out to rescue the youth and in the process discover that his older brother has rigged devices to make him sound like the voice of God rumbling from the sky.

OBSERVATIONS: This segment is a strange cross-pollination of religions as the monotheists here supposedly believe in the one true god although we practically trip over a multitude of Greek gods in every other episode. So how can the monotheists believe in one true god when the Greek gods ably and repeatedly demonstrate their existence and power? In "The Xena Scrolls" (X-34), we're even shown that Ares still exists in the twentieth century. Does this suggest that some future *Xena* episode will have a war between the gods of different cultures?

This episode self-consciously mimics biblical movie epics in its style of cinematography and its background music, which evoke the feeling of such genre pieces as *The Ten Commandments* (1956), *King of Kings* (1961), and *The Bible: In the Beginning* (1966).

In a distinctly non-biblical opening to the segment, viewers are teased by the sight of Xena's breast plate hanging from a tree, then clothes being tossed on the ground while amid laughter we hear Xena's teasing voice saying, "Come on Gabrielle, you've been wanting to do this for ages." Then we see the pair skinny-dipping and learn that what Gabrielle had been waiting for was learning how to catch a fish with her bare hands. The series is filled with playful double entendres like this.

HIGHLIGHTS: Caught unawares in the water and out of her usual war-like costume, Xena dresses in record time and manages to beat up a squad of religious fanatics with a string of fish. In the new Disney *Hercules*

(1997) animated feature movie, Hercules uses a fish as a weapon in a similar manner.

TRIVIA: Karl Urban who plays Mael, the older brother, was apparently well liked by the producers because in season two he plays Julius Caesar in "Destiny" (X-36) and also has the recurring role of Cupid seen mostly on episodes of *Hercules*.

# X-20: TIES THAT BIND

CREDITS: Teleplay by Adam Armus and Nora Kay Foster; directed by Charles Siebert

GUEST STARS: Tom Atkins (Atrius), Kevin Smith (Ares)

SUPPORTING CAST: Heidi Anderson (Slave Girl), Nancy Broadbent (Areliesa), Sonia Gray (Rhea), Lutz Halbhubner (Tarkis), Robin Kora (Village Elder), Stephen Lovatt (Kirilus), John Manning (Ranch Hand #1), James Marcum (Warrior #3), Mark Perry (Warrior #1), Jonathon Whittaker (Andrus), Tony Williams (Warrior #2)

STORY LINE: Xena and Gabrielle are on the road when they encounter a man who claims to be Xena's father, which she seriously doubts.
In later encounters Xena finds herself manipulated into defending the stranger and then further manipulated into a raging anger at some villagers who try to hang him. Furious at such a betrayal, she moves to attack the village herself. In the midst of a warrior fugue, however, she suddenly understands that this was all a set-up by the god Ares to try to turn her back into the fearsome warrior princess of old.

OBSERVATIONS: It has been mentioned previously in the series that Xena never knew her father, which makes it easy for this story line to take place. In this case it was Ares who was using his powers to manufacture events that would manipulate Xena into turning back to her dark side, just as he did in his first *Xena* appearance in "The Reckoning" (X-6). However, rather than Ares being just a one-note character, he profits from his mistakes. In "Intimate Strangers" (X-31), for example, Ares realizes that Callisto (who's now dead) would be much better as his emissary, but he doesn't reckon with the fact that Callisto is insane, which makes her rather difficult to control. In "Ten Little Warlords" (X-32), the Ares saga continues as he realizes the error of his ways after his sword of power is stolen and he's reduced to being a mortal and dependent on Xena for help. By that segment's finale there seems to be something of a truce between these two persistent adversaries. Apparently something in their shared future shatters that peace, which is implied in "The Xena Scrolls" (X-34) where Ares is angling to get out of a tomb in which he has been imprisoned for thousands of years. Xena, of course, is the one who imprisoned him.

All in all, Ares is a multidimensional character who is most interesting when he is shown to have human weaknesses as in "Ten Little Warlords" when he experiences his first hangover. (Gods, of course, don't have hangovers, only mortals do.)

HIGHLIGHTS: When Xena goes into her warrior haze because she believes that the villagers have murdered her father, Gabrielle takes her life in her hands by swatting Xena across the back to knock some sense into her. In reality she is counting on Xena's feelings for her to help snap her friend out of her perilous trance.

# X-21: THE GREATER GOOD

CREDITS: Teleplay by Steven L. Sears; directed by Gary Jones

GUEST STARS: Peter McCauley (Talmadeus), Robert Trebor (Salmoneus)

SUPPORTING CAST: James Adam (Kalus), Jonathon Hendry (Ness), Natalya Humphrey (Photis), Timothy David Mitchell (Gorney), Kenneth Prebble (Old Man)

STORY LINE: When called upon to aid Lord Seltzer (who proves to be the good-natured but sometimes inept Salmoneus), Xena is struck by a poison dart. Afraid that if the warlord learns that she is injured, he'll complete his attack on the village, Xena has Gabrielle disguise herself as the warrior princess.

However, the ruse doesn't work and all are soon captured. The warlord almost gets to the point of having Xena's body drawn and quartered before retribution strikes.

OBSERVATIONS: Salmoneus, the recurring comedic foil on *Hercules*, returns here doing double-duty on *Xena* until Joxer is introduced in the following episode. Although Salmoneus essentially disappears from *Xena*, he makes a surprise return in the second season's "Here She Comes...Miss Amphipolis" (X-35).

Periodically, something happens where either Xena thinks that Gabrielle is dead or Gabrielle believes that Xena is dead, which leads them each in turn to become overwrought with emotion. These emotional displays of concern make one wonder why Gabrielle gets miffed at her friend now and then to the point of running off and going solo for sixty minutes.

HIGHLIGHTS: When Xena's horse Argo is threatened, she wakes up, regains her senses instantly, and beats up the bad guys.

# X-22: CALLISTO

CREDITS: Teleplay by R. J. Stewart; directed by T. J. Scott

GUEST STARS: Hudson Leick (Callisto), Ted Raimi (Joxer)

GUEST CAST: Patricia Donovan (Old Woman), Michael Hallows
    (Tall Villager), Ian Hughes (Melas), Kenneth McGregor
    (Akteon), Toby Mills (Tall Man), David Te Rare (Theodorus),
    Henry Vaeoso (Fat Warrior)

STORY LINE: Xena and Gabrielle come upon a village that is under attack by a woman masquerading as Xena. The woman, Callisto, vows to destroy everything that is important to Xena. Later she dispatches Joxer the Mighty to capture and kill Gabrielle. However, Joxer, the new comic foil, is more talk than action and can't do it.

The episode ends in a bizarre acrobatic battle in which Xena is triumphant, but the unrepentant Callisto vows that allowing her to live is a mistake that Xena will soon regret.

OBSERVATIONS: This episode marks the introduction of both Callisto and Joxer, both of whom return repeatedly on the show. It's interesting that in the course of events, Xena admits that everything Callisto says is true. While the fire that killed Callisto's family was unintentional, it happened because Xena's army was pillaging the village. Thus, Xena was to blame. Not only that, but the fire killed innocent women and children, which violated Xena's warrior code.

Concerned by what she sees in Callisto, Gabrielle wants Xena to promise never to revert to her old ways should anything happen to her, which indicates just how strong their characters' friendship has developed.

As events will prove, Callisto becomes Xena's greatest enemy and even death does not end their feud. Callisto will be on hand once again in "Return of Callisto" (X-29), "Intimate Strangers" (X-31), "Ten Little Warlords" (X-32), and "A Necessary Evil" (X-38). Over the course of time, Hudson Leick, who plays Callisto so effectively, has become quite popular with fans.

Ted Raimi as Joxer has also become an audience favorite, so much so that an episode was crafted to spotlight him in "For Him the Bell Tolls" (X-40). Ted Raimi is the brother of *Xena* producer Sam Raimi and has appeared on various TV series such as the mid-1990s' *seaQuest DSV*.

TRIVIA: Ian Hughes (Melas) played Diomedes earlier in the first season in "The Black Wolf" (X-11). The producers must have liked him to bring him back so quickly in a different role.

# X-23: DEATH MASK

CREDITS: Teleplay by Peter Allan Fields; directed by Stewart Main

GUEST STARS: Joseph Kell (Toris), Michael Lawrence (Cortese)

SUPPORTING CAST: William Davis (Malik), Doug McCaulay (Aescalus), Peter Needham (Village Elder), Elizabeth Skeen (Sera)

STORY LINE: In this episode Xena meets up with her older brother, Toris. Some time before, they had had a falling out when Cortese, a warlord, attacked their home. Xena had the village fight back, which cost her younger brother his life. Cortese is once again ravaging the countryside, and Toris plans to kill him to avenge his brother's fate.

Xena and Toris agree to join forces against Cortese. Xena springs a trap that forces Cortese to reveal to his subjects that he has been betraying them all along, taxing the people to raise an army to fight the bandits while being the leader of the outlaws himself!

OBSERVATIONS: This installment has an interesting opening teaser in which Gabrielle wants to learn how to catch arrows just like Xena. Xena insists that the skill is merely something one's body knows, not something one can be taught. At this very moment an assassin's arrow arcs towards Xena and Gabrielle nimbly catches it!

In addition we learn here much more about Xena's emergence as the warrior princess. A threat of invasion once posed to her homeland by Cortese led her to become a warlord in order to conquer neighboring lands to create a safety zone. Unfortunately, this goal soon expanded into Xena's desire for conquest for its own sake. Coming on the heels of "Callisto" (X-22), we have two episodes in a row in which Xena's past returns to haunt her.

HIGHLIGHTS: Gabrielle catching the arrow in the teaser is a real eye-opener.

TRIVIA: This episode introduces Xena's surviving brother, Toris, and explains that she once had a younger brother, Lyceus, whom viewers have the opportunity to meet during the second season in "Remember Nothing" (X-26).

## X-24: Is There a Doctor in the House?

CREDITS: Teleplay by Patricia Manney; directed by T. J. Scott

GUEST STARS: Danielle Cormack (Ephiny), Ray Woolf
     (Marmax)

SUPPORTING CAST: Tony Billy (Mitoan Warrior), Andrew Binns (Hippocrates), Harriet Crampton (Hysterical Woman), Simon Farthing (Democritus), Geoff Houtman (Gangrene Man), Paul McLaren (POW Leader), Adam Middleton (Blind Soldier), Charles Pierard (Thessalian Guard), Ron Smith (Galen), Deane Vipond (Head Wound Man)

MYTHOLOGICAL BASIS: Two characters, not from mythology but historical ancient Greece, appear in this episode: Galen, or Claudius Galenus, who was a Greek physician and writer of medical literature and lived in the period from 130 to 200 A.D. and Hippocrates, known as the father of medicine, who lived in the period from 460 to 360 B.C.

STORY LINE: Xena and Gabrielle are in a war-torn region where they encounter the Amazon chieftain who is pregnant. Xena takes her to a healing temple where she meets Hippocrates who is learning healing techniques from Galen. As the civil war moves closer to the temple, Xena has her hands full, particularly when the Amazon gives birth to a baby Centaur.
    When Gabrielle is injured and goes into convulsions, a near-hysterical Xena fears her friend is dying. When Gabrielle starts breathing normally again, Xena takes her friend in her arms and kisses her on the forehead.

OBSERVATIONS: This episode is a true season finale. Some TV shows insist that a cliffhanger is the way to end a year. But isn't it much better simply to create an episode that is so good and so engaging that viewers will be eager to see more new episodes the next year?

HIGHLIGHTS: Xena fears that Gabrielle is dying and really loses control of her emotions.

# CHAPTER FOURTEEN

# XENA:
# WARRIOR PRINCESS
## SEASON TWO (1996–97)

The episodes created for the television series are all sixty minutes long, the standard length for a drama-adventure series.

## PRODUCTION CREDITS

Created by John Schulian and Robert Tapert; developed by R. J. Stewart; producer: Liz Friedman; producer: Eric Gruendemann; supervising producer: Steven L. Sears; co-executive producer: R. J. Stewart; executive producer: Sam Raimi; executive producer: Robert Tapert; coordinating producer: Bernadette Joyce; New Zealand producer: Chloe Smith; story editor: Chris Manheim; unit production manager: Chloe Smith; first assistant director: Paul Grinder; second assistant director: Neal James; director of photography: Donald Duncan; editor: Jim Pryor; visual effects: Kevin O'Neill; production designer: Robert Gillies; costume designer: Nigla Dickson; New Zealand casting: Diana Rowan; stunt coordinator: Peter Bell; additional visual effects: Flat Earth Productions, Inc.; music: Joseph LoDuca

## REGULARS

Lucy Lawless (Xena), Renee O'Connor (Gabrielle)

## RECURRING

Ted Raimi( Joxer)

# X-25: ORPHAN OF WAR

CREDITS: Teleplay by Steven L. Sears, directed by Charles
  Siebert

GUEST STARS: David Taylor (Solon)

SUPPORTING CAST: Mark Ferguson (Dagnine), Paul Gittins
  (Kaleipus)

STORY LINE: Nine years earlier, Xena and her husband, Borias, had a
son. When Borias died, Xena gave the baby to the Centaurs to raise,
promising never to return. However, now that an evil Centaur is rising in
power, Xena's help is needed.
   This episode centers around the evil Centaur's search for a magical
crystal. The story is complicated when Xena's son, Solon, is kidnapped,
which results in the villain finding the crystal and transforming him into a
monstrous Centaur that Xena must battle.

   OBSERVATIONS: Although many story lines in the Xena series contain
light humor, the dramatic episodes are the most effective. The writers have
a deft sense of characterization and both Lucy Lawless and Renee O'Connor are more than up to the challenge of conveying subtle emotions.
   Xena meets alone with Solon, wanting to reveal that he is her son. However, she can't bring herself to do it because it would break the boy's heart
to be abandoned by his mother once again. Besides, she knows that he
would never be safe with her. With her heart breaking, she says good-bye
to Solon, promising that she will always be his special friend. The freeze-
frame at the conclusion here as Xena walks away from her young son is particularly effective as her face reflects all of her unspoken pain and turmoil.
   The introduction of Solon comes as just as big a surprise to Gabrielle
as it does to the viewer. Because tragedies dog these characters (e.g.,
Gabrielle's lover was slain by Callisto, Xena's former lover Marcus was
murdered), one hopes that if Solon returns that he is spared being the victim of any violence.
   The depth of Xena's personal conversion is exemplified by her wish
that Solon not become a warrior, and at the conclusion of this segment the
boy agrees with her pacifist philosophy.

HIGHLIGHTS: Once again we see Xena leap straight up into the air when she escapes from Dagnine's tent. If her agile somersaults seem extraordinary, leaping eight feet or more straight up makes her look like a superhero. Also, in one fight scene we observe Gabrielle get flipped over a warrior's back and it's clear that it is the actor Renee O'Connor herself doing this stunt.

# X-26: REMEMBER NOTHING

CREDITS: Teleplay by Steven L. Sears and Chris Manheim; directed by Anson Williams

GUEST STARS: Aaron Devitt (Lyceus), Robert Harte (Maphias)

SUPPORTING CAST: Mark Ferguson (Krykus), Stephen Tozer (Mezentius)

MYTHOLOGICAL BASIS: In Greek mythology the Fates (Clotho, Lachesis, and Atropos) are the three daughters of Erebus and Night who, with Zeus, control the time between the birth and death of each mortal. Clotho spins, Lachesis measures, and Atropos cuts the threads of life.

STORY LINE: The Fates grant Xena's wish to return her to the time when her brother Lyceus was still alive. They warn her that should she ever shed blood in anger, all will be undone and time will resume its previous course.

Xena's joy at being reunited with her brother is tempered by the fact that in this version of time her village has been conquered by a cruel warlord, her mother is dead, and Gabrielle is a slave girl in the marketplace. Xena can only take so much, and when she sees Gabrielle's life threatened by her slave master, Xena fights back, causing time to resume its course to what it had been before the Fates altered its path.

OBSERVATIONS: This episode is virtually old home week as characters whom Xena slew in previous episodes are present and getting into mischief. Mezentius, for instance, whom Xena killed in "The Path Not Taken" (X-5), is ultimately destroyed by Gabrielle here in the alternate past, which causes Xena to throw caution to the wind, say farewell to her brother, and do the misdeed that leads to her return to the life of the warrior princess. Also here is Krykus, previously seen in "Hooves and Harlots" (X-10), from whom Xena successfully defended the Amazons and Centaurs. But without Xena's intervention, Krykus triumphs over the Amazons and Centaurs in the altered timeline.

The aspect of Xena's mother in the altered timeline is also interesting. In the original timeline Xena's mother blamed her for the death of Lyceus, but in the altered version she dies of a broken heart because Amphipolis has been conquered. Xena still feels that in the old timeline her evil ways brought shame to her family, which doesn't happen in the altered version of events.

At the finale when Xena hugs Gabrielle, it's clear that she has no regrets for turning her back on the altered timeline. This episode demonstrates once again how well the series handles straight drama.

HIGHLIGHTS: Xena decides that there is just so much she can take, and with a wicked gleam in her eye she picks up a sword and attacks her enemies.

# X-27: Giant Killer

CREDITS: Teleplay by Terence Winter; directed by Gary Jones

GUEST STARS: Todd Rippon (Goliath), Anthony Starr (David)

MYTHOLOGICAL BASIS: Once again, this series draws upon the Old Testament and melds it with a touch of Greek mythology in order for Xena to play a role in ancient world affairs.

STORY LINE: Xena meets with her old friend Goliath. Nearby Gabrielle encounters the Philistines who have hired Goliath to defeat their enemies, the Israelites.

Xena tries to convince Goliath that he's on the wrong side, but the giant only wants the Philistines' money. Xena goes to King Saul of the Israelites and suggests a winner-take-all contest between her and Goliath, revealing that she knows how to kill giants.

Xena and David, an Israeli hero, decide upon a scheme to get Goliath to remove his protective helmet. David hurls the fateful stone that slays Goliath.

OBSERVATIONS: This is another solemn episode about people having to deal with the consequences of their actions. When Goliath picks the side in a conflict just for the sake of money, it is he who must pay the price.

In this episode there is a scene where Gabrielle finds Xena alone, watching a distant storm. She puts her arm around Xena and soon is holding Xena's hand to which the warrior maiden responds.

HIGHLIGHTS: Most noteworthy is the battle with Goliath, which the Israelites win, but which only brings sorrow to Xena. Later Xena visits the giants' graveyard, expressing her regret over the death of her old friend.

## X-28: GIRLS JUST WANNA HAVE FUN

CREDITS: Teleplay by Adam Armus and Nora Kay Foster; directed by T. J. Scott

GUEST STARS: Matthew Chamberlain (Orpheus), Anthony Ray Parker (Bacchus), Ted Raimi (Joxer)

SUPPORTING CAST: Kim Kristalk (Bacchae #1), Daniel Parker (Thief #1), David Donovan (Thief #2)

MYTHOLOGICAL BASIS: Bacchus is the Roman name for the Greek god Dionysus, the son of Zeus and one of his many lovers, Semele. When Semele angers Zeus, he kills her, but Hermes takes her unborn fetus and sews it into Zeus' thigh so that the child will still be born. After Dionysus' rather unusual birth, Zeus' wife hates the child, so Zeus has Hermes transform him into a ram. It is at this point that Dionysus goes to live with the nymphs on Mount Nysa where he invents wine and becomes the object of worship by Centaurs and Satyrs.

Orpheus was one of the Argonauts and was said to be a talented poet and musician. Perhaps the best known part of his myth is his journey to the Underworld to bring back his wife, Eurydice. He so entertains Hades,

Charon, and the dead that he is allowed to take his wife back to the world of the living but can only do so if he does not look back at her as they journey up from the Underworld. Orpheus can't keep himself from glancing over his shoulder to see if Eurydice is following him, however, and she dies for a second time.

Because Orpheus thereafter shuns the company of women, he is killed by either Thracian women or Maenads, and his head and lyre are thrown into a river and float out to sea and all the way to the island of Lesbos. Orpheus becomes the object of a death cult, and his head continues to make prophesies until Apollo objects to the rest of the gods that it is stealing his worshippers.

Dryads are nymphs that live in oak trees and who are often identified with Eurydice.

STORY LINE: Bacchus has stolen the head and body of Orpheus because the lyre that Orpheus plays can control the wolf-like vampire women called Bacchae. Xena agrees to help get the lyre and Orpheus's body back and defeat Bacchus.

Xena, Gabrielle, and Joxer go to a Dryad graveyard to get bones which can kill the otherwise invulnerable Bacchae. Just when all seems to be going well, Gabrielle turns into a Bacchae and flees into the catacombs. Before Xena can confront Bacchus, she finds that she must let Gabrielle bite her, transforming her into a Bacchae too. In the end she defeats Bacchus and gives Orpheus back his body.

OBSERVATIONS: This is a Bacchus unlike any ever seen before. A large, red, devil-like character, he is reminiscent of Darkness, the demon in the movie *Legend* (1985), but Bacchus is even more fearsome! His harem of Bacchae (which are portrayed as vampire women) are pretty fearsome as well. They can transform into wolves and even fly!

The scene with Xena and Gabrielle fighting the Dryads is quite impressive. This scene seems to be giving a nod to both Ray Harryhausen's skeleton warriors and Harpies in *Jason and the Argonauts* (1963).

Whenever the Bacchae are shown in action, there is a pixilated approach to the photography as though they're moving so fast that we can only see them moving in a jerky, twisted, distorted approximation of reality. It's a very clever visual touch. This episode is easily the closest thing to the horror genre that *Xena* has offered, and although bloodless, it is pretty intense by television standards.

In this installment Joxer isn't quite as useless as before and actually lives up to his word even if he does cower a bit. When he claims he can play the lyre, it turns out he's really telling the truth. We're so used to his false boasts that we certainly expected it to be a lie.

HIGHLIGHTS: The sudden, unexpected transformation of Gabrielle into a Bacchae and Xena sacrificing herself by allowing Gabrielle to turn her into a Bacchae are the two most memorable scenes offered here.

## X-29: RETURN OF CALLISTO

CREDITS: Teleplay by R. J. Stewart; directed by T. J. Scott

GUEST STARS: Hudson Leick (Callisto), Ted Raimi (Joxer)

SUPPORTING CAST: Scott Garrison (Perdicus), David Te Rare (Theodorus)

STORY LINE: Gabrielle's old boyfriend asks her to marry him and she accepts. Xena departs to pursue Callisto, but a fresh clue soon leads Xena back to Gabrielle, only to find that Callisto has killed Gabrielle's husband.

Callisto captures both Xena and Gabrielle and prepares to burn them at the stake, but Joxer's intervention helps Xena escape. Xena chases Callisto into the woods where both fall into quicksand. Xena escapes and then watches as Callisto sinks below the surface to her death.

OBSERVATIONS: Xena and Gabrielle have now each become involved with men who've died soon after the relationship was consummated. You'd think they'd learn from their sad experiences.

While Gabrielle learns to wield a sword in this episode, we never see her with one again. Apparently Gabrielle is still determined to live up to her personal code of not taking a life, and since her arch enemy Callisto is now dead, she can put her sword aside.

HIGHLIGHTS: Callisto chews up the scenery as only she can.

TRIVIA: Actually quicksand only sucks you down if you struggle. It has a layer of water on the top that allows people to swim out if they stop moving and wait until the natural buoyancy of the human body lets them float on the surface. Callisto obviously didn't know this.

# X-30: WARRIOR ... PRINCESS ... TRAMP

CREDITS: Written by R. J. Stewart; directed by Josh Becker

GUEST STARS: Ted Raimi (Joxer)

SUPPORTING CAST: Norman Forsey (King Lias), Lucy Lawless (Meg/Princess Diana), Iain Rea (Philemon)

STORY LINE: This is a sequel to "Warrior...Princess" (X-15), but where the previous episode had one Xena look-alike, this one has two! Princess Diana's father is near death and fears chaos unless Xena is there to smooth the transition of rule.
   A villain who is conspiring to block Diana from the throne has a comrade named Meg who also looks like Diana. Gabrielle lets Meg into the palace when she thinks the newcomer is Xena. When the real Xena arrives, Meg, who was disguised as Xena, is now pretending to be Diana. Xena finds out that there is a Xena-Diana double on the loose. So Xena disguises herself as Meg disguised as Diana and after a lot more disguises and counter-disguises, the story works itself out.

OBSERVATIONS: This really is an odd episode! Granted, it's hilarious to see Lucy Lawless playing three different characters whose interposition of identities is a triumph of scripting in that they actually keep everything in order (albeit complicated) in the viewer's mind. However, it becomes tiresome attempting to keep up with all of the many changes and counterplots.
   Seeing Joxer as the object of affection of Meg, the Xena double, is pretty jarring, and Xena isn't thrilled at the concept of Joxer having made love to someone who looks just like her. Meg, however, is perfectly

matched with Joxer because they're both inept. When Meg tries to practice with her sword, for example, she draws it so quickly from her scab-
bard that it flies out of her hand and into the ceiling. She also has a cheap,
wooden chakram that she keeps breaking.

Gabrielle really takes an emotional beating here when she thinks that
Xena has first had her imprisoned and then is back to treating her like a
useless little tagalong as she did many adventures before in "Sins of the
Past" (X-1).

HIGHLIGHTS: Joxer makes advances toward Xena and her immediate reaction is, "Are you suicidal?!" Diana, disguised as Xena, refers to the
chakram as a "shamrock," and Meg, disguised as Xena, refers to the
chakram as her "round killing thing."

## X-31: INTIMATE STRANGERS

CREDITS: Teleplay by Steven L. Sears; directed by Gary Jones

GUEST STARS: Hudson Leick (Callisto/Callisto as Xena), Ted
    Raimi (Joxer), Kevin Smith (Ares)

SUPPORTING CAST: Darien Takle (Cyrene), David Te Rare
    (Theodorus), Erik Thomson (Hades)

STORY LINE: With the help of Ares, Callisto is able to confront Xena
in the dreamscape. When Xena opens her eyes, she discovers that she is
trapped in Callisto's body in the Underworld. Meanwhile, Gabrielle does
not realize that the Xena with her is really Callisto whose spirit has possessed Xena's body.

The true Xena convinces Hades that Callisto has escaped and he sends
her to the surface world to set things right. When Xena confronts Callisto,
Callisto fades away into the dream realm. When Xena awakens she finds
that she's still in Callisto's body and knows no way to undo the enchant-
ment.

OBSERVATIONS: As this segment proves, Hudson Leick makes a
great Callisto, but an even better protagonist. She is an actress of tremendous range and we've seen her portray all the extremes in this series, from

evil to good and even to anguish in "A Necessary Evil" (X-38). While this episode is a direct sequel to "Return of Callisto" (X-29), it seemed unlikely to expect that it would continue into yet another follow-up episode. However, in the next installment of this ongoing story, "Ten Little Warlords" (X-32), Hudson Leick does her best Xena imitation while Gabrielle experiences further anguish at being close to the apparent killer of her husband even though she knows she's really with Xena.

The god Ares is once again at the bottom of Xena's trouble, but when he decides that Callisto is the right choice for his consort, he finds that he has taken on more than he had bargained for.

This episode also includes Joxer, but his role is not as vital as it has been in other plot lines.

HIGHLIGHT: Callisto is confronted by the many ghosts of her troubled past.

## X-32: TEN LITTLE WARLORDS

CREDITS: Teleplay by Paul Robert Coyle; directed by Charles Siebert

GUEST STARS: Hudson Leick (Xena/Callisto), Kevin Smith (Ares), Ted Raimi (Joxer)

SUPPORTING CAST: Charles Siebert (Sisyphus), Jason Kennedy (Carus), Bruce Hopkins (Tegason), Chris Ryan (Virgilius)

MYTHOLOGICAL BASIS: As noted earlier, in Greek mythology Sisyphus, the ruler of Corinth, is a cunning businessman, a thief, and a murderer who tricks Hades and escapes Tartarus on two occasions before he is caught by Hermes and returned to the Underworld.

STORY LINE: Thanks to Ares Xena is still trapped in the body of Callisto. As luck would have it, Ares has lost his godhood due to the theft of his sword of power. Xena and Ares form a reluctant alliance and he agrees to restore her to her real body when he regains his weapon.

Sisyphus has escaped from the Underworld and stolen the sword of

Ares. He announces a contest where the sword of Ares will be given to the winner. Xena (who still looks like Callisto) and nine warlords kill each other off until only Xena and Ares remain.

Ares regains his sword, Sisyphus is returned to the realm of Hades, and while Xena and Gabrielle are walking along the beach, Xena suddenly regains her own body.

OBSERVATIONS: Seeing "Callisto" as a protagonist is quite a revelation. She is entertaining to watch, especially since Lucy Lawless doesn't come back onto the scene until the conclusion of this segment. In this installment Leick does both a characterization of Xena and of Callisto whom Xena feels she must act like to keep others from suspecting that there is something wrong with her. It's unusual to see such fine acting in an action series.

HIGHLIGHT: Ares gets his comeuppance. As a mortal he suffers from a hangover, something he had never experienced as an immortal. We actually feel sorry for him. How the mighty have fallen.

TRIVIA: This episode features the simultaneous return of no less than four recurring characters: Callisto, Ares, Sisyphus, and Joxer. This may be a record for the most encore engagements in a single episode of *Xena*. On *Hercules* the record is held by "The Wedding of Alcmene" (H-34).

## X-33: A Solstice Carol

CREDITS: Teleplay by Chris Manheim; directed by John T. Kretchmer

GUEST STARS: Joe Berryman (Senticles), Peter Vere-Jones (King Silvus)

MYTHOLOGICAL BASIS: This episode of Xena may have some Greek mythological basis, but it is much closer to the Northern European legend of Saint Nicholaus, with a little Charles Dickens thrown in for good measure.

STORY LINE: It's winter solstice, Xena and Gabrielle are shopping when a young boy steals Xena's chakram. Xena tracks him to an orphanage where her weapon is being used as a decoration on the top of a tree. Soldiers burst in to evict everyone from the orphanage. In this kingdom celebration of the season is a punishable offense.

Xena and Gabrielle set out to teach the king the meaning of the season. Along the way they reenact a tale about a king visited by three Fates—a thinly veiled parallel to Dicken's *A Christmas Carol*, and they encounter Senticles, a toy-maker, who disguises himself in a red suit and a white beard to take toys to the orphanage.

OBSERVATIONS: This holiday tale is a mix of a great number of Christmas stories. (Xena and Gabrielle even encounter a couple en route to Bethlehem where the woman is going to have a baby.)

HIGHLIGHTS: The king is visited by three Fates, one of whom is Gabrielle hanging outside a window pretending to be the king's departed wife. She has to ad-lib quickly when she realizes that the king's spouse didn't die, but merely left him.

# X-34: THE XENA SCROLLS

CREDITS: Story by Robert Sidney Mellette; teleplay by Adam Armus and Nora Kay Foster; directed by Charlie Haskell

GUEST STARS: Ted Raimi (Jacques S'Er/Jack Kleinman/Ted Raimi), Kevin Smith (Ares), Renee O'Connor (Janis Covington), Lucy Lawless (Melinda Pappas)

SUPPORTING CAST: Mark Ferguson (John Smythe), Robert Tapert (Robert Tapert)

STORY LINE: At an archeological dig Melinda Pappas (Lucy Lawless) arrives looking for Janis Covington (Renee O'Connor), a sort of female Indiana Jones type. They are searching for the legendary Xena scrolls. Soon other searchers descend on the site including a Frenchman named Jacques S'Er (Ted Raimi).

Once inside the tomb, Melinda accidentally finds the scrolls and half of a chakram. Before you know it a tomb door magically opens and Ares emerges from a sarcophagus.

What follows is a series of clips from prior episodes that conclude with Melinda fighting Ares and once again trapping him in the tomb.

The episode closes with a scene-shift to fifty years later where the phony Frenchman's descendent is pitching the idea for a series about Joxer and Xena, based on scrolls he found in his attic, to Robert Tapert. Tapert appears to be interested.

OBSERVATIONS: This entry is another economical clip show, but what a clip showcase! This sly takeoff on the Indiana Jones trilogy is filled with in-jokes for regular Xena fans. It also serves as a good introduction for new enthusiasts of the series because the flashback scenes highlight important events and characters, clearly establishing just who Xena, Gabrielle, Joxer, and Ares are. There's even a shot from the now classic first battle with Callisto.

Ted Raimi demonstrates here his chameleon-like knack for portraying any character when he first plays a Frenchman with an almost impenetrable Inspector Clouseau accent, then reverts to his true self, a New Jersey brush salesman who was rated 4F by the army. Determined to fight the Nazis in any way possible, he chose to work to keep the Xena scrolls out of Nazi hands. The flashback showing Joxer along with Jacques, Jack, and then the final scene with Jack's modern day descendent showcases Raimi in four different roles (even if Jacques and Jack are just two sides of the same coin).

Ares is more hostile than when we last saw him, but being imprisoned in a tomb for two thousand years can do that even to a god. How was he imprisoned and who did it? That's not explained here, but the fact that a descendent of Xena must free him tends to point to her as the likely culprit.

The recycled footage isn't just limited to Xena episodes. For example, when Jacques claims to have battled the supernatural himself, we see clips from what appear to be old Spanish horror movies featuring a mummy and a werewolf.

HIGHLIGHTS: There are many good moments in this story. Renee O'Connor as a female Indiana Jones in the teaser is amazing, but then so is Xena's fight with Ares in the tomb.

TRIVIA: Robert Tapert plays himself in the last scene of this episode.

## X-35: HERE SHE COMES...MISS AMPHIPOLIS

CREDITS: Teleplay by Chris Manheim; directed by Marina
    Sargenti

GUEST STARS: Robert Trebor (Salmoneus)

SUPPORTING CAST: Karen Dior (Miss Misini), Geoff Gann
    (Artiphys), John Sumner (Lord Clairon)

MYTHOLOGICAL BASIS: Hermaphroditus is the double-sexed child
that results from the union of Hermes and Aphrodite. Hermaphroditus is
described as "a youth with womanish breasts and long hair."

STORY LINE: Salmoneus is putting on a beauty pageant to celebrate a
year of peace, but it appears that someone is trying to use the pageant to
break the truce. So Salmoneus wants Xena to enter the contest and be a
spy from the inside.
    Once inside the palace where the pageant is being held, Xena figures
out who the culprit is. Xena (disguised as Miss Amphipolis) also realizes
what apparently none of the other women do—that Miss Artiphys is
really a hermaphrodite who is declared the winner by a grateful, if per-
plexed, Salmoneus.

OBSERVATIONS: Here we have a surprise guest appearance by
Salmoneus! Once again, he's involved in an outrageous business enterprise
—this time the world's first beauty pageant. Such things have been sati-
rized before, but this one has both comic and dark undertones. (One of the
sponsors whips the woman he is sponsoring, for example.)
    In addition there's something different here: a story about a hermaph-
rodite. At first he is sure that Xena plans to expose his secret, but she surprises
him and us. His name is Artiphys (pronounced *artifice,* get it?). When Miss
Artiphys kisses Xena at the end, Gabrielle looks distinctly jealous.

HIGHLIGHTS: Xena is seen practicing with swords as her talent in the beauty contest. It gets even better when Xena somersaults across the stage, kicks a cobra out of danger, and catches it in her arms! Talk about upstaging someone!

# X-36: DESTINY

CREDITS: Story by Robert Tapert; teleplay by R. J. Stewart and
    Steven L. Sears; directed by Robert Tapert

GUEST STARS: Nathaniel Lees (Nicklio), Ebonie Smith (M'Lila),
    Karl Urban (Julius Caesar)

SUPPORTING CAST: Mark Perry (Vicerius), Grant Triplow (Brutus)

MYTHOLOGICAL BASIS: Historically, Julius Caesar was a Roman general, statesman, and historian who lived in the period from 100 to 44 B.C.

STORY LINE: When Xena is gravely injured she tells Gabrielle that only a certain healer can save her. Gabrielle sets out to take Xena to the distant healer. While unconscious, Xena flashes back to when she captured Julius Caesar, loved him, and then released him. And how Caesar returned to have her crucified on a cross.
    The flashback also explains how Xena learned her magical fighting techniques from a woman who later saved her from crucifixion and died protecting her.
    In the present Gabrielle locates the healer but he says that it is too late to save Xena who dies in spite of Gabrielle's heartfelt pleas.

OBSERVATIONS: This is one of the most dramatic episodes of *Xena* yet and is certainly one of the most complex. A TV producer (from a different and very inferior series) related that flashbacks generally don't work in TV shows because the viewer gets too easily confused by them. Yet, in this particular Xena segment the story crosscuts from the past to the present in the same manner that a novel would intercut to different events in a story. This is complicated storytelling and viewers are given credit for having the intelligence to comprehend what's going on without having to have the story continually explained to them.

Here we see Xena as she was at the height of her evil ways. Even though she takes the captured Julius Caesar to her bed, she still holds him for ransom. As a result, it should not have come as a complete surprise when he betrayed her trust and took her prisoner.

This *Xena* episode shines from the standpoint of the writing, the acting, and the production values. The scenes in which Xena is shown aboard her ship are exceptionally well handled, particularly when we see the vessel on the high seas. There's no skimping here. And the fact that the story within the story has Xena brutally crucified demonstrates that the show isn't afraid of taking risks.

HIGHLIGHTS: Xena not only is crucified on a cross, but Julius Caesar also orders that her legs be broken because he recognizes the strength of this superior warrior princess.

TRIVIA: The secret origin of the "Xena touch" and of her fighting abilities is, at long last, revealed.

# X-37: THE QUEST

CREDITS: Story by Steven L. Sears; teleplay by Chris Manheim, Steven L. Sears, and R. J. Stewart; directed by Michael Levine

GUEST STARS: Bruce Campbell (Autolycus/Xena)

SUPPORTING CAST: Melinda Clarke (Velasca), Danielle Cormack (Ephiny), Michael Hurst (Iolaus)

MYTHOLOGICAL BASIS: Autolycus, the noted thief, and the substance ambrosia, which was said to be the food of the gods, have both been mentioned in previous episodes.

STORY LINE: In this sequel to the previous episode the spirit of Xena takes over the body of Autolycus, the king of thieves. Gabrielle, who has Xena's body in a coffin, encounters Amazons who insist they give Xena a proper Amazon funeral. When Autolycus appears, he tries to hide Xena's body to prevent it from being put on the funeral pyre, and finally manages to convince Gabrielle that Xena is within his body.

A challenger to the position of queen pursues them to a temple where ambrosia is hidden. In the battle some ambrosia is secured while the renegade Amazon seemingly falls to her death. The ambrosia is placed in Xena's mouth, magically returning her to life.

OBSERVATIONS: This episode is somewhat odd because it is largely a light-hearted action segment that is part two of the story begun in "Destiny" (X-36), a very dark and dramatic episode. The spirit of Xena occupying the body of Autolycus is played strictly for laughs except for the scene when Gabrielle connects with Xena on the dreamscape and they kiss. The kissing scene is done coyly because even though Gabrielle is clearly aware that she is kissing Xena spiritually, physically she is kissing Autolycus and even opens her eyes to find herself in his arms (and with one of his hands on her butt!). This scene is reminiscent of the scene in the movie *Ghost* (1990) in which Demi Moore kisses Patrick Swayze when his spirit is in the body of Whoopi Goldberg.

The two installments "Destiny" (X-36) and "The Quest" (X-37) are a turning point in what has long been the growing on-camera closeness between Xena and Gabrielle. Their friendship has blossomed throughout the series and although it has been made clear that they've each had men as lovers, their horizons are plainly wider than that.

HIGHLIGHTS: Autolycus goes through the motions of being Xena because her spirit is in his body and this adds a lot to the humor of this episode. Also, there is the spirit-plane kiss between Xena and Gabrielle, which has become the series' most talked-about moment.

TRIVIA: This segment has a lot of returning characters in it including the reappearance of the Amazons in a sequel to "Hooves and Harlots" (X-10) and the return engagement of ambrosia, the substance first seen in "A Fistful of Dinars" (X-15). Finally, there is the re-return of Autolycus who was introduced on *Hercules* but has now become a recurring player on *Xena*.

## X-38: A NECESSARY EVIL

CREDITS: Teleplay by Paul Robert Coyle; directed by
    Mark Beesley

GUEST STARS: Melinda Clarke (Velasca), Hudson Leick
    (Callisto)

SUPPORTING CAST: Danielle Cormack (Ephiny), Jodie Dorday
    (Solari)

MYTHOLOGICAL BASIS: An explanation of the history of the Amazons, the female warriors who are featured in this episode, appears in earlier notes.

STORY LINE: This is a continuation of the story line from the two prior episodes and centers around the return of the evil Amazon who has stolen Ambrosia. She eats the Ambrosia, and in a blinding flash is transformed into a goddess.
    Xena and Gabrielle need someone who can help kill a god. Xena's only choice is to seek assistance from Callisto who is now immortal but trapped in the cave where Hercules imprisoned her in "Surprise" (H-49). Callisto agrees to help, but she demands that Xena publicly confess how her actions resulted in the death of Callisto's family.
    After much double-dealing and fighting the final confrontation takes place on a rope bridge where both the Amazon goddess and Callisto, who has also been transformed into a goddess, battle one another until Xena knocks the two goddesses into the lava below, rescuing Gabrielle just in time.

OBSERVATIONS: This is the conclusion of what has become known as the "Destiny" trilogy. While each episode tells a complete story, the first two end with cliffhangers resolved in the subsequent installments.
    When Xena confesses her crimes in public, it is an extremely dramatic moment because there is genuine emotional impact in her open confession. It is one more example of how this series can continually surprise its viewers with plot twists.
    When Callisto agrees to describe what she felt when she heard Xena's confession, she tells Gabrielle to remember what it was like when she was

a child and her family was everything. "Now kill them," she says poignantly. But Callisto can't let her humanity show too long so she mockingly asks Gabrielle how long it took Perdicus to die after she cut him open.

HIGHLIGHTS: Xena confesses her past crimes in public. One can actually feel sorry for Callisto for this brief moment when we see her soul bared.

TRIVIA: This episode is a sequel to multiple episodes including the *Hercules* segment entitled "Surprise" (H-49) and *Xena*'s "Hooves and Harlots" (X-10), as well as being the third part in the trilogy begun with "Callisto" (X-22) and "Return of Callisto" (X-29) and the trilogy that includes "Destiny" (X-36) and "The Quest" (X-37).

# X-39: A Day in the Life

CREDITS: Teleplay by R. J. Stewart; directed by Michael Hurst

GUEST STARS: Murray Keane (Hower), Jim Ngaata (Gareth)

SUPPORTING CAST: Alison Wall (Minya)

STORY LINE: Xena and Gabrielle have two problems: a marauding warlord in one direction and a giant attacking a village in the other. The two women flip a coin and choose to go with the man pleading for help with the giant. The man develops an instant crush on Xena, much to the consternation of the man's girlfriend.

The giant threatening the village turns out to be Gareth, the huge one Goliath was saving up money to go and slay in "The Giant Killer" (X-27), so for Xena this mission has now become personal. After Xena contrives to have the giant destroy the warlord, she takes care of the giant using a kite and a handy thunderstorm. The villager's girlfriend dresses up like Xena to win her boyfriend back.

OBSERVATIONS: In spite of the various threats of pending fights as well as the obligatory battle of strength in the teaser, this segment is essentially a character study. They fish and bicker and Gabrielle complains that

Xena broke their frying pan over some guy's head while saving their lives, so now they need a replacement.

The scene in which Gabrielle is shocked over how Xena uses a piece of one of her scrolls because she can't find a handy leaf when nature calls is also priceless. Nothing like a little scatological humor between friends.

Later, Xena and Gabrielle share a hot tub together and Gabrielle kisses Xena, again, but this time on the cheek.

# X-40: FOR HIM THE BELL TOLLS

CREDITS: Teleplay by Adam Armus and Nora Kay Foster; directed by Josh Becker

GUEST STARS: Ted Raimi (Joxer)

SUPPORTING CAST: Mandie Gillette (Ileandra), Craig Parker (Sarpedon), Karl Urban (Cupid), Alexandra Tydings (Aphrodite)

MYTHOLOGICAL BASIS: This episode is loosely based on the Greek god Eros, whom the Romans gave the name Cupid. Eros is Aphrodite's son and is known to be wild and capricious, recklessly shooting his arrows that stir up sexual passion in whomever they hit.

STORY LINE: Aphrodite (a true valley girl) is against a marriage Cupid has arranged because it will unite two kingdoms that consequently will knock down her temples. To break up the romance, Aphrodite casts a spell on Joxer that turns him into a brave warrior whenever he hears the sound of a bell. When one of the king's daughters sees Joxer, she is immediately smitten with him.

News of her infatuation gets back to the two kings and their alliance is threatened. Joxer is captured and sentenced to immediate execution. Gabrielle arrives just in time to find a way to ring a bell and Joxer takes on every warrior in sight.

OBSERVATIONS: This episode is easily the strangest, and funniest, of the Joxer segments. While Joxer has had major supporting parts in other episodes, he's the actual co-star of this story as Xena is elsewhere for most of the narrative. We even see Joxer in a love scene. When Joxer kisses Gabrielle, the magic begins to work on her until she slaps herself, looks startled, and says, "Scary!"

Just as in "The Xena Scrolls" (X-34), Ted Raimi displays his fine acting abilities as he slips back and forth between the idiotic Joxer and the Ancient Greeks' answer to swashbuckling movie star Errol Flynn. He's so convincing as Joxer the Mighty that it was probably a relief for him to play something close to a genuine leading man since this actor is usually tapped for character roles.

HIGHLIGHTS: Joxer says to the princess, "My sword is always ready to pleasure you."

TRIVIA: This episode is actually a tribute to the Danny Kaye movie *The Court Jester* (1956) in which a clown is given a post-hypnotic suggestion that turns him into a master swordsman at the snap of anyone's fingers. In this case it's a bell. The disclaimer at the end acknowledges the similarity by stating, "The producers wish to acknowledge the inspiration of Danny Kaye and pay tribute to the classic motion picture *Court Jester.*"

## X-41: The Execution

CREDITS: Teleplay by Paul Robert Coyle; directed by Garth Maxwell

GUEST STARS: Tim Thomerson (Meleager), Tony Blackett (Arbus)

SUPPORTING CAST: Douglas Kamo (Sullus), Ranald Hendricks (Elysha), Ann Baxter (Old Woman)

MYTHOLOGICAL BASIS: Meleager, the invincible warrior, has been introduced in an earlier episode.

STORY LINE: Xena and Gabrielle arrive in a town in time to learn that Meleager has just been tried and found guilty of homicide. When Meleager claims that a one-eyed man can provide him with an alibi, Gabrielle helps him escape so that he can return with his witness.

When Gabrielle threatens to attack Xena to defend Meleager, he steps in and admits that he's guilty and there is no one-eyed witness. Meleager acknowledges that he was drunk at the time. However, when Meleager describes the stranger and his sword, Xena recognizes the man and comes up with a way to save Meleager and punish the guilty.

OBSERVATIONS: This is another offbeat installment in that Gabrielle actually chooses Meleager over Xena and is prepared to fight her for this choice. Only Meleager's intervention prevents the quarrel from escalating into something serious. While her decision demonstrates Gabrielle's overwhelming devotion to a friend, she seems awfully quick to take Meleager at his word and willing to turn on Xena to defend him.

HIGHLIGHTS: Xena's clever rescue of Meleager when he is, indeed, hanged by the neck is a real surprise.

TRIVIA: Meleager is another character making a return appearance. He was first seen in "The Prodigal" (X-18).

# X-42: BLIND FAITH

CREDITS: Teleplay by Adam Armus and Nora Kay Foster; directed by Josh Becker

GUEST STARS: Jeremy Callaghan (Palaemon)

SUPPORTING CAST: Chris Bailey (Apex), Sydney Jackson (Vidalus), Graham Lauder (Lagos)

STORY LINE: Xena and Gabrielle are in a marketplace when Gabrielle is kidnapped by the henchmen of a mysterious warrior. Xena challenges the warrior, defeats him, ties him up, and forces him to take her to Gabrielle. However, during the fight poisonous oil splashed in Xena's eyes, and she is slowly going blind. Along the way the stranger comes to understand that Xena is not the vicious killer he'd believed.

Xena and the warrior crash in just as Gabrielle is about to be cremated and they save her just in time. A servant prepares a potion to save Xena's eyesight. The warrior, who had wanted to fight Xena to the death to make a name for himself, decides that perhaps being a hero is better than being a dead warrior.

OBSERVATIONS: This isn't a bad episode, but the kidnapping of Gabrielle and her imperative rescue by Xena seems like the stuff of the program's first season. The meat of the story is really in Xena's temporary blindness and the warrior she meets who turns out to be more than he seems.

The segment's finale has a very strange bit in which the servant-hairdresser of the king decides he wants to be the sidekick of the warror, and they go off together. There's a distinct intimation that the hairdresser is gay and looks forward to being the warrior's pal in the way that Gabrielle is Xena's special friend.

HIGHLIGHTS: Suspense is built up when Xena must do battle while a coffin containing Gabrielle slowly enters a crematory furnace.

# X-43: ULYSSES

CREDITS: Teleplay by R. J. Stewart; directed by Michael Levine

GUEST STARS: John D'Aquino (Ulysses), Rachel Blakely
    (Penelope)

SUPPORTING CAST: Tim Raby (Meticles), Carl Bland (Layos)

MYTHOLOGICAL BASIS: Ulysses is the name that the Romans gave to Odysseus, the son of the illicit union between Sisyphus and Autolycus's daughter, Anticleia. Ulysses marries Penelope, becomes one of Agamemnon's soldiers, and goes off to fight in the Trojan war where he conceives of the plan for the Trojan horse. The return of Ulysses (Odysseus) is the the central theme of Homer's *Odyssey*. His journey is filled with wild adventures, one of which is the blinding of the Cyclops Polyphemus, which is referred to in this episode.

Another part of the classic myth woven into this *Xena* episode is what happens when Ulysses' ship passes by the island of the Sirens. Sirens are mythological creatures with bird-like bodies and beautiful, human, female faces. They have voices so beautiful and enchanting that sailors passing their island hear their singing and become so distracted they lose course and crash on the rocky coast.

Ulysses instructs his crew to stop-up their ears with wax so they will not steer onto the rocks while he has himself tied to the mast so that he can hear the song of the Sirens.

STORY LINE: Xena and Gabrielle encounter Ulysses on his way home to Ithaca. They learn that Poseidon opposes his passage because Ulysses blinded a Cyclops who was one of Poseidon's sons. Xena and Gabrielle agree to help Ulysses.

During the voyage Ulysses reveals that he'd recently learned that his wife, Penelope, has died. Xena and Ulysses start getting to know each other better and romantic sparks begin to fly. When they come close to the island of the Sirens, Gabrielle and Xena tie up Ulysses, but he knocks Gabrielle out and escapes to answer the call of the Sirens. Only Xena's quick thinking saves Ulysses from certain death when she sings a song that drowns out the lure of the Sirens.

On reaching Ithaca Ulysses discovers that his wife is not dead after all. The news of her death was merely a cruel trick played by Poseidon.

OBSERVATIONS: There's a memorable scene when Gabrielle, who is seasick, can't sleep and overhears Xena and Ulysses cementing their warm friendship. The look on her face is one of great sadness. Later when Xena explains her romantic feelings for Ulysses to Gabrielle, Gabrielle says that whatever makes Xena happy makes her happy, which is exactly what Xena tells Gabrielle before she marries Perdicus in "Return of Callisto" (X-29).

This episode has three knock-down, drag-out fight scenes that are some of the best high-action sequences seen on a TV show since the 1960s. In the 1970s the networks quietly introduced censorship standards that allowed only two acts of violence per hour, which is why the original *Kung Fu* series had two fights per episode and why Bruce Banner only became *The Incredible Hulk* twice each week. Only in modern non-network (syndicated) programs such as *Xena* and *Hercules* has the violence quotient been raised to the level it was on television three decades ago.

HIGHLIGHTS: When Ulysses is about to be lured to his doom by the Sirens, Xena sings her own enticing song to cancel them out. Homer left that part out when he wrote the *Odyssey*! Also, in the famous sequence in which Ulysses must bend his bow to string it, Xena secretly helps him.

TRIVIA: The scene of Poseidon rising up out of the sea next to a rocky outcropping was originally created for the episode's opening to establish the fantasy atmosphere to come.

# X-44: THE PRICE

CREDITS: Written by Steven L. Sears; directed by Oley Sassone

GUEST STARS: Paul Glover (Menticles), Charles Mesure (Mercer)

SUPPORTING CAST: Tamati Rice (Garel), Mark Perry (Galipan), Austin Curry (G'Kug)

STORY LINE: Xena and Gabrielle find themselves pursued by a tribe of vicious primitive warriors, but make it to a nearby fort that is under seige by the marauders.

Xena takes charge, devises a battle strategy, and proves ruthless in dispensing food and water. When Gabrielle leaves the fort to give water to wounded enemy soldiers, the enemy regards the act as the sign that they can retrieve their wounded.

Xena offers to fight their greatest warrior with the understanding that whoever is the victor wins the war. She confronts an ax-wielding giant of a man, defeats him, and turns her back on him in contempt. When the warrior moves to attack her from behind, three of his comrades kill him. Xena realizes that being ruthless isn't the only trait needed in battle.

OBSERVATIONS: This is the most violent *Xena* episode to date. The story unfolds like a combination of the movie *Drums Along the Mohawk* (1939) and the Robert E. Howard Conan story "Beyond the Black River." Xena reverts to the ways of the old, ruthless Xena. At one point she admits this, stating that she never thought she'd have need of "that Xena" again.

The fights between the soldiers in the fort and the warriors of the forest are truly brutal. They employ wicked-looking axes, and the bitter fights are all to the death.

While Gabrielle is the voice of compassion here, the death and violence all around her is so barbarous that one wonders how she can have any genuine compassion for the enemy. At one point Xena uses her oar to block a hurled ax that otherwise would have hit Gabrielle in the head. The sequence in which they run for their lives (which in and of itself is unusual for Xena and underlines how deadly she regards their adversaries) is so intense that one would think that Gabrielle would be in shock from the horrifying experience.

HIGHLIGHTS: The flight down the river has death at every turn. The real highlight is Xena's battle with the champion of the forest men.

# X-45: LOST MARINER

CREDITS: Written by Steven L. Sears; directed by Garth Maxwell

GUEST stars: Tony Todd (Cecrops), George Henare (Hidsim), Nigel Hebrow (Basculis)

SUPPORTING CAST: Michael Hallows (Tig), Edward Campbell (Altrech), Frank Iwan Jr. (Colfax)

MYTHOLOGICAL BASIS: In Greek mythology the name Cecrops is famous as that of the first king of Attica. In some versions of the myth he has no father but is the son of Mother Earth and is part man, part serpent. Cecrops also indirectly figures in a myth that involves a quarrel between Athena and Poseidon who each claim to be the patron of Attica. The gods are called in as arbiters to decide which of the two is the giver of the finest gift. Poseidon strikes the earth with his trident and brings forth a salt-water spring; Athena simply plants an olive tree of peace. The arbiters choose Athena.

The Cecrops who appears in this episode is based on this myth in that he claims Poseidon cursed him because of the arbiters' choice.

STORY LINE: When Xena and Gabrielle are shipwrecked in a storm, Gabrielle is rescued by the cursed vessel of Cecrops the mariner. (The curse of Cecrops is that he cannot touch land again until love redeems him.)

Xena has landed on a nearby island and after fighting off some pirates, she races to catch up to the ship and hurls herself in a series of somersaults onto the deck. Even Gabrielle laughs at these outrageous acrobatics.

The pirate ship follows too close, is caught in a giant whirlpool, and is swept away, and inadvertently Cecrops learns the true meaning of the curse and redeems himself.

OBSERVATIONS: It's odd that Poseidon would put a curse on Cecrops that could be broken in such a positive way. Tony Todd as Cecrops is excellent.

Interestingly, the pirates see Xena board the ship and are smart enough to realize that if anyone can defeat the curse, Xena can, and so they wait to see what happens next. It turns out, however, that their vessel is sucked into a whirlpool, which allows for nice special effects.

HIGHLIGHTS: Xena runs the gauntlet of pirates to get to Gabrielle. If you thought Xena had shown us seemingly impossible jumps that made it look like she could fly before, this one outdoes them all.

Gabrielle conquers her sea sickness and munches down on squid.

TRIVIA: Tony Todd (Cecrops) previously appeared in the *Hercules* episode "The Gladiator" (H-20) as Gladius, a fighter who was held in bondage to an evil king until he was freed by Hercules.

# X-46: A COMEDY OF EROS

CREDITS: Written by Chris Manheim; directed by Charles Siebert

GUEST STARS: Ted Raimi (Joxer), Jay Laga'Aia (Draco), Karl Urban (Cupid)

SUPPORTING CAST: Cameron Russel (Bliss), Anthony Ray Parker (Pinullus), Barry Te Hira (Craigan)

MYTHOLOGICAL BASIS: Cupid, the name the Romans gave to the Greek god Eros, has been introduced in previous episodes.

STORY LINE: Xena and Gabrielle are looking for Draco who is threatening the Hestian virgins. Cupid's baby is discovered nearby indiscriminately firing arrows. Draco rides up as one of Cupid's arrows hits Xena. She kisses Draco and the two of them cross swords and fight to a draw.

Xena tries to talk Draco out of kidnapping the virgins. Always the deceiver, he pretends to go along with her wishes and then leaves to kidnap them anyway. Gabrielle is also hit with Cupid's arrow and falls in love with Joxer, which even he thinks is peculiar. When Xena finds out that Gabrielle loves Joxer, she simply can't believe it.

Draco falls in love with Gabrielle after being shot with an arrow. Xena rescues the virgins and all of them are shot with Cupid's arrows. They set their sights on Draco's men who run away because they know that Draco will kill them if they defile any virgins. Finally, Cupid appears and puts everything right again.

OBSERVATIONS: Obviously, this is a humorous episode that unfortunately comes across as old hat. This is also the first excursion with Joxer in which he's more silly than amusing.

HIGHLIGHTS: Gabrielle and Joxer sing Joxer's theme song together.

TRIVIA: The second season thus ends with the return of Draco who first appeared in the first episode of the first season, "Sins of the Past" (X-1).

# PART

# 4

✧❖✧

# APPENDICES

# EPISODE GUIDES
## HERCULES: THE LEGENDARY JOURNEYS

TELEFILMS

HM-1: Hercules and the Amazon
    Women
HM-2: Hercules and the Lost
    Kingdom
HM-3: Hercules and the Circle of Fire
HM-4: Hercules and the Underworld
HM-5: Hercules and the Maze of the
    Minotaur


TELEVISION SERIES

**First Season**

H-1: The Wrong Path
H-2: Eye of the Beholder
H-3: The Road to Calydon
H-4: The Festival of Dionysus
H-5: Ares
H-6: As Darkness Falls
H-7: Pride Comes Before a Brawl
H-8: The March to Freedom
H-9: The Warrior Princess
H-10: The Gladiator
H-11: The Vanishing Dead
H-12: The Gauntlet
H-13: Unchained Heart

**Second Season**

H-14: The King of Thieves
H-15: All That Glitters
H-16: What's in a Name?
H-17: Siege at Naxos
H-18: Outcast
H-19: Under the Broken Sky
H-20: The Mother of All Monsters
H-21: The Other Side
H-22: The Fire Down Below

H-23: Cast a Giant Shadow
H-24: Highway to Hades
H-25: The Sword of Veracity
H-26: The Enforcer
H-27: Once a Hero
H-28: Heedless Hearts
H-29: Let the Games Begin
H-30: The Apple
H-31: The Promise
H-32: King for a Day
H-33: Protean Challenge
H-34: The Wedding of Alcmene
H-35: The Power
H-36: Centaur Mentor Journey
H-37: Cave of Echoes


**Third Season**

H-38: Mercenary
H-39: Doomsday
H-40: Love Takes A Holiday
H-41: Mummy Dearest
H-42: Not Fade Away
H-43: Monster Child in the Promised
    Land
H-44: The Green-Eyed Monster
H-45: Prince Hercules
H-46: A Star To Guide Them
H-47: The Lady and the Dragon
H-48: Long Live the King
H-49: Surprise
H-50: Encounter
H-51: When a Man Loves a Woman
H-52: Judgment Day
H-53: The Lost City
H-54: Les Contemptibles
H-55: Reign of Terror
H-56: The End of the Beginning
H-57: War Bride
H-58: A Rock and a Hard Place
H-59: Atlantis

# XENA: WARRIOR PRINCESS

## First Season

X-1: Sins of the Past
X-2: Chariots of War
X-3: Dreamworker
X-4: Cradle of Hope
X-5: The Path Not Taken
X-6: The Reckoning
X-7: The Titans
X-8: Prometheus
X-9: Death in Chains
X-10: Hooves and Harlots
X-11: The Black Wolf
X-12: Beware of Greeks Bearing Gifts
X-13: Athens City Academy of the
    Performing Bards
X-14: A Fistful of Dinars
X-15: Warrior...Princess
X-16: Mortal Beloved
X-17: The Royal Couple of Thieves
X-18: The Prodigal
X-19: Altared States
X-20: Ties That Bind
X-21: The Greater Good
X-22: Callisto
X-23: Death Mask
X-24: Is There a Doctor In the House?

## Second Season

X-25: Orphan of War
X-26: Remember Nothing
X-27: Giant Killer
X-28: Girls Just Wanna Have Fun
X-29: Return of Callisto
X-30: Warrior...Princess...Tramp
X-31: Intimate Stranger
X-32: Ten Little Warlords
X-33: A Solstice Carol
X-34: The Xena Scrolls
X-35: Here She Comes...Miss
    Amphipolis
X-36: Destiny
X-37: The Quest
X-38: A Necessary Evil
X-39: A Day in the Life
X-40: For Him the Bell Tolls
X-41: The Execution
X-42: Blind Faith
X-43: Ulysses
X-44: The Price
X-45: Lost Mariner
X-46: A Comedy of Eros

# FAN CLUBS AND WEB SITES

## HERCULES-RELATED FAN CLUBS

If you would like more information on Hercules, you may send a self-addressed stamped envelope to one of the following fan clubs.

Official Hercules: The Legendary Journeys Fan Club
411 North Central Avenue, No. 300
Glendale, CA 91203
e-mail: outback@primenet.com

Kevin Sorbo Fan Club
Kevin Sorbo
P.O. Box 410
Buffalo Center, IA 50424

Michael Hurst Fan Club
Michael Hurst Fan Club
P.O. Box 49622
Algood, TN 38506

Robert Trebor Fan Club
Palindrome Pals
3352 Broadway Boulevard, no. 538
Garland, TX 75043

## XENA-RELATED FAN CLUBS

Lucy Lawless Fan Club
P.O. Box 279
Pendleton, IN 46064
web site: http://www.ansa.siplenet.com/jett

Renee O'Connor/Gabrielle Fan Club
P.O. Box 180435
Austin, TX 78718

# INTERNET WEB SITES FOR HERCULES AND XENA

Please note that the URLs for Internet Web#sites frequently change.

Alpha-Omega Sena Plus Fantasy & Scifi Cyberspace Guide:
http://www.hurricane.net/~wastor/aodir/xena2.htm

alt.culture: Xena:
http://pathfinder.com/altculture/aentries/x/xena.html

AvondaleGuy's Xena Page:
http://ansa.simplenet.com/avondaleguy/

Canoe.Com:
http://www.canoe.com/Search/home.html

Hercules: Ultimate Guide:
http://msmoo.simplenet.com/guide/hug.htm

The History of Xena: Warrior Princess:
http://www.xenite.org/xenahist.htm

International Fan Club: Xena: Warrior Princess:
http://www.concentric.net/~Loisanne/

International Xena Club Homepage:
http://personal.riverusers.com/~xenafan/

Jill's Xena Page:
http://funnelweb.utcc.utk.edu/~jtdybka/xena.htm

Logomancy: Xena Fandom:
http://plaza.interport.net/logomanc/xena.html

Mac's Xena "Extra" Page:
http://mattbrent.simplenet.com/Xena/Extra.html

Midnight Xenites:
http://edweb.concord.wvnet.edu/~deanca/xena/

Pazsaz Entertainment Network:
http://www.pazsaz.com/hercules.html
http://www.pazsaz.com/xena.html

TeddyR's TV show and Movie Page:
    http://users.arn.net/~syousif/hollywood.html

A Tribute to Hercules and Xena:
    http://ourworld.compuserve.com/homepages/cchaves_2/mari
    ahca.htm

Universal Channel:
    http://www.mca.com/tv/xena/

Universal Studios:
    http://www.universalstudios.com/tv/xena/

Universal Studios: Netforum:
    http://univstudios.com/tv/netforum/read/mca.tv.hercules/
    http://univstudios.com/tv/netforum/read/mca.tv.xena/

Xena Dungeon:
    http://www.wcnet.org/~timothy2/xena/

Xena Information Page:
    http://xenite.simplenet.com/index.html

Xena's Web Page:
    http://members.aol.com/Randy3456/Xena.html

# MERCHANDISE

Spin-offs from the *Hercules* and *Xena* TV series exist in the form of many licensed products. The five two-hour movies that launched Hercules have been released on home video along with the direct-to-video animated feature film (1997), which uses the voices of Kevin Sorbo, Lucy Lawless, and the other series regulars.

## Action Figures

A whole line of *Hercules* action figures has existed for some time, and mixed in with the *Hercules* line were a few *Xena* action figures (in boxes listing her as being part of *Hercules: The Legendary Journeys*), but those have remained very difficult to find. This situation will change when the separate line of *Xena* action figures finally appears. Universal has been behind in merchandising *Xena*, but that began to change in 1997. Lucy Lawless was less than pleased with the original *Xena* action figures. She told *Entertainment Weekly*: "It looks like they put my head on a He-Man's body! It's got these enormously muscular arms. They could shave a few bloody cubic inches off that dolly!"

## CD-ROMs

Early in 1997 came the release of the *Hercules/Xena* Multi-media CD-ROM from Software Sculptors (SSHX-4000), which retails for $35.00 and has graphics, sound effects, a partial episode guide to the two series, and bloopers. Each episode listed on the CD-ROM includes live action scenes from the episode, which only runs about five seconds. For some reason most scenes are fight scenes, and it gets a bit repetitious after the third time Xena is seen quaffing a mug of brew and exhaling it across the flame of a torch to blast some opponents off their feet. Do they think fans only watch the show for the fights?

## Books

There are also separate *Hercules* and *Xena* novels for those fans who can't get enough with one hour of each show every week. These books are original novels, not adaptations of any of the TV series episodes. The *Hercules* books include:
*By the Sword* by Timothy Boggs (Boulevard Books)
*Serpent's Shadow* by Timothy Boggs (Boulevard Books)
*Eye of the Ram* by Timothy Boggs (Boulevard Books)
*The First Casualty* by David L. Seidman (Boulevard Books)

The Xena books include:

*The Empty Throne* by Ru Emerson (Boulevard Books)
*The Huntress and the Sphinx* by Ru Emerson (Boulevard Books)
*The Thief of Hermes* by Ru Emerson (Boulevard Books)
*Prophecy of Darkness* by Stella Howard (Boulevard Books)

Boulevard Books is an imprint of the Berkley Publishing Group. These books are available by contacting the publisher directly at: The Berkley Publishing Group, 390 Murray Hill Pkwy, Dept. 8, East Rutherford, NJ 07073. The cost per book is $5.99 plus $1.75 postage. They can also be ordered at any major retail bookstore. For younger readers there are two juvenile books:

*Queen of the Amazons* by Kerry Milliron (ISBN 0679882960). This picture book is an adaptation of the first-season *Xena* episode "Hooves and Harlots" (X-10).

*Princess in Peril* by Kerry Milliron (ISBN 0679882596). This book is an adaptation of the first-season *Xena* episode "The Path Not Taken"(X-5).

# Comic Books

Topps Comics publishes a *Hercules* comic book and just added a *Xena* comic book. The first issue of the *Xena* comic book offered two different cover options—a cover illustrated with a comic-book-style drawing and a cover illustrated with an action photograph. Topps also has a set of *Hercules* bubble gum cards that include a few *Xena* cards from her *Hercules* episode appearances.

# Soundtracks

A Xena CD soundtrack album has been released recently on Varese Sarabande Records. It contains the fine musical score of series composer Joseph LoDuca.

# Videos

On June 17, 1997, Universal Studios Home Video released the four *Hercules* TV movies at a low price of $14.98 each. The ninety-minute films (on TV they were two hours with commercials) are *Hercules and the Amazon Women* (HM-1), *Hercules and the Lost Kingdom* (HM-2), *Hercules and the Circle of Fire* (HM-3), and *Hercules in the Underworld* (HM-4).

# BIBLIOGRAPHY

Blincow, Neil. "Big Bonus for Xena." *New Zealand Women's Weekly* (February 10, 1997).

Brennan, Steve. "Uni action heats up worldwide—Xena, Hercules int'l sales account for big chunk of revenue." *Hollywood Reporter* (March 29, 1997).

"Celebrity Circle with Lucy Lawless." *America Online, Inc.:* (1996).

"Celebrity Circle with Kevin Sorbo." *America Online, Inc.:* (April 1, 1997).

"Celebrity Circle with Renee O'Connor." *America Online, Inc.:* (1997).

"Cybertalk—Xena's Lucy Lawless on AOL." *Entertainment Weekly* (February 7, 1997).

Flaherty, Mike. "Xenaphilia." *Entertainment Weekly* (March 7, 1997).

Graham, Jefferson. "Xena makes Lawless an accidental action star." *USA Today* (February 15, 1996).

Helmer, George. "Steve Reeves Interview." *Cult Movies* #18 (1996).

"Hercules, Xena tops in top markets." *Daily Variety* (February 4, 1997).

Hontz, Jenny. "U Muscle Pushes 'Trek' From Top." *Daily Variety* (April 3, 1997).

Hontz, Jenny. "Xena hits a season zenith, tops all syndie action hours." *Daily Variety* (March 6, 1997).

Jacobs, A. J. "Gimme Some Skin" by Ken Tucker; "Toys In Babeland." *Entertainment Weekly* (November 24, 1995).

Kenny, Glenn. "Xena-phobia? No, we love her." *TV Guide* (September 30, 1995).

Knutzen, Erik. "Wild at Heart." *Cleo Magazine* (January 1997).

"Lesbians Love Xena!" *National Enquirer* (March 25, 1997).

Littlefield, Kinney. "Kevin Sorbo of hit action series `Hercules' is TV's coolest macho man." *Orange County Register* (1996).

"Lucy Lawless Just Flawless." *New Zealand TV Guide* (February 7, 1997).

McCaughey, Brian F. "Fight On! The Official Hercules: The Legendary Journeys and Xena: Warrior Princess Convention." *Axcess* (April 1997).

McHaney, Dennis. *Barbarian Cinema: The Films of Steve Reeves* (November/December, 1992).

Nazzaro, Joe. "Creating Xena." *SFX* #19 (December 1996).

Nazzaro, Joe. "Xena: Warrior Princess." *Starlog* #237 (April 1997).

Pescovitz, David. "Hollywood's War On The Fans."*The Web Magazine* (May 1997).

"Prime-Time Syndicated Series—Xena: Warrior Princess."*TV Guide* (September 16, 1995).

Reid, Craig. "Xena Warrior Princess." *Sci-Fi Universe* (January 1997).

Rensin, David. "The Woman Behind the Warrior." *TV Guide* (May 3, 1997).

Saltarelli, Mario. "Hercules and Beyond." *Cult Movies* #20 (1997).

Scapperotti, Dave. "Xena: Make War, Not Love." *Femme Fatales* (February, 1997).

Shapiro, Marc. "The Labors of Hercules." *Starlog* #211 (February 1995).

Sheff, David. "Xena, Web Princess."*Yahoo Internet Life* (May 1997).

Spelling, Ian. "Hercules humble at heart." *The Denver Post* (December 27, 1996).

Spelling, Ian. "Kevin Sorbo Speaks." *Starlog* #238 (May 1997).

Stewart, Susan. "Xena Versus Hercules." *TV Guide* (January 20, 1996).

"Summer Movie Preview: Hercules." *Entertainment Weekly* (May 16, 1997).

Szebin, Frederick C. "Lucy Lawless: Warrior Princess." *Femme Fatales* (January 1996).

Thomas, Bob. "More surfer dude than classical hero, Sorbo soars as TV's Hercules." *Roanoke Times* (April 13, 1996).

Tucker, Ken. "Macho, Macho Man." *Entertainment Weekly* (June 2, 1995).

"20 Questions—Lucy Lawless." *Playboy* (May 1997).

Wedlan, Candace A. "Not Even A Horse Can Throw Xena for a Loop." *Los Angeles Times* (March 26, 1997).

Wedlan, Candace A. "A Regimen Fit for a Hercules." *Los Angeles Times* (April 2, 1997).

Weinstein, Steve. "Forget 'Baywatch': The Action's With 'Hercules,' 'Xena'." *Los Angeles Times* (February 17, 1996).

Williams, Stephanie. "Hercules: The Man Behind the Myth." *TV Guide* (February 1, 1997).

Wilner, Richard. "Tie-ins create 'Xena' money machine." *New York Post* (March 20, 1997).

"Xena: Coming On Strong." *New Zealand Women's Day* (January 6, 1997).

"Xena's back in the saddle." *Globe* (April 15, 1997).

# INDEX

265

# ABOUT THE AUTHOR

James Van Hise has made his living from writing and editing since 1974. Born and raised in a suburb of Buffalo, New York, he fled the bitter winters of western New York State for Florida in 1970. In 1978 he relocated to California where he intends to remain.

In the 1970s he edited and published the small press magazines *RBCC* and *Enterprise Incidents*.

In the 1980s he began freelance writing for such magazines as *Starlog* and *Cinefantastique*. He also edited the national newsstand version of *Enterprise Incidents* (which later became *S.F. Movieland*) for twenty-four issues. In addition, he edited the magazines *Movieland* and the last few issues of *Monster Land*. During that period he also wrote *The Art of Al Williamson* (1983) for Blue Dolphin Books of San Diego. Between 1987 and 1995 he wrote more than sixty published books for Pioneer Books on a variety of film- and TV-show-related subjects, from *Star Trek* to old movie serials, not to mention two volumes devoted to the works of Stephen King and Clive Barker.

In 1988 he co-founded and co-edited *Midnight Graffiti* magazine with Jessie Horsting, which spawned the 1992 Warner Books *Midnight Graffiti* anthology. He also wrote some fifty published comic book stories for such titles as *The Green Hornet, Ghostbusters*, and *Twilight Zone*. He also created his own science fiction comic book series called *Tyrannosaurs Tex*.

In the 1990s he has authored books on such American pop culture subjects as *Pulp Heroes of the Thirties* (1994), *Pulp Masters* (1996), *Edgar Rice Burroughs Fantastic Worlds* (1996), and *The Fantastic Worlds of Robert E. Howard* (1997).

He continues covering modern films for *Cinefantastique* and other magazines and recently wrote a 23,000-word production piece on the making of *Spawn* as well as the longest article to appear anywhere on the highly acclaimed 1996 independent film *The Whole Wide World*.

James Van Hise lives in the Palm Springs area with his wife and far too many cats.

BOOKS